Lobel's Prime Time Grilling

SINCE 1840

Lobel's

Prime Time Grilling

RECIPES AND TIPS FROM AMERICA'S #1 BUTCHERS

Stanley, Leon, Evan, Mark, and David Lobel

BICENTENNIAL
1807
WILEY
2007
BICENTENNIAL

Published by Wiley Publishing, Inc., Hoboken, New Jersey
Published simultaneously in Canada

For general information about our other products and services, please contact our Customer Care Department within the United States at (800) 762-2974, outside the United States at (317) 572-3993 or fax (317) 572-4002.

Wiley also publishes its books in a variety of electronic formats. Some content that appears in print may not be available in electronic books. For more information about Wiley products, visit our website at www.wiley.com.

Library of Congress Cataloging-in-Publication Data:
Prime time grilling / Stanley Lobel ... [et al.]. -- 2nd ed.
    p. cm.
    Includes index.
    ISBN   978-0-471-75682-8 (cloth)
    1. Barbecue cookery. 2. Cookery (Meat) I. Lobel, Stanley.
    TX840.B3P74 2007
    641.5'784--dc22
    2006014217

Printed in the United States of America
10 9 8 7 6 5 4 3 2 1

To my dear wife, Evelyn, my partner in life, who makes each day brighter than the day before; to my wonderful children, David, Mark, and Carla, of whom I am very proud; and to my dear, sweet grandchildren, Brian, Jessica, Michael, and Scotty, who keep me smiling. I dedicate this book to you all with enormous love and devotion. To my brother, Leon, whom I worked so closely with for more than 50 years and whose loving memory will stay with me forever. I will miss you. Thank you God for blessing me. Thank you Mom and Dad.

Stanley Lobel

This book is dedicated to my father, Leon, who taught me through his example, that the capacity to love is boundless. Although I miss his hugs and endless smile, I will feel his love and remember him forever.

Evan Lobel

To my dear wife, Carla, my best friend and inspiration in life. To my dear children, Brian and Scotty, whom I cherish with all my heart. You bring so much joy and laughter into my life. To my wonderful parents, Evelyn and Stanley, whose love and support are endless. And to my Uncle Leon, whose love, guidance, and support I will so sadly miss but will remember fondly forever.

Mark Lobel

With love, I dedicate this book to my dear children, Jessica and Michael, who are a constant source of pride and countless blessings to me. To my wonderful parents, Stanley and Evelyn, whose love, support, and wisdom are limitless and priceless. And to my Uncle Leon, whose love and guidance I will carry with me in my heart forever. Thanks for all of your help.

David Lobel

Contents

Acknowledgments

Many people contributed to this book: our respective families and friends, who offered encouragement and advice along the way; our clientele, who enthusiastically asked when "our next book" was coming out; our employees, who happily put in a little extra time while we worked on the manuscript.

There are a few people we would like to thank individually, for without them this book would not have been possible:

Mary Goodbody, who worked closely and caringly with us to shape the words and recipes into a book that makes us proud.

Susan Lescher, who worked with us and John Wiley & Sons to make this book a reality.

Linda Ingroia, Adam Kowit, and the team at Wiley, who took such good care of the manuscript and transformed it into the great book it is. Thanks so much to all of you.

Deborah Callan, who cheerfully helped with the new recipes. And to those who helped with the book now and years ago when it was first published: Lisa Thornton, Francine Fielding, and Elizabeth Wheeler.

To everyone at Cookshack, Inc., who enhanced our knowledge of smoking meat and poultry, and whose terrific smokers made all the difference.

Finally, we want to thank our loyal customers who, over the years, have made it possible for us to run the kind of shop where the art of butchery is practiced still, and where true quality meat and poultry, as well as dedication to service, are appreciated. Without you, there would be no Lobel's.

Introduction

For us, grilling is a family affair. Not only do we come from a long line of butchers, but we come from a long line of accomplished cooks with a love of meat—and what better way to cook meat than on the grill? Obviously, our grandfathers didn't have the efficient outdoor grills that we do today, but from the day we tasted our first grilled steak, we were hooked. Undoubtedly, our grandfathers and great-grandfathers would have been, too.

There are five names on the front of this book, which represent two brothers and their sons. Leon and Stanley learned the butcher business from their father Morris, and have, in turn, taught it to their sons, Evan, Mark, and David. All of us relish good food and the enjoyment that comes with its preparation and serving, and nowhere do we get more of this pleasure than when we stand in our own (or each other's) backyards and man the grill. More recently, we have become enamored with the idea of smoking meat and poultry and so, when we revised this book, we included some recipes for smoked foods that we know you will love as much as we do.

Why We Love to Grill

Above all, we consider grilling good fun. If it's not, something is wrong. It's a joyous type of cooking if ever there were one. The aroma of the smoke alone signals a good time. When meat or poultry is sizzling on the grill, everyone gathers around, eagerly anticipating the meal to come.

For the grill cook, it's as important to feel relaxed and loose as it is to tend properly to the food. For this, we usually find ourselves with a few friends by our sides and a glass of wine or bottle of beer nearby, although a tall glass of iced tea or lemonade is as welcome. The point is to enjoy the process and never consider it a chore. Kick back! Have fun! It's a party!

Nevertheless, grilling is a serious method of cooking. It's important to know how to build a good fire and maintain the heat, when to cover the grill, and when to use it as a brazier (open grill). Equally important is buying the best meat and poultry for cooking on the grill, and in the following chapters we will go more deeply into it. For example, the finest beef and veal you can buy is prime. If you can acquire it, it will unquestionably taste better than other grades (we talk more about grades of meat, including prime, later in the book). Because prime meat is dear, it must be treated with respect both before and during grilling. Of course, once it's off the grill, it's every man for himself.

We explain at the opening of each chapter how to select and then handle the meat or poultry, and later, in individual recipes, offer our best advice for grilling and smoking success. In the opening chapter of the book, we discuss different grills and smokers, how to build a fire, how to maintain the heat, and what tools you will need. In short, how to conquer the logistics of being a backyard grill warrior. But also remember that grilling and smoking, like all types of cooking, are personal. Once you find the style that appeals to you, go with it. The more often you fire up the grill, the better you will get at it. No fire, whether fueled by charcoal or gas, burns exactly the same. Every grill is a little different, and so cooking times will vary. The weather plays a role, too, in determining the intensity of the fire. We have been "grillmeisters" for decades and still learn something new every season. As we have spent more time with our smokers, we have found that the same applies to them, too.

Why We Wrote This Book

All the Lobels love to grill. We appreciate expertly prepared meat and poultry, and want to share our knowledge about buying, preparing, and cooking it. However, equally important to us is that grilling signals family time. A book written by five people with the same last name speaks loudly of our belief in the importance of family ties.

Sunday afternoon, for example, is a great time for an outdoor get-together with loved ones. These parties are the ideal events to gather old and new friends, invite children and grandparents, fill a cooler with soda and beer, and then fire up the grill in anticipation of great eats. Grilling is most fun in the warm weather, but even if the mercury drops, grilling a whole chicken or rack of lamb outdoors can turn an indoor meal into a casual, festive occasion.

Over the years we have noticed obvious changes in our customers' buying habits. Forty years ago, customers bought far more roasts, joints for braising, and other large cuts; today they buy steaks, ground meat, chops, boned chicken breasts, and pork tenderloins. Our informal customer surveys (those we conduct over the counter as we wrap up the meat for our clientele or look over the orders for our mail-order business) inform us that during the summer, at least 75 percent of these purchases end up on a grill. This indicates to us that the grill is not just an occasional tool for outdoor cookouts but an everyday method of cooking everything from steak to vegetables. We've seen this growth firsthand, as friends, neighbors, and family members have invested in bigger and better grills, bought freestanding smokers, and built impressive backyard "kitchens" alongside patios and decks. We have also noticed that more indoor ranges have built-in grills and nearly every kitchen, even tiny New York City ones, seems to be equipped with a countertop grill, such as the George Foreman Grill.

Such observations make sense. As Americans have less and less time for cooking, it's natural for grilling to take center stage. It's quick and easy, and requires little cleanup. It also lends itself to advanced preparation in terms of marinating or rubbing the meat with spices. These techniques also beckon to the creative cook in all of us.

Any and all methods of grilling make sense to us. We simply love to grill.

How We Became Butchers

We almost had no choice. We come from generations of men in the meat business, beginning with Leon and Stanley's great-grandfather who with his son (their grandfather) ran beef cattle near Czernowitz, which was part of the Austrian Empire from 1775 to 1918. This grandfather added a slaughterhouse to the business and because he knew so much about cattle, was able to apply this knowledge to the art of butchering. His son, Morris, learned the business from him so that by the time Morris was 14 years old, he was buying and selling his own cattle. At the age of 17 Morris, like so many other young men of that era, emigrated to the United States to start life in the New World.

Morris's career began in Boston. He eventually found his way to New York where he established a butcher business, first in the Bronx and later on the Upper East Side of Manhattan, where we still do business today at 1096 Madison Avenue, near the corner of East Eighty-Second Street. We wonder if Morris would recognize the business as it is run today. Granted, aged prime meat still hangs in the meat locker, but there are cooked meat and poultry dishes for sale. These include whole roasted chicken and beef stew—and smaller cuts ready for smaller families and the changing needs of the modern-day cook. We also market our own bottled barbecue sauce (on page 221 you'll find a recipe for Madison Avenue Barbecue Sauce, which is very similar). Along with the sauce, we sell our meats and many of our store's other goods on our website, too. Clearly, this is marketing for the twenty-first century.

This is how we think it should be. We pass our knowledge on to our children, who in turn incorporate it even as they evolve the business to meet the demands of the times. But one thing never changes. We understand and revere good butchering.

Butchering is a lost art. Today, meat is butchered at the wholesale location, wrapped in Cryovac (air-tight plastic) and shipped to its destination, and while there are some exceptions where Cryovac serves an important function, we miss the old days when meat was handled differently. Hanging meat for aging seems to be a thing of the past, except among a small group of dedicated butchers. Aging itself is an art and can mean the difference between a good- and a great-tasting piece of meat. We age our meat for four to six weeks in coolers where the temperature is maintained at 34° to 36°F, until we judge it has reached perfection and is ready to sell.

We respect these time-tested traditions and deliberately take the best of the old and combine it with the requirements of the present and future. We also believe it is crucial to treat our customers fairly and pleasantly, to sell only quality meat, and to answer every question. Because of this dedication to our customers, we have grown and changed, and along the way have learned even more about meat and meat cookery. This is knowledge we have happily shared with customers and with anyone else who asks.

Our customers are among the most famous and influential people in the world. We have advised private chefs and restaurant chefs on how to cook our prime meat for world leaders, captains of industry, glamorous film stars, artists, and Broadway legends. But the majority of our customers are our neighbors, people who appreciate good meat and good service and with whom we have developed warm and lasting relationships over the years. We would like this book to become an extension of just this sort of relationship. Once you begin cooking from it and gain a greater understanding both of your grill and of how best to prepare meat and poultry, we truly hope you will come to think of us as butchers and grill experts you can trust.

A BUTCHER'S EYE VIEW OF GRILLING BASICS

Before the grill, before the fuel, before the perfect summer afternoon, you need good meat. This is our first and most important piece of advice: Buy the best you can afford, handle it with care, and then, when the fire is hot enough, when the meat has been allowed to come to cool room temperature, and when you start to get hungry, carefully lay it on the grill rack and anticipate an outstanding meal. Our second rule is: Use a grill you enjoy and trust.

Various grill experts tout the virtues of a particular kind of grill. We admit to having our favorites, but when you get right down to it, what you have or what you like is the best grill for you. Make sure the grill is large enough, that neither the grill rack nor the firebox is rusted, and that you are comfortable cooking on it. If these criteria are not met, perhaps it is time to consider buying a new grill. For instance, there's no good reason to hold onto a flimsy tabletop grill with short, stubby legs if you would be more at ease with a waist-high standing grill.

Grills

Some aficionados swear by brazier-style grills with racks that can be raised or lowered, but we prefer grills with covers and stationary (but removable) grill racks. By opening the cover, you can use the grill as a brazier and by replacing the lid, you can raise the temperature of the cooking chamber and thus affect the cooking time. Opening and closing the vents in the lid can influence cooking temperatures, too.

Charcoal Grills

Covered charcoal grills can be round or rectangular. Very few are equipped with racks that move up and down, so all food is cooked about six inches from the fire. We tested the recipes in this book with such grills, as well as with gas grills. We have observed that a majority of charcoal grills available at hardware stores and large discount chains are either covered grills, hibachis, or inexpensive tabletop grills—the sort you might take to the beach but that are next to useless for serious grilling, although for a few burgers or some hot dogs they are just fine.

With covered grills, the grill lid traps the smoke, which infuses the food with outdoorsy flavor, while at the same time smothering flare-ups. But don't think for a minute that the smoke "smokes" food (which in fact is a form of cooking) the way a smoker does. Most covered charcoal grills have vents, or dampers, on both the top of the lid and the bottom of the grill, making it easy to control the heat. If the fire is burning too slowly, open a bottom vent to add a little oxygen to feed the fire. If the food is cooking too quickly, open a top vent to allow some heat to escape.

The most popular covered grill is the kettle-style grill, which is round with a domed lid that, rather than being hinged, lifts off completely. The round kettle reflects and deflects the heat evenly, which is particularly advantageous when you are cooking large pieces of meat such as turkey breasts, standing rib roasts, or even whole chickens.

Covered grills are small or large, with some table-top models suitable for balcony or boat-deck grilling. With these versatile grills, you can cook over direct heat or not, depending on how you arrange the coals. You can sear the meat on the open rack, marking it nicely with grid lines and sealing in the juices, and then cover the grill to keep the fire hot and the food cooking evenly. At the end of cooking, remember to remove the lid so that the meat develops a crispy crust.

Hibachi Grills

Hibachis are small, Japanese-style brazier grills that are generally well made and just about perfect for some grilling needs. If you have a small backyard and a small family, there is a lot that you can cook perfectly well on a hibachi. These approximately 10 × 15–inch iron grills are excellent for grilling steaks, chops, and chicken breasts that need hot, direct heat. For success, lay the pieces of food close together on the grill rack so that they nearly touch and cover the rack almost completely to hold in heat. When the party is over, move the hibachi to a protected place—it will rust in the rain.

Gas Grills

Gas grills have surpassed charcoal as the most popular kind of grill for backyard cooking. Their prices have dropped since we worked on the first edition of this book and although they still cost significantly more than charcoal grills, they are affordable for most families, particularly since with care they last for years. Even as we confess to a slight preference for charcoal grills because of the flavor imparted to the food, we admit that we grill on gas grills all the time. Why? They are so convenient! A gas grill essentially is an outdoor gas stovetop. The fire is lit and the heat is controlled by the turn of a knob, and because there are always at least two burners or grates—and sometimes more—it is an easy matter to move food to the "cooler part of the grill" for slow cooking and push it back to the hottest part of the fire when necessary. You just turn one burner down or off and leave the other going full blast or less. Most gas grills don't burn quite as hot as the hottest charcoal fire, but they reach temperatures more than adequate for backyard grilling needs (the exception to this are gas grills with very high Btu, as explained below). Grill makers now also offer what they call hybrid grills, which are gas grills that serve as sizable, standard backyard grills and are relatively easy to carry with you for grilling in the park or at the beach.

Some gas grills are connected to the main gas line coming into the house, making them as ready to use as the kitchen stove. These often are built into the patio or deck as a feature for an outdoor kitchen, a concept that is growing in popularity, especially in warmer climates. However, most gas grills are fueled by canned propane gas. The propane is inexpensive—usually you refill the common 20-pound cans at a local gas station or hardware store—and one can lasts for up to nine hours of grilling, or for 20 to 25 meals. For some folks, this means only one or two fill-ups during a summer, while for others (like us!) it can mean multiple trips to the gas station. We have two cans that fit our grills, and keep the second one filled and on hand in case the first one runs out while the turkey is roasting or the burgers are sizzling. This is safe. Keep the filled propane can out of the sun and away from house, just as you do the grill.

What to Look For in a Gas Grill

Big, sleek gas grills can be extremely fancy, with multiple grates (burners) and side burners (similar to those you have on the stove) suitable for keeping the sauce warm or boiling the marinade. Others are pretty basic: two burners and removable grill racks. The higher priced gas grills might have built-in thermometers; removable pans for wood chips, charcoal, or liquids that you might want to use to flavor food; warming racks; storage cabinets; side tables; removable ash pans; infrared burners for quick searing; built-in coolers for beer and soda; and enough Btu to fuel a small rocket ship!

British thermal units (Btu) are a measure of the heat output. The most basic gas grills have 20,000 to 25,000 Btu, while the high-end grills can go much higher. Some boast 12,000 Btu for each burner (with four burners, or grates, that means 48,000 Btu). A burner that puts out 12,000 Btu reaches temperatures of 1,600°F, while a single burner on most gas grills reaches about 600°F. When you cook on a grill with very high Btu, you will sear a thick steak in no time, but you could also incinerate a more delicate duck breast before you know it.

But don't obsess about Btu! Instead look for a grill's versatility. This means the size of the grill and its cooking surface, the configuration of the grates (they should be close together so that food does not slip through them), and the material used to make them. We recommend porcelain-coated cast-iron grates, although porcelain-coated steel and plain stainless steel are also good. The coated cast iron conducts heat beautifully, which is why it gets an enthusiastic nod from us.

Finally, when you invest in a gas grill, remember that what is right for your neighbor may not be exactly right for you. Only you can decide what features on a grill will enhance your own cooking style and the needs of your family.

Fuel

Charcoal grills need charcoal, and when you meander down the supermarket aisle these days you may be astounded by the variety available. This is good news because it means it is now easy to buy our fuel of choice, hardwood lump charcoal, which may also be called natural charcoal. We like it because it burns hotter, longer, and cleaner than standard briquettes, and although it is irregularly shaped and so a little clumsy to use, we go for it every time. These lumps are made from hardwoods such as oak, maple, cherry, mesquite, and hickory. Some people wrongly assume that burning mesquite or hickory charcoal will give their grilled food a distinctive flavor. On the contrary, these charcoals may smoke a little more than other types of coals, but any perceptible imparted flavor will be subtle at best.

If a noticeable wood-smoke flavor is your goal, buy hardwood chunks. These are pieces of wood—not wood that has been compressed into charcoal. The wood requires a good 40 or 45 minutes to get hot enough for grilling, burns more quickly than charcoal, and never reaches the same high temperatures—but the flavor of the wood is easily discernible on the food without being unpleasant. Wood also produces more smoke than charcoal. For these reasons, charcoal is generally the favorite fuel of the backyard chef. Experimenting with wood, however, can be fun. For a distinctly smoky flavor, you need to smoke the food. We address smoking later in the chapter.

None of this is to say that standard briquettes are not good fuel. They are evenly shaped and less expensive than hardwood lump charcoal—two attributes that many folks appreciate. But they burn more quickly and a little cooler than hardwood lump charcoal, so you may need more briquettes if you are grilling for any length of time—such as cooking a roast or large whole chicken. Unless you buy the super-duper discount special (the cheapest you can find), standard briquettes burn evenly and cleanly. However, we caution against extremely cheap charcoal. It burns "dirty," partly because it has been made with fillers such as second- or third-rate sawdust, and it also burns quickly, so you will need more, which can quickly counteract any financial savings.

We also do not recommend self-lighting briquettes, which are saturated with chemicals so that they ignite with a match as easily as a wad of newspaper. This convenience product imparts an unappetizing oily flavor to the food. The manufacturer may claim that the chemicals "burn off" once the charcoal reaches cooking temperatures, and while many do, we can't help but notice a residual flavor—even if it's only in our imaginations.

Like wood chunks, wood chips provide real wood flavor. However, these cannot be considered fuel, but merely flavoring agents. They may be labeled "smoking chips" and commonly are from woods such as oak, cherry, maple, aspen, hickory, apple, and—the all-time favorite—mesquite. Some companies even market wine-infused chips. The small pieces of wood, sold everywhere from gourmet specialty markets to hardware stores, smoke just enough to give food a mild, smoky flavor. The chips must be soaked in water to cover for 20 to 30 minutes before they are scattered over the hot coals or the hot heating elements in a gas grill to produce a good smoke cloud. Too many chips can dampen the fire or extinguish it completely, so use wood chips judiciously. Also, it's important to use only recommended hardwoods for chips or for chunks—soft woods such as pine, spruce, or cedar produce billows of bitter, acrid smoke. Don't confuse the smoke from wood chips used in a charcoal or gas grill with smoking. Smoking is a completely different cooking method, which we discuss on page 11.

Water-soaked fresh herb sprigs, citrus peel, and cinnamon sticks also can be used to make aromatic smoke. However, don't expect any of these smoke makers to flavor the food very much. They are no replacement for spice rubs and marinades. But they make the air smell wonderful and enhance the entire grilling experience—which is why we love them.

Building and Lighting the Fire

When figuring the amount of coals you will need for most grilling, estimate that about five pounds of standard briquettes or three to four pounds of hardwood lump charcoal are adequate for 30 or 40 minutes of grilling in a standard-size kettle grill. Another way to figure this amount is to spread the briquettes in a single layer in the firebox so that the surface area is slightly larger than that of the food. If you will be grilling for longer than 30 or 40 minutes, you will need to add six or seven fresh coals to the fire to maintain the temperature and then add more every 25 or 30 minutes after that.

There are several ways to light coals. One of the most popular is to use a chimney starter. To use these sturdy, inexpensive metal cylinders, pile the charcoal in the larger, top section of the chimney, stuff crumbled newspaper in the bottom, and light the paper. The coals ignite as the heat from the paper fire sweeps up the chimney. When the top briquettes are barely covered with gray ash, pour them into the firebox, and spread them out for direct cooking or stack them for indirect cooking. (The firebox is the bottom portion of the grill that safely contains the coals during cooking and then, when you are done, as they cool.)

Electric starters are effective, too, although the grill must be close to an electric outlet. The looped heating element is attached to a heatproof handle. To use, spread briquettes in the firebox, lay the electric starter over them, and then pile more briquettes over it. In a very short time, the coals near the starter will be smoldering. Remove the starter and push the coals into a mound until all are covered with gray ash. Some charcoal grills come equipped with a built-in electric starter, which makes the chore of starting the coals easier than ever. Any grill with an electric starter or electric cooking elements needs a nearby outlet.

You can also use solid starters, which are small blocks of pressed wood fibers that are saturated with flammable chemicals and ignite quickly. Unlike self-lighting briquettes, the amount of flammable chemicals is so tiny that the starters impart no unpleasant flavors.

Liquid starter, or charcoal lighter fluid, is the most popular ignition agent in America. If not used correctly, it is a backyard accident waiting to happen. To use a liquid starter properly, pile the briquettes in the center of the firebox and sprinkle evenly and thoroughly with the lighter fluid (read the instructions on the bottle for best results). Let the fluid permeate the coals for about one minute, and then light the coals in several places with long safety matches. When the coals are covered with gray ash, spread them out for grilling. Some people complain that liquid starters make the food "taste funny," but in fact, the starters burn off long before the coals are ready and no residual flavor remains. However, they do smell oily while they are burning, which may be the cause for the complaint.

Liquid starters turn dangerous when impatient grill chefs squirt them onto already hot coals to "speed up the process" or if they are not sure the coals actually ignited. Too often this results in scary flare-ups and perhaps singed eyebrows, or worse. For this reason, never let children use liquid starters and never use gasoline!

Direct and Indirect Grilling

You may be perplexed by these terms, although they are quite logical. Because the heat of a grill cannot be regulated by the turn of a knob as it can on the stove, backyard cooks have come up with two basic ways to cook: on hot grills and on not-so-hot grills. It's as simple and sensible as that, and as you become accustomed to your grill and your own likes and predispositions, you will probably find yourself using these methods or combinations of them without really thinking about them.

For most grilling, the ignited coals are spread in a single layer under the food. This is called direct grilling and represents the way most people grill. The single layer of coals emits even, steady heat, whether the grill is open or covered. For more control, pile some of the coals at one side of the grill where they will emit intense heat. You can move the food around on the grill, setting it over the very hot coals when you want to sear it or when a thick piece needs to cook a little more quickly.

For some grilling needs, you will want to use indirect grilling. This method is for long, slow cooking in a covered grill, and when it is appropriate, it is indicated in the recipes. For indirect cooking, the coals are piled two or three coals deep on one side of the grill, or divided and piled on two sides. This leaves an empty space next to the coals or between them. If you are grilling on a gas grill, only one or two burners are lit. Food cooked over indirect heat often is started over direct heat and then moved to the cooler (empty) part of the grill for even, slow cooking. To make the heat as even as possible, construct two piles of coals or leave the center gas burner off and light those on either side of it. Do not prepare the gas grill for indirect grilling by preheating only one or two burners. Let the grill preheat with all burners on high as usual, and then turn off one or more.

Many grill cooks place a metal drip pan in the empty space beside or between the coals, which is filled with water, wine, beer, broth, or a combination. Set the food directly above the drip pan. This will add a little extra moisture to the cooking environment and also catch dripping juices and fat, which makes cleanup a little easier and reduces the chance of flare-ups. (Remember to keep a spray bottle filled with water on hand to extinguish flare-ups.) Generally, we don't use drip pans, finding them cumbersome and irrelevant except in very specific instances, but you may want to try them.

Once you get used to the indirect method, you may prefer to use it for more grilling tasks than we specify in the recipes. Although it may take a little longer, it is an excellent cooking style, a sure way to prevent the food from burning, and a good way to promote even cooking.

The Heat of the Fire

In our recipes we call for the coals to be "hot," "moderately hot," or, most often, "moderately hot to hot." Occasionally, we call for "moderately cool" coals. There is a "flame" graphic at the top of each recipe specifying the heat of the fire, too—just in case you miss the heat level description in the recipe! But what do these terms mean?

The Heat of the Coals

Heat of Coals or Heating Elements	Seconds You Can Hold the Palm of Your Hand 4 Inches Above the Coals	Temperature Range (°F)	Visual Cues
HOT COALS	2	400 to 450	Barely covered with gray ash; deep red glow
MODERATELY HOT TO HOT COALS	3	375 to 400	Thin coating of gray ash; deep red glow
MODERATELY HOT COALS	4	325 to 375	Significant coating of gray ash; red glow
MODERATELY COOL COALS	5	300 to 325	Thick coating of gray ash; dull red glow
HEATED WOOD CHUNKS OR CHIPS FOR SMOKING	—	200 to 225	Check smoker's thermometer

No doubt you have read grilling books and pamphlets that talk about gray ash and the red glow of the coals. These are valid visual descriptions. Hot coals are those that are barely covered with gray ash and are deeply glowing red underneath. Moderately hot to hot coals are covered with a thin layer of gray ash and are glowing deep red. Moderately hot coals are covered with a little more gray ash and still glow. Moderately cool coals are covered with a thick layer of gray ash and glow only slightly. With hot coals, you can hold the palm of your hand four inches above them for only two seconds before it feels uncomfortably hot—for moderately cool coals you can hold the palm of your hand over the coals for a full five seconds.

When you use a chimney starter, pile as many pieces of charcoal into the chimney as it holds, ignite them, and when the top coals are covered with ash and glowing red, dump the coals into the firebox. Add more raw coals to the burning ones, piling them on top. When they reach the desired stage of heat, spread them out and start cooking. It takes 15 to 30 minutes to build a charcoal fire. It takes only about 10 minutes to preheat a gas grill.

The Heat of Indoor Grills

If you decide to grill on an indoor grill, such as a countertop model or the grill built into your stove, its highest heat probably is comparable to moderately hot coals on a charcoal grill. This temperature will work for most grilling needs. Some of the less expensive countertop grills have no controls: they are on or off. You will have to experiment with these but assume that when they are heated up (and they take about 5 minutes to preheat), they are moderately hot.

Thermometers

We think instant-read meat thermometers are one of the greatest inventions for the backyard grill cook and smoker. It's reassuring to know that the interior of the chicken has reached 170°F for white meat, or the pork is indeed 150° to 155°F, which means it will reach 160°F after it rests for a few minutes and will be thoroughly cooked without being dry. And when the interior of the steak is 130°F, you feel confident that the meat will be gloriously rare and juicy. These thermometers are sold everywhere: in supermarkets, in hardware and cookware stores, and through cooking catalogs and websites. They are made of sturdy metal or plastic, and have a sharp point for inserting in the meat, and offer the temperature in a matter of seconds, either on an easy-to-read analog dial or a digital screen.

Internal Temperatures for Meat and Poultry (°F)

Beef and Veal	130 for rare meat
	140 for medium-rare meat
	150 for medium meat
	160 for well-done meat
Lamb	140 for rare meat
	145 for medium-rare meat
	150 for medium meat
	160 for well-done meat
Pork	160*
Chicken and Pheasant	170 for white meat
	180 for dark meat
Turkey	170 for white meat
	180 for dark meat
Duck	145 for medium-rare breast meat
	170 for well-done breast meat
	180 for thighs and legs
Venison	145 for medium-rare meat
	160 for medium meat
	170 for well-done meat
Rabbit	165 for well-done meat

*Cook pork until the temperature is 150° to 155°F and then let the meat rest for 5 to 10 minutes. The internal temperature will rise to 160°F but the meat will not be overcooked.

Many gas grills and some high-end charcoal grills are fitted with thermometers to gauge the interior temperature of the cooking chamber. Smokers nearly always are so equipped. Neither grilling nor smoking is an exact science, and so the precise temperature of the coals or cooking chamber is not as crucial as it might be for a culinary activity such as baking—although it is important to maintain the temperature of the smoking chamber. If your grill does not have a thermometer, do not despair. We like the visual cues and open-hand test described on page 8 as much. However, place an accurate oven thermometer under the lid of a covered grill, or insert a thermometer through the vents in the lid to read the temperature if it gives you more confidence.

Using Vegetable Oil Cooking Sprays on Grill Racks

It's a good idea to grease grill racks so that the meat does not stick to them, making it easier to turn and move the meat around on the rack. A well-oiled grill makes cleanup easier, too. Be sure to oil the grill rack lightly before lighting the fire to avoid flare-ups. (Keep a spray bottle of water nearby when you grill to extinguish flash fires.)

We have found that pressurized vegetable oil cooking sprays are efficient for the task of grilling. They are inexpensive, easy to use, and can be kept with the rest of the grilling tools so that they are always on hand. However, if you prefer, brush the grill with oil, using a broad-bristle brush or wadded-up paper towels.

Smoking Explained

Smoking, or barbecuing, is an ancient method in which the food is cooked at a low temperature in a closed chamber. Hardwood chips, chunks, pellets, or charcoal produce smoke that envelops the food, which slowly cooks a significant distance from the heat source. This may or may not be "over" the heat. In some smokers, the heat source is off to the side and in some it's down below—so it's not exactly accurate to speak of food as "over" the heat. During the relatively long cooking time, the food absorbs both smokiness and the flavor of the wood. The entire process results in incredibly tender, fall-off-the-bone meat that is moist and full-flavored. Once you try it, you will likely develop a hankering for smoked food. You'll very quickly discover how easy it is to prepare, too. At first, the terminology sounds foreign, but like anything, it makes perfect sense once you do it.

In case you haven't noticed, we never refer to grilled food as barbecued food. Food cooked on a grill is grilled; food cooked in a smoker is, authentically speaking, barbecued. Of course, you are free to call the food anything you like! Barbecue masters from Tennessee, Texas, North Carolina, and other locales where barbecue is king build elaborate, customized smokers in which they maintain their fires and smoke output as the food cooks "low and slow." The best of these 'quers find themselves at barbecue contests such as Memphis in May, their barbecuing apparatus in tow. We've been to the Memphis in May celebration and, take our word for it, the aroma wafting from the cookers stationed along the Mississippi River is positively intoxicating.

Tips for Smoking Success

Since putting out the first edition of *Prime Time,* we've become big-time aficionados of smoking, and we've added recipes to every chapter for smoked meat, poultry, and game. Here are few tips to help you achieve success with all our smoking recipes:

- Whether you've rubbed it with spices, soaked it in a brine or marinade, or left it plain, you should pat the meat and poultry dry with paper towels before smoking it.

- It might be easier to handle smaller cuts of food for smoking to cut down on cooking time. Cutting a large piece of meat in half (as we suggest for Smoked Brined Turkey Breast, page 190) will shorten cooking time but will not cut it in half.

- We like to leave the skin on fowl when we smoke it. It keeps the meat from shrinking more than it needs to. You can remove it before serving.

- If you can, include wings and backbones when you smoke poultry pieces. You can use them to add a wonderful smoky flavor to soups and bean dishes.

- If you smoke sausage, make sure you begin with raw sausage and not any that is partially cooked or already smoked.

- A lot of barbecue experts brine meat and poultry to make them even moister before adding them (patted dry) to the smoker. Whether you rinse it or not after brining depends on the recipe.

- Smoked meat and poultry cooks at "low and slow" temperatures and will not overcook. Instead, it will become incredibly tender.

- Use the amount of wood chunks or chips suggested in the instructions that come with your smoker. Even if sounds like too little, try it before you increase the amount.

- Too much wood produces a lot of smoke, which can impart an unpleasant flavor or appearance. Chicken, for example, will turn an unappealing gray.

- Try different hardwoods. The most common and easiest to find are alder, apple, hickory, maple, and mesquite. In some parts of the country, pecan is used for smoking.

- Be sure the wood chips or chunks are completely cool before you dispose of them.

- Use an accurate instant-read thermometer to tell when meat is thoroughly cooked.

- Barbecue sauce is meant to flavor the meat after it's smoked. In a few instances it's mopped on the meat during the final hour or so of smoking but usually it's prepared separately and passed at the table.

Smokers

Like grills, smokers come in many different sizes and shapes. There are large, expensive smokers that make their presence very much known, and then there are smaller ones better suited for small families, occasional smoking, or perhaps storing at a weekend or vacation house. You can smoke small amounts of food in kettle grills and some of the more elaborate gas grills have smoking capabilities in that they have pans for wood chips, but this is not authentic smoking. If you plan to "get into" smoking, it's a good idea to invest in a good, freestanding smoker, also called a cooker. Food smoked in a kettle grill or a gas grill will taste good and be appealingly tender, but it will never rival the food you prepare in an actual smoker. Plus, tending to the low fire in a grill is time consuming and fussy and you may decide it's not worth the trouble.

If you decide to invest in a smoker, buy the best one you can afford, because we guarantee that once you start smoking food, you will be hooked, and a good smoker makes a difference as far as convenience and ease. Every smoker operates a little differently, so it's important to read the instructions that come with your particular model. Some require preheating, others don't. Some have more shelves than others. All have temperature gauges that let you know the internal temperature of the cooking chamber and all have chimneys so that you can tell if the wood is smoking nicely. Most will smoke up to 50 pounds of food, which makes them great for party planning.

The aroma that seeps from the cooker is one of the best fringe benefits of smoking. It whets the appetite like nothing else and adds to the overall enjoyment of the meal in astounding ways. When you light up the smoker, even the neighbors will comment on the glorious smells wafting from your backyard.

Smoking results in moist cooking. Even the leftovers are moister than grilled leftovers, and when mixed with other foods impart delicious smokiness to them. We also appreciate the fact that while you must tend to the food when it's in the smoker, you don't have to watch over it as closely as you do when you grill.

Other Useful Grilling Equipment

Grill manufacturers gladly will sell you any number of accessories for the outdoor grill. If you like gadgets, collect them to your heart's content. But for the rest of us, there are only a few pieces of equipment that are almost crucial.

Every backyard chef should have long-handled tongs, spatulas with heatproof handles, as well as several long-handled, soft-bristle brushes for brushing marinades and sauces on the meat. Using tongs to turn meat is preferable over a fork because it prevents piercing the meat and releasing juices. We also like mesh grill screens and perforated silicone mats, which can be laid on the grilling grid and used to grill delicate foods, such as ground-chicken burgers or anything that might slip through the grates. Lots of grill cooks like grilling baskets or grate toppers with slanted sides for vegetables and small pieces of meat, too.

While we believe the joy of grilling lies in its simplicity, we also know that the right tools make all the difference. Other than the above-mentioned, you might want to consider any of the following accessories to make your grilling experience better than ever:

- A grill mat to protect your deck or patio from drips
- A heavy-duty plastic grill cover to protect the grill from rain (it will look nicer and last far longer than the cheaper varieties)
- A tool caddie or utensil rack
- Skewer holders for kabobs
- A lid holder that hangs from the side of the kettle grill
- A stainless-steel or silicone basting brush
- Firm-bristle brushes to clean the grill
- A fork with a temperature probe (doubles as an instant-read thermometer)
- A metal smoker box for wood chips
- An indicator to gauge the gas level in the propane tank
- An extra propane tank

Smokers, which are self-contained and freestanding, require less equipment than grills. Primarily, other than the cooker and the wood, you need heavy-duty aluminum foil and some disposable aluminum pans to catch the drippings—a better choice for placing in a smoke-filled cooker than your best bakeware. Regardless of how delicious the smoked food is, the pans will darken in the smoker and be tricky to clean. The smoke's residue will cling to the surface of the pans, so unless you want your next batch of brownies to taste like smoked pork, we suggest disposable pans when a pan is recommended.

For both grilling and smoking, we recommend you invest in long, heavy oven mitts and, as previously mentioned, an accurate instant-read thermometer. Calibrate the thermometer and if you're the least bit unsure of its accuracy, buy a new one. They are easy to find and not expensive.

Along with some good, sharp knives, which every good cook likes to have, and large cutting boards, that's about it. As butchers, we pay careful attention to our knives and recommend you do the same. Invest in good knives with high-carbon stainless-steel blades. Choose knives that feel right in your hand and build your collection as you go along and become a more accomplished grill cook. For most home cooking and grilling needs, you should have a cleaver, a 10- or 12-inch chef's knife, an 8-inch chef's knife, a 6-inch utility knife, a slicing knife, a boning knife, and a serrated knife. They don't need to match, and the choice of wood, plastic, or rubberized handles is yours, as long as the steel extends all the way through the handle. Poultry shears are terrific investment, too.

Don't put your knives in the dishwasher but instead hand wash and dry them. Use a sharpening steel every time you use them and refine the edge every so often with a sharpening stone or send them out to be professionally sharpened. Butchers and chefs reach for the sharpening steel without thinking about it; home cooks should get into the habit as well.

We have a large wood butcher block in the store and we use wood cutting boards at home, too. Plastic and rubberized ones are also good. The important thing is that they protect (and don't dull) the knife blade.

We also suggest you stock the kitchen with shallow glass or ceramic dishes for marinating or with several large rectangular, inflexible plastic containers with tight-fitting lids, or both. Heavy-duty resealable plastic bags are handy for marinating, too.

For kabobs, have six or more 10- to 12-inch-long metal skewers. Metal skewers get very hot on the grill and have to be handled carefully with oven mitts and long-handled tongs, but they are reusable, lasting virtually forever. Bamboo skewers are esthetically pleasing to many people, and when you are grilling numerous kabobs or short kabobs, they may be preferred because they are inexpensive and disposable. The short bamboo skewers are also useful for skewering chickens and quail when preparing them for the grill. Bamboo skewers must be soaked in cool water for at least 20 to 30 minutes, until they are saturated. They must then be drained just before the food is threaded on them. This helps prevent the bamboo from scorching on the grill.

Cleaning the Grill

It is important to keep the grill and the grill rack clean. For this, you'll need a stiff metal bristle brush for scrubbing the rack. Scouring pads are also good for keeping the racks clean. If you aren't too busy enjoying the meal, brush the grill rack while it is still warm—any burned-on food will come off easily. Spray the grill rack with vegetable oil cooking spray before you light the grill. This keeps the food from sticking and so helps with cleanup.

The firebox does not need frequent scrubbing, although the built-up ashes should be emptied out and the inside periodically sprayed clean with a hose and left to dry in the sun or wiped dry with paper towels.

Buy Meat Cold, Cook It at Room Temperature

Always buy cold meat and poultry. In supermarkets, meat is stored in refrigerated cases and in butcher shops some is displayed in chilled cases, but most is held in the meat locker. When shopping for groceries, buy the meat last and when you get home, unpack it first and transfer it directly to the refrigerator or freezer. Remember that summer humidity and higher temperatures are hard on meats, so in warm weather, plan to grill the meat soon.

Keep the meat or poultry in the refrigerator until just before you are ready to cook it—30 minutes at most, less if it's a warm day. You may have taken it from the refrigerator to marinate or rub it with a seasoning mix, but we advise returning it to cold storage as soon as it has been prepped. It is simply not safe to hold meat or poultry at room temperature for extended periods of time.

Meat, in general, should be at room temperature when you grill it, because it cooks more evenly than chilled meat. Take it from the refrigerator about 30 minutes before you are ready to grill. In hot weather or with small cuts of meat like chicken breasts, the meat may only need 15 or 20 minutes to come to cool room temperature. As soon as it no longer feels cold to the touch, put the meat on the grill. If for some reason your timetable changes, return the uncooked meat to the refrigerator. Ground meat is the exception and should be cooked when still chilled, for two reasons: the greater surface area of ground meat would make it more susceptible to bacteria at room temperature, and on the plus side, ground meat patties or meatballs will keep their shape better when previously chilled.

A Word on Food Safety

It is just as important to maintain sanitary conditions when cooking meat and poultry outside as it is in the kitchen. Clean the cutting board and all utensils that have been in contact with uncooked meat or poultry with warm soapy water. Wash your hands, too, after working with uncooked food (chicken, in particular) to avoid salmonella contamination.

Many grill cooks continually slather the grilling meat or chicken with its marinade. This is not a good idea except during the very early stages of cooking. The marinade can contain bacteria from the raw meat and poultry, and the heat of the fire will not have time to render the bacteria harmless if the marinade is brushed on the food in the final stages of grilling. If you want to brush the food with the marinade, make a little more than the recipe requires. Keep it separate and then use it to baste the food with a little extra flavor.

Grilling is a casual and relaxing way to cook and entertain. Once you have the basics in hand, don't worry. Half the fun is improvising when necessary—but the best part is eating the delicious food that comes from your grill.

Practical Freezing

We prefer to grill fresh meat and poultry, but we appreciate the fact that meat freezes well, which is a practical consideration for many people. Although we never sell meat that has been frozen, we are well aware that our customers often freeze the meat we sell—and because we want them to enjoy their purchase, regardless of whether they eat it right away or freeze it, we have some suggestions for successful freezing.

If you plan to freeze meat or poultry, do so as soon as you get home. If it's wrapped in supermarket plastic, leave it in the original packaging. The same goes for butcher paper. Wrap another layer of sturdy plastic wrap around the package, making sure it is well protected. Do not use foil for over-wrapping, because it becomes brittle in the freezer and can rip. Put the package inside a heavy freezer-quality resealable plastic bag, making sure the bag is large enough to hold the meat comfortably. Press as much air from the bag as you can before sealing it so that it collapses around the meat. Clearly mark the bag, making sure to date it. Stash the bag in the far reaches of the freezer, which is the coldest part. When it is frozen solid, you can shift it around to make room for other foods.

If you are concerned that your freezer may not be cold enough for meat, consider this: If it is cold enough to freeze ice cream hard, it is cold enough to freeze meat and poultry. But even having the coldest freezer does not mean you can leave the meat in it indefinitely. For the best texture and quality, do not leave meat in the deep freeze for longer than 30 days in the winter, or 15 days in the summer.

Let meat thaw slowly in the refrigerator. This can take from one to two days, depending on the time of year and the size and cut of the meat. If you are planning to slice the meat for kabobs or stew, keep in mind that it is easier to slice when partially frozen.

Even with careful wrapping, sometimes food develops freezer burn. We don't advise grilling the damaged meat, but don't discard it, either. Cut it up and stew or braise it.

Leftover Strategy

Who doesn't love leftovers? Especially grilled or smoked leftovers? The charred or smoky flavor remains with the meat or poultry, making it nearly as enticing the next day as it was right off the grill. For this reason, cook extra when you can. You will never regret it.

As soon as you realize you will have some leftovers, put the food away in the refrigerator. It is never a good idea to leave any food, even cooked food, at room temperature for more than an hour, and this is particularly true in the hot summer months when we tend to fire up the grill and smoker most often. Room temperatures are the most dangerous for food because it is at these temperatures that bacteria thrive. Wrap the leftovers well in plastic or put them in rigid plastic storage containers with fitted lids. Eat them within a day or two, at the most.

If you want to reheat the leftover meat on the grill, wrap it in foil first. The coals should be arranged for indirect cooking and they should be only moderately hot. However, most grilled meat and poultry tastes terrific cold. Slice it for sandwiches or salads. To heat up leftover smoked food, sprinkle it with a little liquid and heat it in the microwave, low oven, or a saucepan.

BURGERS

Hamburgers are an American summertime tradition. But thanks first to diners and then to fast-food restaurants, they are also a symbol of what many people don't know about quality meat. Truth be told, a good burger can be as good as it gets when it comes to casual eating—juicy and tender, bursting with robust meat flavor. On the other hand, an inferior burger can be a disappointing meal at best.

Most people buy ground meat in the supermarket, reserving the butcher shop for the "better" cuts. But we think it's far wiser to buy ground meat from a reliable butcher. When you walk into the butcher shop or approach the meat counter in a larger store, don't buy the ground meat on display, particularly if you have not developed a relationship with the butcher. That meat can be ground from any part of the animal, including trimmings. It's far better to ask the butcher to grind the meat for you, and ask him to trim most of the fat before he puts the meat through the meat grinder. Let him know you will be using the meat for grilled burgers and ask him to grind it quite fine so that it can be formed into compact patties. If you do buy ground, packaged beef or other meat, make sure it is rosy colored, without browned sections, and evenly mixed with creamy white particles of fat.

Beef is the most popular burger meat, but we urge you to try using ground lamb, veal, pork, turkey, and chicken, too. Other than ground beef and lamb, other ground meats do best when mixed together. When you experiment with other ground meats you will be happily rewarded with new taste experiences as well as expanded choices when it's time to eat.

The secret to successful grilled burgers is to make the patties firm and large so they neither fall apart on the grill nor slip through the grill rack onto the smoldering coals. As mentioned, using meat that is evenly ground helps, as does, in some cases, working bread crumbs and other ingredients into the meat. Some of our burgers are nothing but lightly seasoned meat; others incorporate more ingredients. To avoid crumbly burgers, open your fingers slightly when handling the meat and forming the patties; don't squeeze the meat and try not to overhandle it.

Make sure the fire is hot enough before you put the burgers on the grill, and that the grill rack is lightly sprayed with vegetable oil cooking spray. These steps are important for all grilling, but particularly for burgers. Nothing ruins a burger faster than the bottom sticking to the grill. And your mood won't be great, either, when you have to scrape the charred mess off the grill rack. Both a hot fire and an oiled grill prevent this. During grilling, turn the meat only once. If you flip-flop the burgers (as you would a thin steak), they run the risk of crumbling. And resist the urge to press on the burger with the flat of a metal spatula. That only presses valuable juices out of the meat and leaves it dry.

We suggest cooking burgers until they are medium—although chicken, turkey, and pork burgers should be cooked until medium-well. Some folks like rare beef burgers and if you feel confident about the source of your meat, you can still enjoy them red and juicy in the center. However, as a rule, it's better to cook them until they are at least pink all the way through to be sure that any harmful bacteria have been killed. Use an instant-read thermometer to determine if the burgers are cooked. For beef, we like medium-rare to medium, 140° to 150°F, but the USDA recommends well-done, which is 160°F. For pork, it should register 150° to 155°F, and for all poultry it should be at least 160°F.

Keep in mind that grilling is an inexact science—even more so than cooking on a stove. The heat of the fire will vary from grill to grill and depend, among other things, on the fuel you use and the ambient temperature of the day. Use the times provided in the recipes as guides. Our burgers may be fatter or rounder than yours and, therefore, will take longer. Once you know your own grill and your style of cooking, you will be able to determine the time it takes to cook the perfect burger perfectly.

Grilled burgers are great on their own, but you can load them onto lightly grilled or toasted hamburger rolls, kaiser rolls, or any soft bun. Top them with red onions, lettuce, garden-fresh tomatoes, ketchup, flavored mayonnaises, bold salsas (see pages 248 to 250 and pages 231 to 234 for some great mayonnaise and salsa recipes), mustard, or anything else you particularly like, and then sit back and enjoy the exquisite delight of a really great burger.

Storing and Grilling Ground Meat

Store ground meat in the refrigerator. As with all meat, do not unwrap it and rewrap it in your own plastic wrap or waxed paper. Doing so unnecessarily exposes the meat to the air. If it is leaking, wrap an overlay of paper over the butcher's wrap. Meat is best stored in the rear of the lowest shelf of the refrigerator, which for most refrigerators is the coolest spot. Nevertheless, plan to cook the ground meat within one day of purchase.

Uncooked ground meat freezes well. Put the meat, still in its store wrapping, in a freezer-quality resealable plastic bag, extract as much air as possible from the bag, and freeze the meat in the back of the freezer until frozen solid. After it is solid, you can shift it around in the freezer to make room for new additions. For more on freezing ground and other meat, see page 17.

One you've removed fresh or thawed ground meat from the refrigerator, form the meat into patties and then grill them as soon as you can. Unlike other meat, successful burgers do not depend on the meat coming to room temperature before grilling. In fact, we advise using chilled meat to season and shape the patties and then refrigerating it again before grilling, which helps keep the burgers from crumbling. In every burger recipe, we instruct you to refrigerate the formed patties "until ready to grill." Don't remove it from the refrigerator until the grill or smoker is hot and ready—even if the refrigeration is only for 10 or 15 minutes. The formed patties can be refrigerated for up to four or five hours.

Ground Beef Explained

Buy high-quality ground beef. The ground beef you find in a store usually comes from these parts of the beast:

- Ground chuck, from the forequarter
- Ground round, from the rump
- Ground sirloin, from the hindquarter

We think ground chuck is the best for burgers, although we like the flavor of burgers made with a combination of chuck and sirloin or round. When you buy ground sirloin, make sure it's lean. It may be labeled as 90 or 80 percent lean; the choice is yours. Either, when mixed with chuck, makes a superior burger. We always recommend to our customers a mixture of half chuck, half sirloin or half chuck, half round. If chuck is the only meat available, go for it because of its fat content. The fat guarantees a juicy burger. Ground round is not as desirable on its own. Regardless of the type of ground meat, avoid overhandling; otherwise, the meat can toughen up.

Grinding Your Own

To ensure that you get the best possible ground meat, grind your own at home. Trim the meat of all fat, gristle, silver skin (for red meat), and skin (for poultry), and grind it in a meat grinder or a food processor fitted with a metal blade just until finely ground. If you use a meat grinder, pass the meat through the grinder three times until finely ground. A food processor can pulverize the meat, so take care that it does not become too mushy. And remember to handle the meat gently after grinding to avoid toughening.

Most butchers will grind the meat for you if you buy a whole cut. Ask yours to trim the fat before grinding the meat. Be sure to specify you want the meat finely ground so that it will be easy to form into juicy burgers.

When Americans think hamburger, they think beef. We agree. Very little surpasses a great grilled beef burger—there are times when nothing else hits the spot. For the best, juiciest burgers, we suggest combining equal weights of ground sirloin and ground chuck. The sirloin provides good flavor, and the chuck, with its higher fat content, provides all the juiciness you could desire. The only other cuts of beef we think should be ground are round and tail of porterhouse, which is the section of the steak that extends from its eye (tenderloin). Both round and porterhouse should be mixed with chuck for gloriously juicy results. Of course, if you can find a hanger steak and want to grind it for a burger, you will be rewarded with a terrific meal, too! When working with ground beef, handle the meat gently to avoid toughening.

Classic Hamburger   *Serves 6*

HEAT =

1 POUND GROUND BEEF SIRLOIN

1 POUND GROUND BEEF CHUCK

SALT AND FRESHLY GROUND BLACK
    PEPPER TO TASTE

VEGETABLE OIL COOKING SPRAY

BAJA-STYLE TOMATO SALSA (PAGE 233;
    OPTIONAL)

1. Combine the beef and salt and pepper in a bowl. Using your hands, mix well. Form into 6 patties. Refrigerate until ready to grill.

2. Prepare a charcoal or gas grill: Lightly spray the grill rack with vegetable oil cooking spray. Light the coals or heating elements, and let them burn or heat until hot.

3. Grill the burgers for about 5 minutes. Turn and grill for 4 or 5 minutes longer for medium-well burgers. Serve with the salsa, if desired.

note: To make a cheeseburger, use 3 ounces of sharp Cheddar or Pepper Jack, cut into 6 slices, instead of salsa. After turning burgers, place cheese on top and grill for the remaining 4 to 5 minutes.

Depending on the type of blue cheese you prefer, you may not be able to slice the cheese into firm slices. Most blue cheese crumbles and you will have to scatter the crumbled cheese over the burgers. Blue cheese melts nicely and its flavors blend seductively with the beef and the onions.

Blue-Cheese Burgers with Grilled Onions *Serves 6*

HEAT =

1 POUND GROUND BEEF SIRLOIN

1 POUND GROUND BEEF CHUCK

SALT AND FRESHLY GROUND BLACK
　　PEPPER TO TASTE

VEGETABLE OIL COOKING SPRAY

SIX ½-INCH-THICK SLICES WHITE ONION

CANOLA OIL

3 OUNCES BLUE CHEESE, CUT INTO 6
　　SLICES OR CRUMBLED

1. Combine the beef and salt and pepper in a bowl. Using your hands, mix well. Form into 6 patties. Refrigerate until ready to grill.

2. Prepare a charcoal or gas grill: Lightly spray the grill rack with vegetable oil cooking spray. Light the coals or heating elements, and let them burn or heat until hot.

3. Brush the onion slices with oil and season each with salt and pepper. Grill on the outer edge of the grill for 5 or 6 minutes until the onions begin to soften. Turn and grill for 8 to 9 minutes on the other side, until tender and lightly browned. Lift from the grill, set aside, and keep warm.

4. Grill the burgers for about 5 minutes. Turn and place a slice of cheese or crumble about ½ ounce cheese on top of each burger. Grill the burgers, covered, for 4 to 5 minutes longer, until the cheese melts and the burgers are medium-well. Top with the onions and serve.

We love the idea of putting the cheese inside the burger, rather than on top of it. Make this with chuck alone for a juicier burger, although if you opt for sirloin alone, the cheese-mushroom filling will provide some moisture.

Stuffed Cheeseburger Deluxe *Serves 6*

HEAT =

1 OUNCE DRIED MUSHROOMS (SEE NOTE)

½ CUP VERY HOT WATER

1 POUND GROUND BEEF SIRLOIN

1 POUND GROUND BEEF CHUCK

2 TABLESPOONS WORCESTERSHIRE SAUCE

2 TEASPOONS DRIED MARJORAM

2 TEASPOONS FRESHLY GROUND BLACK PEPPER

4 OUNCES GORGONZOLA CHEESE, CRUMBLED

4 SCALLIONS, WHITE AND GREEN PARTS, FINELY SLICED

1 TEASPOON SALT

VEGETABLE OIL COOKING SPRAY

1. Put the mushrooms in a small bowl and add the hot water. Cover and set aside for about 20 minutes for the mushrooms to hydrate.

2. Combine the beef, Worcestershire sauce, marjoram, and pepper in a bowl. Set aside.

3. Squeeze the mushrooms dry and discard the soaking liquid or reserve it for another use. Mince the mushrooms and combine the mushrooms with the cheese, scallions, and salt. Divide the cheese mixture into 6 equal portions, flattening each into a thick patty about 2½ inches in diameter.

4. Divide the meat into 12 portions and flatten each into a thin patty. Set a cheese patty on 6 of the beef patties and top with the remaining beef patties. Press the edges of the patties closed to seal tightly and hold in the juices during grilling. Refrigerate until ready to grill.

5. Prepare a charcoal or gas grill: Lightly spray the grill rack with vegetable oil cooking spray. Light the coals or heating elements, and let them burn or heat until moderately hot to hot.

6. Grill the burgers for about 5 minutes. Turn and grill for 4 or 5 minutes longer for medium-well burgers. Use a large spatula when turning the burgers, taking care that they do not split.

note: Dried mushrooms are sold in packages containing several different kinds. This mixture works well here, or buy loose dried mushrooms.

For this burger, which has become what we call a "pub favorite" in America, we again combine ground chuck with ground sirloin. If you prefer, you can use one or the other, but remember that a burger made with chuck alone with be juicy but lack the deep flavor of sirloin, while a burger made with sirloin alone will be a little drier. However, the bacon, although cooked, and the mushrooms add a little moisture. For truly spectacular flavor, use Apple Wood Double-Smoked Bacon, page 139, for these burgers.

Bacon-Mushroom Burger   *Serves 6*

HEAT =

6 SLICES BACON (ABOUT 3 OUNCES
   TOTAL)
1 POUND GROUND BEEF SIRLOIN
1 POUND GROUND BEEF CHUCK
1/4 CUP PLUS 2 TABLESPOONS CHOPPED
   ONION
1/4 CUP PLUS 2 TABLESPOONS CHOPPED
   WHITE MUSHROOMS
SALT AND FRESHLY GROUND BLACK
   PEPPER TO TASTE
VEGETABLE OIL COOKING SPRAY

1. Cook the bacon over medium heat in a skillet until cooked but not crispy. Drain on paper towels and when cool enough to handle, tear or chop into small pieces.

2. Combine the beef, bacon, onion, mushrooms, and salt and pepper in a large bowl. Using your hands, mix well. Form into 6 patties. Refrigerate until ready to grill.

3. Prepare a charcoal or gas grill: Lightly spray the grill rack with vegetable oil cooking spray. Light the coals or heating elements, and let them burn or heat until hot.

4. Grill the burgers for about 5 minutes. Turn and grill for 4 or 5 minutes longer for medium-well burgers.

Sausage varies wildly in quality and seasonings. Buy your favorite hot Italian sausage from a butcher or shop you know and like. If you prefer, use another kind of sausage meat, flavored as you prefer, but use the best money can buy.

Spicy Sausage Burgers   *Serves 6*

HEAT =

10 OUNCES GROUND BEEF CHUCK

½ POUND GROUND BEEF SIRLOIN

¾ POUND HOT ITALIAN SAUSAGE MEAT,
   CASINGS REMOVED

SALT AND FRESHLY GROUND BLACK
   PEPPER TO TASTE

VEGETABLE OIL COOKING SPRAY

1. Combine the chuck, sirloin, sausage meat, and salt and pepper in a bowl. Using your hands, mix well. Form into 6 patties. Refrigerate until ready to grill.

2. Prepare a charcoal or gas grill: Lightly spray the grill rack with vegetable oil cooking spray. Light the coals or heating elements, and let them burn or heat until hot.

3. Grill the burgers for about 5 minutes. Turn and grill for 4 to 6 minutes longer for medium-well burgers. Be sure the burgers reach 155°F so that the pork is thoroughly cooked.

If you haven't tried smoked burgers, or even dreamed of them, you are in for a treat. We were knocked over by how extraordinarily good these were—deeply smoky but still tasting very much of beef—and have decided they are our current favorites. Burgers require less than an hour in the smoker, which qualifies as "quick cooking" on the barbecue circuit! We used hickory wood to flavor the burgers, but mesquite would envelop them in equally delicious smoke. When you mix ground sirloin and ground veal—both lean meats—with ground chuck, which is a little fattier, the result is the moistest, most delectable burger you've ever tasted. Ask the butcher to grind veal shoulder or neck meat for these. We suggest our own easy-to-make salsa to top the burgers, along with some mild cheese, but you could vary the condiments to suit your taste.

Smoked Southwest Sirloin Burgers *Serves 6*

HEAT =

BURGERS

¾ POUND LEAN GROUND SIRLOIN

¾ POUND LEAN GROUND CHUCK

½ POUND GROUND VEAL

ONE 4½-OUNCE CAN MILD GREEN
  CHILES, DRAINED AND DICED
  (ABOUT ⅓ CUP)

2 TABLESPOONS MINCED GARLIC
  CHIVES, SCALLIONS, OR ORDINARY
  CHIVES

1 TEASPOON CRUMBLED DRIED OREGANO

1 TEASPOON FRESHLY GROUND BLACK
  PEPPER

1. Make the burgers: In a large bowl, mix ground beef and veal with the chiles, chives, oregano, and pepper. Using your hands, mix well. Make 6 patties about 1 inch thick, and refrigerate until ready to smoke.

2. Prepare and preheat the smoker according to the manufacturer's instructions. We used hickory chips for our burgers.

3. Put the patties directly on the smoker's rack and smoke at 200°F for 40 to 45 minutes for medium-rare (140°F on an instant-read thermometer), or 50 to 55 minutes for medium (registers 150°F). (The times are guidelines only. Test the burgers during cooking to determine how quickly they are cooking.)

4. Meanwhile, make the salsa: In a mixing bowl, combine the tomatoes, green bell pepper, cilantro, onion, lime juice, salt, and pepper. Stir and adjust the seasonings. You will have about 1 cup of salsa. Cover and set aside.

SALSA

2 MEDIUM PLUM TOMATOES, SEEDED
   AND FINELY DICED (ABOUT ¾ CUP)

2 TABLESPOONS MINCED GREEN BELL
   PEPPER

1 TABLESPOON MINCED FRESH
   CILANTRO

1 TEASPOON GRATED SWEET ONION,
   SUCH AS A VIDALIA OR OTHER
   MILD ONION

½ TEASPOON FRESH LIME JUICE

¼ TEASPOON COARSE SALT

FRESHLY GROUND BLACK PEPPER

6 ONION ROLLS OR OTHER HAMBURGER
   ROLLS

8 OUNCES MONTEREY JACK OR
   CHEDDAR, SLICED

6 LARGE LEAVES CRISP LETTUCE

5. Shortly before the burgers are cooked, split and lightly toast the rolls.

6. While they are still in the smoker, top the burgers with cheese slices. Cover or close the smoker and heat 3 to 4 minutes longer, or just until the cheese begins to soften. If you leave the cheese-topped burgers in the smoker for too long, the cheese will ooze and turn oily.

7. Assemble the burgers on the rolls with the lettuce and salsa.

ASK THE BUTCHER

What does it mean if raw beef looks brown? Should it be avoided?

Beef should be pink, never brown and never deep, dark red. Do not buy two-tone meat (pink and brown, for instance). Any beef, whether it's ground or a single steak, will turn brown with extended exposure to oxygen. While this will not hurt you, it is not optimal. If beef has been handled and packaged properly, it will have a desirable, healthy pink appearance.

Ground veal should be from the shank, neck, or shoulder, because these cuts are moist and sweet-flavored. Veal is lovely grilled and lends itself to gentle seasonings—and even when formed into burgers, retains its elegance.

Veal-Mushroom Burgers *Serves 6*

HEAT =

1 TABLESPOON OLIVE OIL

1¼ CUPS FINELY CHOPPED WHITE
    MUSHROOMS

1 LARGE CLOVE GARLIC, MINCED

SALT AND FRESHLY GROUND BLACK
    PEPPER TO TASTE

2 POUNDS GROUND VEAL

2 TABLESPOONS CHOPPED FLAT-LEAF
    PARSLEY

VEGETABLE OIL COOKING SPRAY

ROASTED RED BELL PEPPERS IN OLIVE
    OIL (PAGE 251)

1. Heat the olive oil in a skillet over medium-high heat. Add the mushrooms and cook, stirring, for about 1 minute, until they begin to soften. Add the garlic and salt and pepper and cook for 2 or 3 minutes, until the mushrooms soften. Set aside to cool.

2. Combine the veal, parsley, cooled mushroom mixture, and more salt and pepper in a large bowl. Using your hands, mix well. Form into 6 patties. Refrigerate until ready to grill.

3. Prepare a charcoal or gas grill: Lightly spray the grill rack with vegetable oil cooking spray. Light the coals or heating elements, and let them burn or heat until moderately hot.

4. Grill the burgers for about 8 minutes. Turn and grill for about 6 minutes longer for medium-well burgers. Serve with the red peppers.

When you buy ground lamb, ask that it be ground from the shoulder or shank. A mixture of these cuts is great, too. Ground lamb has enough body and flavor to stand on its own—no need to mix another ground meat with it—although we love seasonings such as garlic and rosemary.

Lamb-Rosemary Burgers   *Serves 6*

HEAT =

2 POUNDS GROUND LAMB

2 TABLESPOONS DIJON MUSTARD

1 TABLESPOON CHOPPED FRESH
   ROSEMARY

1 TEASPOON MINCED GARLIC

1 TEASPOON SALT

1/2 TEASPOON FRESHLY GROUND BLACK
   PEPPER

VEGETABLE OIL COOKING SPRAY

1. Combine the lamb, mustard, rosemary, garlic, salt, and pepper in a large bowl. Using your hands, mix well. Form into 6 patties. Refrigerate until ready to grill.

2. Prepare a charcoal or gas grill: Lightly spray the grill rack with vegetable oil cooking spray. Light the coals or heating elements, and let them burn or heat until hot.

3. Grill the burgers for about 7 minutes. Turn and grill for about 6 minutes longer for medium-well burgers.

Ground lamb can be mixed with all kinds of flavorings, including piquant kalamata olives, and still taste very much like lamb. You can cook the onions and garlic in a skillet in the kitchen or, if you have a gas grill with a side burner, bring the skillet outdoors to cook them.

Greek Lamb Burgers   *Serves 6*

HEAT =

1 TABLESPOON OLIVE OIL

1 CUP DICED ONION

1 LARGE CLOVE GARLIC, MINCED

2 POUNDS GROUND LAMB

2 TABLESPOONS CHOPPED FLAT-LEAF
   PARSLEY

2 TABLESPOONS CHOPPED KALAMATA
   OLIVES

1 TABLESPOON CHOPPED FRESH MINT

VEGETABLE OIL COOKING SPRAY

MINTED SUMMER FRUIT SALSA
   (PAGE 231)

1.   Heat the olive oil in a skillet over medium heat. Add the onions and cook for about 2 minutes, or until they begin to soften. Add the garlic and cook for 2 or 3 minutes longer, until the onions are tender. Set aside to cool.

2.   Combine the lamb, parsley, olives, mint, and cooled onions in a large bowl. Using your hands, mix well. Form into 6 patties. Refrigerate until ready to grill.

3.   Prepare a charcoal or gas grill: Lightly spray the grill rack with vegetable oil cooking spray. Light the coals or heating elements, and let them burn or heat until hot.

4.   Grill the burgers for about 7 minutes. Turn and grill for about 6 minutes longer for medium-well burgers. Serve with the salsa.

Mixing ground turkey with ground pork produces a juicy, flavorful burger that is not overpowered by the pork. By itself, pork is too strong-flavored for burgers.

Spicy Southwestern Pork-Turkey Burgers   *Serves 6*

HEAT =

1¼ POUNDS GROUND TURKEY BREAST

¾ POUND GROUND PORK

⅓ CUP CHOPPED RED BELL PEPPERS

¼ CUP CHOPPED SCALLIONS, WHITE
   AND GREEN PARTS

¼ CUP CHOPPED FRESH CILANTRO

1 JALAPEÑO, SEEDED AND CHOPPED

1 TABLESPOON PLUS 1½ TEASPOONS
   CHILI POWDER

1 TEASPOON GROUND CUMIN

1 TEASPOON SALT

¼ TEASPOON FRESHLY GROUND BLACK
   PEPPER

VEGETABLE OIL COOKING SPRAY

BAJA-STYLE TOMATO SALSA (PAGE 233)
   OR SOUTH-OF-THE-BORDER
   TOMATILLO SALSA (PAGE 232)

1. Combine the turkey, pork, red peppers, scallions, cilantro, jalapeño, chili powder, cumin, salt, and pepper in a large bowl. Using your hands, mix well. Form into 6 patties. Refrigerate until ready to grill.

2. Prepare a charcoal or gas grill: Lightly spray the grill rack with vegetable oil cooking spray. Light the coals or heating elements, and let them burn or heat until hot.

3. Grill the burgers for about 10 minutes. Turn and grill for 7 to 10 minutes longer for medium-well burgers. Serve with a salsa.

A common complaint from customers is that ground turkey breast is dry and tasteless. We agree that it needs moisture, which is why we often combine the turkey with another ground meat and other ingredients. Here, the apples provide flavorful moisture (but don't make it too sweet), while the bread crumbs help hold it in the meat. Mixing the turkey with ground veal helps, too. Serve these with Herbed Mayonnaise (page 250) or Chunky Cranberry Ketchup (page 235).

Turkey-Veal-Apple Burgers   *Serves 6*

HEAT =

1¼ POUNDS GROUND TURKEY BREAST

¾ POUND GROUND VEAL

½ CUP FRESH WHITE OR WHOLE WHEAT
  BREAD CRUMBS

1 FIRM, CRISP APPLE (EITHER SWEET
  OR TART), CORED (BUT NOT PEELED)
  AND DICED

2 TABLESPOONS CHOPPED FRESH THYME

1 TEASPOON CHINESE FIVE-SPICE
  POWDER

1 TEASPOON SALT

1 TEASPOON GROUND WHITE PEPPER

VEGETABLE OIL COOKING SPRAY

1. Combine the turkey, veal, bread crumbs, apple, thyme, five-spice powder, salt, and pepper in a large bowl. Using your hands, mix well. Form into 6 patties. Refrigerate until ready to grill.

2. Prepare a charcoal or gas grill: Lightly spray the grill rack with vegetable oil cooking spray. Light the coals or heating elements, and let them burn or heat until hot.

3. Grill the burgers for 8 to 10 minutes. Turn and grill for 5 to 7 minutes longer for medium-well burgers. The juices will run clear when the burgers are pressed gently with a spatula.

Ground turkey is showing up more and more in butcher shops and supermarket meat departments. When buying it, make sure it's ground from turkey breast. To keep this healthful meat from getting too dry, we've included some lemon juice, which adds a little moisture while accentuating the turkey's mild flavor. Moist hands help when forming these patties, as does well-chilled meat.

Turkey-Sage Burgers   *Serves 6*

HEAT =

2 POUNDS GROUND TURKEY BREAST

4 TEASPOONS CHOPPED FRESH SAGE

1 TABLESPOON FRESH LEMON JUICE

2 TEASPOONS CHOPPED FRESH THYME

SALT AND FRESHLY GROUND BLACK
    PEPPER TO TASTE

VEGETABLE OIL COOKING SPRAY

1. Combine the turkey, sage, lemon juice, thyme, and salt and pepper in a large bowl. Using your hands, mix well. Form into 6 patties. Refrigerate until ready to grill.

2. Prepare a charcoal or gas grill: Lightly spray the grill rack with vegetable oil cooking spray. Light the coals or heating elements, and let them burn or heat until hot.

3. Grill the burgers for 6 to 8 minutes. Turn and grill for 5 to 7 minutes longer for medium-well burgers. The juices will run clear when the burgers are pressed gently with a spatula.

These turkey burgers may be a little more complicated to make than the others, but the zucchini and leek enhance the flavor of the turkey while providing needed moisture. Ground turkey, which is wet when raw, benefits from refrigeration before it is formed into firm patties, but that is not absolutely necessary if the other ingredients are chilled. Moist hands keep the meat from sticking so that the patties are easier to form. Try these with Baja-Style Tomato Salsa (page 233).

Turkey-Zucchini Burgers   *Serves 6*

HEAT =

1 CUP TIGHTLY PACKED, COARSELY
   GRATED ZUCCHINI (ABOUT 1 MEDIUM)
SALT
1 TABLESPOON OLIVE OIL
1 SMALL LEEK, WHITE PART ONLY,
   HALVED LENGTHWISE AND SLICED
   CROSSWISE 1/4 INCH THICK
   (SEE NOTES)
1/2 CUP FRESH BREAD CRUMBS
   (SEE NOTES)
2 TO 3 TABLESPOONS CHICKEN BROTH
1 1/4 POUNDS GROUND TURKEY BREAST
3 TABLESPOONS THINLY SLICED FRESH
   CHIVES
1/8 TEASPOON FRESHLY GRATED NUTMEG
SALT AND FRESHLY GROUND BLACK
   PEPPER TO TASTE
VEGETABLE OIL COOKING SPRAY

1. Put the zucchini in a colander and salt lightly. Mix well and set aside for about 20 minutes, or until it begins to give up its juices. Quickly rinse the zucchini and let it drain, squeezing the moisture from it by the handful. When quite dry, press together into a mass and squeeze again to extract any remaining moisture.

2. Heat the oil over medium heat in a small skillet. Add the leek and sauté for about 5 minutes, or until softened. Add the zucchini and cook, stirring, for 5 or 6 minutes longer, until the zucchini strands separate and any remaining excess moisture evaporates. Remove from the heat and set aside to cool until lukewarm.

3. Add the crumbs and broth to the vegetables and mix well.

4. Combine the turkey, chives, nutmeg, and salt and pepper in a bowl and mix lightly. Add the vegetable–bread crumb mixture and using your hands, mix thoroughly, being careful not to overmix the meat. Cover and refrigerate for about 1 hour until firm.

5. Form the turkey mixture into 6 patties. Refrigerate until ready to grill.

6. Prepare a charcoal or gas grill: Lightly spray the grill rack with vegetable oil cooking spray. Light the coals or heating elements, and let them burn or heat until hot.

7. Grill the burgers for 8 to 10 minutes. Turn and grill for 5 to 7 minutes longer for medium-well burgers. The juices will run clear when the burgers are pressed gently with a spatula.

notes: Leeks must be cleaned thoroughly or they may be gritty. For this recipe, halve lengthwise and soak in a sink of cold water for at least 10 minutes. Drain and rinse well.

To make fresh bread crumbs, process slices of fresh bread in a blender or food processor. We particularly like French- or Italian-style baguettes for crumbs.

Similar in spirit to our Stuffed Cheeseburger Deluxe (page 25), this all-turkey burger is moistened by a stuffing—in this case, a variation of Thanksgiving bread-crumb stuffing. Be sure the edges of the burgers are well sealed so that the moisture does not seep out the sides.

Stuffed Holiday Turkey Burgers with Chunky Cranberry Ketchup *Serves 6*

HEAT =

1 SCANT CUP FRESH WHITE OR WHOLE
   WHEAT BREAD CRUMBS

⅓ CUP CHOPPED FLAT-LEAF PARSLEY

¼ CUP CHOPPED CELERY LEAVES

3 SCALLIONS, WHITE AND GREEN PARTS,
   THINLY SLICED

2 TABLESPOONS UNSALTED BUTTER,
   MELTED

1½ TEASPOONS POULTRY SEASONING
   (SEE NOTE)

1½ TEASPOONS FENNEL SEEDS

1 TEASPOON CHOPPED FRESH THYME

SALT AND FRESHLY GROUND BLACK
   PEPPER TO TASTE

2 POUNDS GROUND TURKEY BREAST

VEGETABLE OIL COOKING SPRAY

CHUNKY CRANBERRY KETCHUP
   (PAGE 235)

1. Combine the bread crumbs, parsley, celery leaves, scallions, butter, poultry seasoning, fennel, and thyme in a bowl. Mix well and season with salt and pepper. Form the stuffing into 6 small patties, each about 2½ inches in diameter.

2. Divide the turkey into 12 portions and flatten each into a thin patty. Set a stuffing patty on 6 of the turkey patties and top with the remaining turkey patties. Press the edges of the patties closed to seal tightly to hold in the juices during grilling. Refrigerate until ready to grill.

3. Prepare a charcoal or gas grill: Lightly spray the grill rack with vegetable oil cooking spray. Light the coals or heating elements, and let them burn or heat until moderately hot to hot.

4. Grill the burgers for 6 to 8 minutes. Turn carefully and grill for 5 to 7 minutes longer for medium-well burgers. The juices will run clear when the burgers are pressed gently with a spatula. Serve with the Chunky Cranberry Ketchup.

note: We used Bell's Poultry Seasoning, which is easy to find in the supermarket spice aisle.

Ground chicken is perhaps the trickiest ground meat to form into burgers because it is so wet, but its mild flavor marries temptingly with the mustard, capers, and herbs into a burger that is out of this world. Chill the meat well—or even partially freeze it—and work with moistened hands to prevent sticking. Because chicken can be so sticky, it helps to cook the burgers on a lightly oiled mesh grill screen that you set directly on the grates.

Chicken Provençal Burgers   *Serves 6*

HEAT =

2 POUNDS GROUND CHICKEN BREAST

¼ CUP DIJON MUSTARD

¼ CUP DRAINED CAPERS (SEE NOTES)

¼ CUP CHOPPED FLAT-LEAF PARSLEY

2 SHALLOTS, CHOPPED

2 TABLESPOONS HERBES DE PROVENCE
   (SEE NOTES)

1 TEASPOON SALT

½ TEASPOON FRESHLY GROUND BLACK
   PEPPER

VEGETABLE OIL COOKING SPRAY

MUSTARD SAUCE (PAGE 230)

1. Combine the chicken, mustard, capers, parsley, shallots, herbs, salt, and pepper in a large bowl. Using your hands, mix well. Form into 6 patties, placing each on a small piece of waxed or parchment paper for easier transfer to the grill. Refrigerate until ready to grill (see notes).

2. Prepare a charcoal or gas grill: Lightly spray the grill rack with vegetable oil cooking spray. Light the coals or heating elements, and let them burn or heat until hot.

3. Grill the burgers for 8 to 10 minutes. Turn and grill for 7 to 9 minutes longer for medium-well burgers. Serve with the Mustard Sauce.

notes: Because the chicken is so moist, it's important that the other ingredients be dry. Drain the capers and pat them dry between sheets of paper towels.

If the chicken seems too moist and you are afraid the patties will break when they are transferred to the grill, put them in the freezer for no longer than 30 minutes to firm but not to freeze them solid.

Herbes de Provence are available in supermarkets, but if you cannot find them, use dried oregano or thyme, or a mixture of the two.

The mild flavors of chicken and veal complement each other, and the veal provides the naturally wet chicken with needed stability. Sherry accentuates the veal's delicate but luxurious flavor.

Chicken-Veal Burgers *Serves 6*

HEAT =

2 TABLESPOONS CANOLA OIL

½ TEASPOON CRUMBLED DRIED
  ROSEMARY

½ TEASPOON FINELY CHOPPED ONION

1 TEASPOON CHINESE FIVE-SPICE
  POWDER

2 TABLESPOONS FINE DRY BREAD
  CRUMBS

2 TABLESPOONS CREAM SHERRY, SUCH
  AS HARVEY'S BRISTOL CREAM
  (OPTIONAL)

SALT AND FRESHLY GROUND BLACK
  PEPPER TO TASTE

1 POUND LEAN GROUND CHICKEN

1 POUND LEAN GROUND VEAL

VEGETABLE OIL COOKING SPRAY

1. Combine the oil, rosemary, onion, five-spice powder, bread crumbs, and sherry, if using, in a large bowl and mix well. Season with salt and pepper.

2. Add the chicken and veal and using your hands, mix well. Form into 6 patties. Refrigerate until ready to grill.

3. Prepare a charcoal or gas grill: Lightly spray the grill rack with vegetable oil cooking spray. Light the coals or heating elements, and let them burn or heat until hot.

4. Grill the burgers for 6 to 8 minutes. Turn and grill for about 5 to 8 minutes longer for medium-well burgers.

BEEF AND VEAL

Without question, beef is the most desired red meat for the grill. In our opinion, it is the best of all meat to grill and apparently backyard chefs across the nation agree, because beef accounts for nearly 45 percent of all meat (including poultry) sold in the country. Granted, much of the beef tossed on the grill is in the form of ground chuck, patted into burgers, but who can deny the glory of a grilled sirloin or perfectly marinated flank steak? For those of us who appreciate high-quality red meat, just the term "char-grilled steak" can set our mouths to watering.

For the retail customer, most beef is sold as prime or choice, grades of beef that denote certain qualities. Other grades exist. These are good, standard, commercial, utility, cutter, and canner—but very few retailers sell any grade below good. Grades are based on tenderness, juiciness, flavor, and cutability (the amount of useable meat on the carcass). Beef is also graded from one to five for cutability.

At our New York City shop and on our website, we sell only prime beef. Considering that only one or two percent of the beef produced in the country makes the grade of prime, you can be sure of getting premium beef when you shop at Lobel's. And we don't stop at insisting on prime beef. We examine every side of beef we buy and reject about 98 percent of them. We look for even, delicate marbling (often called fine-needle marbling or graining), we check the color and texture of the meat, and we look at the color and texture of the fat. Our customers get only the best, but of course, most Americans are not our customers!

Ask your butcher what grade meat he sells and if you are lucky, he will say prime. However, choice beef is excellent and if that is what you can get, there is no need to be disappointed. In fact, Angus beef, a name many Americans know and trust, is choice beef. The top 12 percent of the choice-graded beef is Angus—beef from black Angus cattle. The stocky, short-legged black cattle have become a symbol for great steak (some Angus is sold under the brand name "Black Angus"). High-end choice beef is beautifully marbled and, because of this, has great flavor.

When shopping for beef at the supermarket, look for the words prime or choice on the label (it's unlikely you will find prime meat in the supermarket but no harm in checking). Look for a cut without an excessive amount of outer fat but with good, even marbling (streaks of fat) that webs through the meat. The marbling should not be heavy. The fat should look creamy and moist—not yellowed or gray. The color of the meat should be a healthy-looking cherry red, not a deep, dark red, and it should be evenly hued, not two-toned. Even if the meat is wrapped in plastic, when you press it, the meat should feel firm and finely textured.

Meat is best when aged, although it is not always possible to determine how long a piece of meat in the supermarket has been aged. As we explained earlier, at our shop we age meat for four to six weeks, holding it at 34° to 36°F in coolers with well-circulated refrigerated air. The beef that arrives at most retailers often has only been stored for six to ten days. This is another reason to buy your meat from a reputable butcher with whom you have developed a good relationship. If this is not possible, we suggest ringing the bell at the butcher's counter in the supermarket and asking the butcher who answers the call how long the beef has been aged.

Unlike beef, veal does not require aging. At our shop, we sell veal as fresh as possible and have come to appreciate this delicate meat for its texture and flavor. For the most part, today's veal is raised in open, ventilated pens, so the consumer need not worry about inhumane treatment. Veal is from calves, although most of it comes from animals that are about five months old and weigh 350 to 400 pounds. This is the veal most available to the consumer.

Younger calves, called "vealers" in the trade, are only eight to twelve weeks old and weigh 150 to 250 pounds. Their meat is nearly white, which explains why this tender, mild meat is sometimes described as "milk-fed," although it's not too common. True milk-fed veal is even more rare; only the youngest calves qualify and these are hard to find.

Veal should not be marbled, as the animals do not grow large enough to develop much fat. For this same reason, many cuts of veal are not ideal for grilling; there is not enough fat to keep the meat moist during the fast, dry-heat cooking of grilling. In this book we grill thick veal chops and cut veal sirloin or loin for brochettes and kebobs, and we mix ground veal with other ground meat in the burger chapter, but otherwise we leave veal for slower indoor cooking, or quick sautéing.

Because the quality of veal must be superior, it is a good idea to buy it from a butcher you know. Regardless of its age, veal meat should be white or very light pink. It should look firm, moist, and velvety, and its soft bones should be red, appearing full of blood. While there will be no noticeable marbling, the thin layer of exterior fat should be white.

Preparing Beef and Veal for Grilling

When you get the meat home from the butcher or supermarket, immediately stow it in the coldest part of the refrigerator, which usually is the rear of the lowest shelf. Do not unwrap it; you do not want it to be unnecessarily exposed to the air, and keeping it wrapped in its original packaging is a good idea.

When you are ready to prepare the beef—whether you are marinating it or grilling it virtually unadorned—take it from the refrigerator and let it come to room temperature, which means leaving it on the counter for about 30 minutes, still wrapped. If it is a particularly hot, humid summer day, reduce the counter time. Pat the meat dry with paper towels and then either marinate it, rub it with dry rub, or otherwise prepare it for the grill. In our recipes we do not instruct you to pat the meat dry before marinating, rubbing, or otherwise preparing it, because it is universally appropriate whenever beef, veal, poultry, lamb, or pork is grilled. We do remind you in the recipes for smoking to pat the meat dry with paper towels because if for some reason you forget, the smoking process will not be as effective as it should be.

How to Grill a Perfect Steak

Prime or choice sirloin, club, T-bone, and other high-quality steaks don't need to be marinated. They are flavorful and tender enough to be cooked with no more seasoning than salt and pepper.

After patting the room-temperature meat dry, season it with salt and pepper. Set the steaks over moderately-hot to hot coals. Sear the steaks for 2 or 3 minutes on each side, turning them with tongs to avoid piercing the meat so that none of the precious juices escape. When the steaks are seared on both sides, remove them from the grill, brush the steaks with a little olive oil, and then return the meat to the grill until it is cooked to the desired degree of doneness. See the table on page 44 for grilling times.

Total Grilling Times for Perfect Steaks
(including searing)*

Steak Thickness	Rare	Medium	Medium-Well
1 inch	10 minutes	15 minutes	20 minutes
1¼ inches to 1½ inches	12 minutes	17 minutes	22 minutes
1¾ inches to 2 inches	15 minutes	20 minutes	25 minutes

*For filet mignon steaks, decrease the cooking times by one minute. Times may vary depending on the intensity of the coals.

Flip-Flop Grilling

When grilling steaks that are thinner than one inch, employ the flip-flop method. Grill the steaks to sear them for 2 or 3 minutes on each side over high heat. Then turn them every minute or so until they are cooked to the desired degree of doneness. Sure, this requires standing at the grill for 8 to 10 minutes, but it's not hard work and will avoid the disaster of meat that is burned on the outside and undercooked in the center. When steaks and chops are thicker than an inch, such constant flipping is not necessary. Bone-in chicken parts do best when flip-flopped, too.

Grilling Super-Thick Steaks

If you are fortunate enough to have a steak that is two and one-half inches thick or thicker, do not cook it directly over hot coals. Grill it using the indirect method, as explained on page 7, and take care that it cooks evenly. If using a gas grill, cook it over low heat. Cover the grill, lifting the cover periodically to check for flare-ups. If the steak is engulfed by flames, move it to a cooler part of the grill and when the flames subside, return the meat to the hotter fire. Remove the grill cover during the last 4 or 5 minutes of cooking and move the steak nearer to the heat source, flipping once, so that it will char a little and form a nice crust. Let the meat rest for about 5 minutes before slicing.

With meat this thick, use a meat thermometer to determine when the meat is done. Very rare beef should be 130°F, and medium-rare beef 140°F. Remove the steak from the grill when the thermometer registers a few degrees below these temperatures; the meat continues cooking during resting.

Basting with Beer

On a hot summer day, few things taste as good as a cold beer. We also think that beer tastes good on meat. Regardless of what we are grilling—steak, standing rib roast, butterflied leg of lamb, pork loin, chicken, or game—we often baste the grilling meat with dark beer or ale. Brush some beer or ale on the grilling meat two or three times during cooking to give the meat a subtle yet deep flavor. The beer—which can be at room temperature—also cools the meat momentarily during grilling, which can help moderate cooking.

Selecting Round Steak

When buying round steak, which is cut from the rump section of the hindquarter, ask the butcher to cut it from the front section of the round, called the top round. The first few slices of top round are the most tender and flavorful. Top round has very little fat, which is why it so often is marinated to give it flavor and moisture. Round steak makes good London broil, which should be one of the first cuts of the round. It can also be roasted. Its lack of fat means it has little marbling and so while less expensive than other cuts, it is also less flavorful.

What Is Flank Steak?

There is only one flank steak to a side of beef and it comes from the lower section of the short loin. It is a lean, flat, boneless muscle with fibers that run lengthwise through the meat. Flank steak is best when grilled or broiled—it does not lend itself to slow cooking. Once cooked, flank steak should be cut on the diagonal into thin strips, cutting across the fibers. This brings out its flavor and renders the meat tender. Flank steak is the most common cut used in recipes calling for London broil, although in some instances, top round is also called London broil.

Bison

While bison is popular in some parts of the country, we don't sell a lot of it at our shop in New York City. When we offer it to our customers, we generally sell them fillets or strip steaks. Bison is not as marbled as beef and so should be grilled only until rare or medium-rare. Once it gets past these points, the lean meat tends to toughen. It takes well to most marinades.

Shaped similar to a T-bone, the porterhouse is made up of a large portion of shell steak on one side of the "T" and a smaller portion of tenderloin on the other. However, the porterhouse is cut from the part of the short loin nearest the sirloin and therefore contains a more generous section of tenderloin, which also makes for a larger steak. A single steak is usually 1¼ to 3 inches thick and weighs one and a half to two pounds. One good-sized steak easily feeds four. Porterhouses are also distinguished by their "tail," which is the section of the cut that extends from the tenderloin; it should be folded back against the steak and held in place with a small metal or bamboo skewer for even grilling. The tail can also be removed, ground, and cooked alongside the steak as a burger. When grilling any steak, but particularly a porterhouse steak with a tail, watch for flare-ups when the fat drips on the coals. Extinguish them with a spritz of water from a spray bottle.

Lobel's Classic Grilled Porterhouse Steak   *Serves 4 or 5*

HEAT =

ONE 3- TO 3½-POUND PORTERHOUSE
   STEAK, ABOUT 2 INCHES THICK
½ LEMON
METAL OR BAMBOO SKEWER
2 TABLESPOONS OLIVE OIL
2 CLOVES GARLIC, CRUSHED
2 SCALLIONS, WHITE PARTS ONLY,
   FINELY CHOPPED
SALT AND FRESHLY GROUND BLACK
   PEPPER TO TASTE
VEGETABLE OIL COOKING SPRAY

1. Trim the outer fat from the steak, or ask the butcher to do so. Rub the remaining fat areas with the cut lemon to prevent burning and smoking. Score both sides of the tail of the steak, fold it back toward the main body, and attach it to the meat with a small metal skewer or sturdy bamboo skewer. (If using a bamboo skewer, soak it in water for about 20 minutes first.)

2. Combine the olive oil, garlic, scallions, and salt and pepper in a shallow glass or ceramic dish. Put the steak in the dish and turn several times to coat. Cover and marinate at room temperature for 1 hour or in the refrigerator for as long as 4 hours, letting the meat come to room temperature before grilling. Turn the meat once or twice during marinating.

3. Prepare a charcoal or gas grill: Lightly spray the grill rack with vegetable oil cooking spray. Light the coals or heating elements, and let them burn or heat until moderately hot to hot.

4. Lift the steak from the dish. Discard the marinade. Grill the steak, covered, for 10 to 12 minutes. Turn and grill, covered, for 10 to 12 minutes longer for medium-rare, or until it is cooked to the desired degree of doneness. Let the meat rest for a few minutes before serving.

Grill a boneless sirloin or rib-eye steak with this spicy marinade for a hint of piquancy. The thickness of the steak is important so make sure you buy the meat from a butcher who will cut a two-inch-thick sirloin for you.

Sirloin Steak in Spicy Marinade

Serves 6

HEAT =

ONE 3- TO 3½-POUND BONELESS
   SIRLOIN, ABOUT 2 INCHES THICK
½ CUP SOY SAUCE
¼ CUP FRESH LEMON JUICE
2 TABLESPOONS OLIVE OIL
2 TEASPOONS GROUND CUMIN
1 TEASPOON CAYENNE
2 SCALLIONS, WHITE AND GREEN PARTS,
   THINLY SLICED
1 JALAPEÑO, SEEDED AND SLICED
1 CLOVE GARLIC, MINCED
FRESHLY GROUND BLACK PEPPER TO
   TASTE
VEGETABLE OIL COOKING SPRAY

1. Trim the outer fat from the steak, or ask the butcher to do so.

2. Combine the soy sauce, lemon juice, oil, cumin, cayenne, scallions, jalapeño, garlic, and pepper in a glass or ceramic bowl. Put the steak in a shallow glass or ceramic dish and pour the marinade over the meat. Cover and marinate at room temperature for 30 minutes or refrigerate for as long as 2 hours, letting the meat come to room temperature before grilling. Turn the meat once or twice.

3. Prepare a charcoal or gas grill: Lightly spray the grill rack with vegetable oil cooking spray. Light the coals or heating elements, and let them burn or heat until moderately hot to hot.

4. Lift the steak from the dish. Discard the marinade. Grill the steak, covered, for 10 to 12 minutes. Turn and grill, covered, for 10 to 12 minutes longer for medium-rare, or until it is cooked to the desired degree of doneness. Let the meat rest for a few minutes before serving.

The T-bone is easily identified by the T-shaped bone in the center of the cut. The steak comes from the center section of the short loin, between the porterhouse and the club steak—and while it tastes similar to porterhouse, it has a smaller tenderloin and shorter tail. For this recipe, you can substitute porterhouse or club steak.

T-Bone for Two   *Serves 2 or 3*

HEAT =

ONE 2-POUND T-BONE STEAK WITH TAIL,
   ABOUT 2 INCHES THICK
1 TO 2 TABLESPOONS OLIVE OIL
1 TABLESPOON FRESHLY CRACKED
   BLACK PEPPER
1 TEASPOON DRIED ROSEMARY
VEGETABLE OIL COOKING SPRAY
1 TO 2 TEASPOONS COARSE SALT
MUSHROOM-SAGE SAUCE (PAGE 224)

1. Rub the steak with the olive oil, pepper, and rosemary. Set aside for 20 to 30 minutes until ready to grill.

2. Prepare a charcoal or gas grill: Lightly spray the grill rack with vegetable oil cooking spray. Light the coals or heating elements, and let them burn or heat until moderately hot to hot.

3. Rub the salt into both sides of the steak. Grill for 8 to 10 minutes on each side for medium-rare meat. Let the meat rest for a few minutes and serve with the Mushroom-Sage Sauce.

Filet mignon is one of the most popular steaks for grilling. These are also known as tenderloin steaks. The small, thick steaks, perfect for individual servings, are soft and tender, which is appealing to grill cooks. But filet mignon is not always as flavorful as other steaks. Therefore, we think it's important to rub it with olive oil, salt, and pepper before grilling to enhance the flavor. Here, we serve each one with a pat of melting flavorful butter, too.

Grilled Filet Mignon with Gorgonzola-Scallion Compound Butter *Serves 4*

HEAT =

4 FILET MIGNONS, EACH 1½ INCHES
　　THICK

1 TO 2 TABLESPOONS OLIVE OIL

1 TABLESPOON CRACKED BLACK PEPPER

VEGETABLE OIL COOKING SPRAY

1 TO 2 TEASPOONS COARSE SALT

4 TABLESPOONS GORGONZOLA-SCALLION
　　COMPOUND BUTTER (PAGE 228) OR
　　HORSERADISH-SCALLION COMPOUND
　　BUTTER (PAGE 227)

1. Rub the steaks with olive oil and pepper. Set aside for 20 to 30 minutes until ready to grill.

2. Prepare a charcoal or gas grill: Lightly spray the grill rack with vegetable oil cooking spray. Light the coals or heating elements, and let them burn or heat until moderately hot to hot.

3. Rub the salt into both sides of the steaks. Grill for 5 to 6 minutes on each side for rare meat or for 6 to 7 minutes for medium-rare meat. Brush a little more olive oil on the steaks after they are turned. Place a pat of butter on top of each filet mignon as soon as it comes off the grill so that the butter begins to melt on top of the meat. Let the meat rest for a few minutes before serving.

For a classic steak au poivre, we recommend as fine a steak as you can find, such as shell steak, also known as New York strip, Kansas City strip, and strip loin. Filet mignon is also good for this recipe.

Grilled Steak au Poivre   *Serves 4*

HEAT =

4 BONELESS SHELL STEAKS, EACH
   ABOUT 2 INCHES THICK AND
   WEIGHING 12 TO 14 OUNCES
¼ CUP CRACKED BLACK OR BLACK AND
   WHITE PEPPERCORNS
VEGETABLE OIL COOKING SPRAY

1. Trim the outer fat from the steak, or ask the butcher to do so.

2. Press the peppercorns into the meat on both sides.

3. Prepare a charcoal or gas grill: Lightly spray the grill rack with vegetable oil cooking spray. Light the coals or heating elements, and let them burn or heat until hot.

4. Grill the steaks for 7 minutes. Turn and grill for 8 to 10 minutes longer for medium-rare, or until they are cooked to the desired degree of doneness. Let the meat rest for a few minutes before serving.

Bacon-Mushroom Burger (page 26)

Grilled Sirloin Steak with Green Chile Sauce (page 52)

Sirloin Steak Kabobs with Rosemary-Brushed Potatoes and Red Peppers (page 68)

Tortilla-Wrapped Round Steak (page 63)

Lamb Chops with Grilled Stuffed Mushrooms (page 100)

Southwest-Style Pork Chops with Ancho Chile Powder (page 123)

Grilled Chicken Breasts and Apple Rings with Maple Syrup Marinade (page 162)

Grilled Quail with Raspberry-Cranberry Cumberland Sauce (page 210)

owboy steaks are big, brawny, extra-thick, bone-in rib-eye steaks, weighing in at about two pounds each. We french the rib bone, which means it's stripped of meat and so adds to the steak's robust appearance. These huge steaks, which take a good 30 or 35 minutes to cook, develop a lovely crust during grilling, and while they need no accompaniment, we like them with a dab of zesty chipotle mayonnaise. Make sure the thick steak has time to come to room temperature before grilling and then grill it over indirect heat for all but the initial searing. One will easily serve two people, and probably even three.

Cowboy Steak with Chipotle Mayonnaise   *Serves 2*

HEAT =

STEAKS

ONE 2-POUND COWBOY STEAK, ABOUT
   2½ INCHES THICK
OLIVE OIL
2 TEASPOON CRUSHED FRESH BLACK
   PEPPERCORNS
SALT AND FRESHLY GROUND BLACK
   PEPPER
VEGETABLE OIL COOKING SPRAY

MAYONNAISE

1 SMALL CHIPOTLE CHILE IN ADOBO
   SAUCE, WIPED DRY AND CHOPPED
   FINE (ABOUT 2 TABLESPOONS; SEE
   NOTE ON PAGE 000)
½ CUP MAYONNAISE, STORE-BOUGHT
   OR HOMEMADE
1 SMALL CLOVE GARLIC, MINCED
1 TABLESPOON CHOPPED FRESH CILANTRO
1 TABLESPOON FRESH LEMON JUICE
SALT AND FRESHLY GROUND BLACK
   PEPPER

1. Make the steaks: Rub both sides and the sides of the steak with olive oil. Sprinkle the crushed peppercorns on both sides of the steak, pressing them lightly into the meat. Season lightly with salt and pepper.

2. Prepare a charcoal or gas grill for indirect cooking (see page 7): Lightly spray the grill rack with vegetable oil cooking spray. Light the coals or heating elements, and let them burn or heat until hot.

3. Grill the steak over the hottest part of the grill for about 5 minutes. Turn and sear for 5 minutes on the other side. Move the steak to the cool part of the grill and grill, covered, for 15 minutes. Turn and grill for 15 to 20 minutes longer for medium-rare or until it is cooked to the desired degree of doneness.

4. Prepare the chipotle mayonnaise: In a small bowl, stir the chile into the mayonnaise. Add the garlic, cilantro, and lemon juice, stir gently, and season to taste with salt and pepper. Cover and refrigerate if not using within 30 minutes.

5. Let the meat rest for a few minutes before serving with the mayonnaise on the side.

In this recipe, note that the chiles for the sauce can be lightly grilled over the fire before you grill the steak. Be sure to have all the other sauce ingredients ready so that you can prepare the chiles and finish the sauce while the steak grills—or as soon as it is lifted from the grill. If you have a gas grill with a gas burner, use it to cook the sauce.

Grilled Sirloin Steak with Green Chile Sauce   *Serves 6*

HEAT =

STEAK

3³⁄₄- TO 4-POUND BONELESS SIRLOIN,
   ABOUT 2 INCHES THICK

1 TABLESPOON OLIVE OIL

¹⁄₂ TEASPOON CRUSHED CUMIN SEED

1 TEASPOON DRIED OREGANO

1 TEASPOON DRIED THYME LEAVES

1 CLOVE GARLIC

SALT AND FRESHLY GROUND BLACK
   PEPPER TO TASTE

VEGETABLE OIL COOKING SPRAY

1. Trim the outer fat from the steak, or ask the butcher to do so.

2. Rub the entire surface of the meat with the olive oil. Combine the cumin, oregano, thyme, garlic, and salt and pepper in a small bowl. Using your fingers, rub evenly on both sides of the steak and put the steak in a shallow glass or ceramic dish. Cover and refrigerate for at least 1 hour or overnight, letting the meat come to room temperature before grilling.

3. To make the sauce, prepare a charcoal or gas grill or preheat the broiler. If using a grill, the coals should be moderately hot to hot. Set the chiles over the heat or under the broiler and grill or broil for about 5 minutes on each side until lightly charred and fragrant. Remove from the grill or broiler and set aside in a paper bag or cover with a thickness of paper towels to cool. When cool enough to handle, peel the skin using your fingers or a dull knife. (Do not peel the chiles under running water or their flavor will be diluted.) Cut off and discard the stems and caps. Slit the chiles, scrape out the seeds (don't worry if a few remain), and thinly slice the chiles. You will have about 1 cup of chiles.

4. Meanwhile, if you haven't already, prepare a charcoal or gas grill: Lightly spray the grill rack with vegetable oil cooking spray. Light the coals or heating elements, and let them burn or heat until moderately hot to hot.

SAUCE

6 FRESH ANAHEIM GREEN CHILES

1 TABLESPOON CANOLA OIL

1 YELLOW ONION, HALVED, AND THINLY
    SLICED CROSSWISE

1 LARGE CLOVE GARLIC, SLICED

1 CUP HALF-AND-HALF

3 TABLESPOONS CREAM CHEESE

3 TABLESPOONS SOUR CREAM

SALT TO TASTE

5. Heat the oil in a skillet over medium heat. Add the onions and garlic and cook, stirring, for about 5 minutes, or until the onions are softened. Add the chiles and cook for 3 to 4 minutes longer, until fragrant.

6. Increase the heat to medium-high and add the half-and-half. Cook, stirring, for about 10 minutes, or until the sauce is reduced by half. Cover and set aside to keep warm while grilling the steak.

7. Grill the steak for 10 to 12 minutes. Turn and grill for 10 to 12 minutes longer for medium-rare, or until it is cooked to the desired degree of doneness. Let the meat rest for a few minutes before serving.

8. Set the pan with the sauce over low heat. Add the cream cheese and stir until smooth. Stir in the sour cream and season with salt. While stirring, heat the sauce just until hot. Do not let the sauce boil. Serve immediately with the steak.

ASK ⸛ BUTCHER

What is aged beef? Is it better than beef that is not aged?

Aged beef is superior to unaged beef in texture and flavor. At Lobel's, we dry age all our beef for four to six weeks in humidity-free cold lockers where the temperature is maintained at 34° to 36°F. During this time, enzymes break down the fibers to leave the meat more tender and flavorful. This is an expensive process. Not only do we have to maintain the cold storage areas, but as it hangs, the meat loses moisture and blood and so it shrinks. By the time we trim the meat and offer it for sale, it has lost 30 to 35 percent of its original size. We think it's worth it: The firm beef with its relatively dry appearance is far tastier than unaged beef.

Some butchers "wet age" beef for two to three weeks in the Cryovac wrapping in which they arrive from the packing house. This, more than dry aging, is the industry norm and while it improves the tenderness of the beef, it does little for its flavor. Very few supermarkets age meat in any way. From wholesaler to supermarket, the meat is in Cryovac for 7 to 10 days, tops.

Any tender steak tastes great with a classic teriyaki marinade. In this recipe we suggest porterhouse, but you won't go wrong with sirloin or T-bone. The T-bone comes from the center section of the short loin, between the porterhouse and the club steak, and, although it has a smaller fillet, is very similar in texture and flavor to the porterhouse. If you would rather grill these fine steaks without marinating them first, please do and serve them with the grilled pineapple. Use the marinade, too, on round steak or rib-eye steak. Rib-eye steaks are fattier and less tender than club steaks, which they resemble in appearance. Round steaks are from the rump and are quite lean, which is why they do well when marinated—the lack of fat means the meat is drier than other cuts and so benefits from a good soaking in a flavorful liquid.

Teriyaki Steak with Grilled Pineapple
Serves 6

HEAT =

ONE 3¾- TO 4-POUND PORTERHOUSE
   STEAK, ABOUT 2 INCHES THICK
SMALL METAL OR BAMBOO SKEWER
1 CUP TERIYAKI MARINADE (PAGE 239)
VEGETABLE OIL COOKING SPRAY
SIX 1½- TO 2-INCH-THICK FRESH
   PINEAPPLE RINGS
CANOLA OIL
¼ CUP PACKED LIGHT OR DARK BROWN
   SUGAR

1. Trim the outer fat from the steak, or ask the butcher to do so. Score both sides of the tail of the steak, fold it back toward the main body, and attach it to the meat with the skewer. (If using a bamboo skewer, soak it in water for about 20 minutes first.)

2. Put the steak in a shallow glass or ceramic dish and pour the marinade over the meat, turning several times to coat. Cover and marinate at room temperature for 30 minutes or refrigerate for as long as 2 hours, letting the meat come to room temperature before grilling. Turn the meat once or twice.

3. Prepare a charcoal or gas grill: Lightly spray the grill rack with vegetable oil cooking spray. Light the coals or heating elements, and let them burn or heat until moderately hot to hot.

4. Lift the steak from the dish. Discard the marinade. Grill the steak for 10 to 12 minutes. Turn and grill for 10 to 12 minutes longer for medium-rare, or until it is cooked to the desired degree of doneness. Let the meat rest for a few minutes before serving.

5. Meanwhile, brush the pineapple slices on both sides with a little canola oil and sprinkle each one with about 2 teaspoons of brown sugar. Lay them sugared side down on the outer edge of the grill, away from the hottest heat. Grill for about 7 minutes, turn, and grill for 6 or 7 minutes longer, until lightly browned and tender. Serve set on top or alongside the steak.

ASK THE BUTCHER

Does the thickness of the steak matter when you grill it?

We like to grill steaks that are at least an inch thick and, because we can cut our steaks as thick as we like, we frequently take home two-inch-thick steaks. The thick meat holds more of its natural juices and so comes off the grill deliciously juicy. It also takes long enough to cook to the right internal temperature to give the outside time to develop a nice, charred crust. For thinner steaks, try our flip-flop method explained on page 44.

We rely on a peppery rub to give these already flavorful steaks a mouth-watering jolt. Temper the heat with a crisp green salad and creamy potato salad or mashed potatoes. In our opinion, rib-eye steaks are among the best for the grill, especially if you can find prime beef rib-eyes with heavy, even marbling. High-end choice beef is the next best. Avoid any steaks with ivory colored fat and bright red meat; instead seek out steaks with fine, white, needlepoint marbling and pink meat.

Sizzling Spicy Rib-Eye Steaks *Serves 6*

HEAT =

SIX 12- TO 14-OUNCE BONELESS RIB-
EYE STEAKS, EACH ABOUT 1½
INCHES THICK
2 TABLESPOONS PEPPERY DRY RUB
(PAGE 241)
1 TEASPOON CHIPOTLE OR OTHER CHILI
POWDER
3 TABLESPOONS OLIVE OIL
VEGETABLE OIL COOKING SPRAY

1. Trim the outer fat from the steaks, or ask the butcher to do so.

2. In a small mixing bowl, blend the spice rub with the chili powder. Place the steaks in a single layer in a shallow glass or ceramic dish and rub them on both sides with the oil. Rub the chili mixture thoroughly over them. Cover and set aside at room temperature for 15 to 20 minutes.

3. Prepare a charcoal or gas grill: Lightly spray the grill rack with vegetable oil cooking spray. Light the coals or heating elements, and let them burn or heat until moderately hot to hot.

4. Grill the steaks for 10 minutes. Turn and grill for 8 to 10 minutes longer for medium-rare, or until they are cooked to the desired degree of doneness. For nice looking grill marks and even cooking, turn the steaks once more just before taking them from the grill. Let the meat rest about 5 minutes before serving.

Hanger steak is also known as "butcher's tenderloin" because traditionally butchers saved this full-flavored but unattractive-looking cut for themselves. It "hangs" between the rib cage and the loin cage, which explains its name. All hanger steaks are approximately the same size and weight. In recent years, the cut has become popular with chefs and steak lovers, and once you try one, you will understand why. Hanger steak needs no fancy preparation, just a brushing of oil and a little salt and pepper. You probably will not find hanger steaks in the meat section of the supermarket, but ask a good butcher for one, making sure it is prime or choice beef. (Hanger steak also makes great hamburgers.) It's best to have the butcher remove the center vein, which runs lengthwise down the center of the steak. This leaves the steak in two pieces, neither of uniform thickness, which can make grilling tricky—but well worth the effort.

Grilled Hanger Steak   *Serves 2 or 3*

HEAT =

VEGETABLE OIL COOKING SPRAY
1 HANGER STEAK (ABOUT 1 POUND),
   TRIMMED AND CENTER VEIN
   REMOVED
OLIVE OIL
COARSE OR KOSHER SALT AND FRESHLY
   GROUND BLACK PEPPER TO TASTE

1. Prepare a charcoal or gas grill: Lightly spray the grill rack with vegetable oil cooking spray. Light the coals or heating elements, and let them burn or heat until moderately hot to hot.

2. Brush the steak with olive oil and sprinkle on both sides with salt and pepper. Gently press the salt and pepper into the meat.

3. Sear the meat for about 1 minute on each side and then grill for 12 to 15 minutes for medium-rare, depending on the thickness of the steak. If the thin end of the steak cooks before the fatter end is done, position the steak so that the thin end is on the edge of the grill. Turn the steak frequently during grilling. Let it rest for about 5 minutes before slicing.

Skirt steaks cook in a flash—less than 8 or 10 minutes—but should be marinated first in a brew bolstered by a flavorful acidic ingredient such as the pomegranate juice used here, fortified by the molasses. Although skirt steaks are relatively inexpensive, it's a good idea to buy prime or choice steaks and pay close attention when you grill them. This way you will be guaranteed tender, absolutely delicious meat.

Three-Pepper Pomegranate Skirt Steaks   *Serves 6*

HEAT =

2 TEASPOONS WHOLE BLACK
  PEPPERCORNS

2 TEASPOONS WHOLE GREEN
  PEPPERCORNS IN BRINE, DRAINED
  AND RINSED

2 TEASPOONS COARSE SALT

½ CUP POMEGRANATE JUICE (SEE
  NOTE)

2 TABLESPOONS MOLASSES

2 TABLESPOONS OLIVE OIL

2 LARGE SHALLOTS, PEELED AND THINLY
  SLICED

½ TEASPOON THAI CHILI PASTE

2 TO 2¼ POUNDS SKIRT STEAK (3 OR 4
  PIECES), TRIMMED OF EXCESS FAT

VEGETABLE OIL COOKING SPRAY

1. With a mortar and pestle, roughly crush the black and green peppercorns and the salt.

2. In a small bowl, stir together the pomegranate juice, molasses, oil, shallots, and chili paste. Stir in the crushed pepper mixture; you should have about 1¼ cups of marinade.

3. Lay the steaks in a single layer in a shallow glass or ceramic dish. Pour the marinade over the meat. Turn the meat to coat, cover, and refrigerate for at least 2 hours, letting the meat come to room temperature before grilling, or set aside at room temperature for no longer than 30 minutes before refrigerating or grilling.

4. Prepare a charcoal or gas grill: Lightly spray the grill rack with vegetable oil cooking spray. Light the coals or heating elements, and let them burn or heat until moderately hot to hot.

5. Lift the steaks from the dish, letting most of the marinade drip off. Pat the meat dry and set it aside at room temperature for about 15 minutes.

6. Grill the steaks for 2 to 4 minutes on each side for medium-rare, depending on thickness, or until they are cooked to the desired degree of doneness. Let the steaks rest for about 5 minutes before slicing and serving.

note: Pomegranate juice is sold in most supermarkets in the produce section alongside fresh orange juice, apple cider, and other fresh juices. It requires refrigeration.

ASK THE BUTCHER

What are the best cuts for a perfect grilled steak?

This is one of the most common questions we're asked (along with "How do you cook a perfect steak?") and it's a tough one, primarily because many different cuts do beautifully on the grill and we have supplied recipes for all of our favorites. Thick sirloin, club, rib-eye, porterhouse, and T-bone steaks are great choices, and are even delicious when grilled unadorned. We love shell steaks, too, for their tenderness and flavor. Flank and skirt steaks, marinated to enhance their flavor, are wonderful on the grill. If you are lucky enough to find a good hanger steak, grill it for a superb treat.

Flank steak is lean, flat, boneless meat. Because its fibers run lengthwise, it is best to slice it on an angle, which means perpendicular to the long, fine fibers running through the meat. For six servings, you may have to buy it in two smaller pieces to equal three pounds.

Thai-Style Marinated
Flank Steak   *Serves 6*

HEAT =

¼ CUP RICE WINE VINEGAR

¼ CUP FRESH LIME JUICE

¼ CUP DARK TOASTED SESAME OIL

¼ CUP SOY SAUCE

ASIAN CHILI SAUCE, TO TASTE (SEE
　NOTE)

2 TABLESPOONS CHOPPED FRESH
　GINGER

2 TABLESPOONS CHOPPED SCALLIONS,
　WHITE AND GREEN PARTS

2 OR 3 CLOVES GARLIC, CHOPPED

2 TO 3 TABLESPOONS CHOPPED FRESH
　CILANTRO PLUS EXTRA FOR GARNISH

SALT AND FRESHLY GROUND BLACK
　PEPPER TO TASTE

3 POUNDS 1¼-INCH-THICK FLANK
　STEAK OR LONDON BROIL, TRIMMED

VEGETABLE OIL COOKING SPRAY

1. Whisk together all the ingredients except the steak and cilantro used for garnish in a shallow glass or ceramic dish. Put the steak in the marinade, turning several times to coat. Cover and refrigerate for at least 1 hour and as long as 8 hours, letting the meat come to room temperature before grilling.

2. Prepare a charcoal or gas grill: Lightly spray the grill rack with vegetable oil cooking spray. Light the coals or heating elements, and let them burn or heat until moderately hot to hot.

3. Lift the steak from the dish, letting the marinade drip back into the dish. Grill the meat for 6 or 7 minutes, brushing several times with the marinade during the first 5 minutes of grilling. (The oil in the marinade may cause flare-ups.) Turn the steak and grill for 6 to 7 minutes longer for medium-rare, or until it is cooked to the desired degree of doneness.

4. Let the steak rest at room temperature for about 5 minutes before slicing on the diagonal into thin strips. Serve garnished with cilantro.

note: Asian chili sauce is sold in most supermarkets and Asian markets. It may be Chinese, Thai, or Vietnamese, and will vary in heat and intensity. It usually is made from red chiles, but some are made from green chiles. The kind you use does not matter as much as your own preference.

As with the preceding recipe, you may need to buy two pieces of meat for three pounds of flank steak. London broil and flank steak are practically synonymous—although some London broils are cut from the top round. Either cut is fine for this recipe and for others calling for flank steak or London broil.

Thyme-Mustard Crusted
Flank Steak   *Serves 6*

HEAT =

3 TABLESPOONS DIJON MUSTARD

1 TABLESPOON WHITE WINE

1 TABLESPOON CHOPPED FRESH THYME
   OR 1 TEASPOON DRIED

1 TABLESPOON FRESHLY CRACKED
   PEPPER

2 TABLESPOONS OLIVE OIL

3 POUNDS 1½-INCH-THICK FLANK
   STEAK OR LONDON BROIL, TRIMMED

VEGETABLE OIL COOKING SPRAY

1. Stir together the mustard, wine, thyme, and pepper in a small bowl. Whisk in the olive oil.

2. Place the meat in a single layer in a shallow ceramic or glass dish. Spoon the mustard mixture over the meat, spreading to cover. Turn the meat and coat the other side. Cover and refrigerate for at least 2 hours, letting the meat come to room temperature before grilling, or set aside at room temperature for no longer than 30 minutes.

3. Prepare a charcoal or gas grill: Lightly spray the grill rack with vegetable oil cooking spray. Light the coals or heating elements, and let them burn or heat until moderately hot to hot.

4. Lift the steak from the dish. Grill the meat for 6 or 7 minutes, brushing several times with the marinade during the first 5 minutes of grilling. (The oil in the marinade may cause flare-ups.) Close the lid on the grill and cook for 2 to 3 minutes longer, until the mustard coating turns crispy. Turn the steak, cover, and grill for 6 to 7 minutes longer for medium-rare, or until it is cooked to the desired doneness.

5. Let the steak rest at room temperature for about 5 minutes before slicing on the diagonal into thin strips.

ondon broil is usually flank steak, although the term is used for any thin cut of meat that is broiled or grilled and sliced on the diagonal or bias. Be sure always to slice London broil into thin strips and on an angle to cut across the lengthwise fibers. For six servings, you may have to buy two pieces of meat to get three and a half pounds.

Bloody Mary London Broil   *Serves 6*

HEAT =

2 CUPS TOMATO JUICE

1/4 CUP WORCESTERSHIRE SAUCE

3 TABLESPOONS PREPARED
   HORSERADISH

3 TABLESPOONS DRY SHERRY

2 TEASPOONS CRUMBLED DRIED
   MARJORAM

1 TEASPOON CRUMBLED DRIED BASIL

1 TEASPOON FRESHLY GROUND BLACK
   PEPPER

3 1/2 POUNDS LONDON BROIL, 3/4 TO
   1 INCH THICK, TRIMMED

VEGETABLE OIL COOKING SPRAY

SALT TO TASTE (OPTIONAL)

1. Stir together the tomato juice, Worcestershire, horseradish, sherry, marjoram, basil, and pepper in a small bowl.

2. Place the meat in a single layer in a shallow glass or ceramic dish. Spoon the tomato juice mixture over the meat, spreading to cover. Turn the meat to coat the other side. Cover and refrigerate for at least 2 hours, letting the meat come to room temperature before grilling, or set aside at room temperature for no longer than 30 minutes.

3. Prepare a charcoal or gas grill: Lightly spray the grill rack with vegetable oil cooking spray. Light the coals or heating elements, and let them burn or heat until moderately hot to hot.

4. Lift the meat from the dish. Sprinkle with salt, if desired. Discard the marinade. Grill the steak for 8 minutes. Turn the steak and grill for 7 to 10 minutes longer for medium-rare, or until it is cooked to the desired doneness.

5. Let the steak rest at room temperature for about 5 minutes before slicing on the diagonal into thin strips.

From the rump—also called round, skirt, or flank of the steer—round steak may be sold with a small, round bone or not, depending on the butcher. It is lean and not as juicy as some other steaks, which is one reason it lends itself so well to marinating, slicing thin after grilling, and then serving with other flavorful ingredients, such as tomatoes, jalapeños, and salsa.

Tortilla-Wrapped Round Steak   *Serves 6*

HEAT =

1 ½ POUNDS ROUND STEAK, ABOUT 1 ½
   INCHES THICK, TRIMMED

1 ½ CUPS TOASTED CUMIN MARINADE
   (PAGE 238)

VEGETABLE OIL COOKING SPRAY

1 LARGE WHITE ONION, CUT INTO
   ½-INCH SLICES

2 TO 3 TABLESPOONS CANOLA OIL

COARSELY GROUND BLACK PEPPER TO
   TASTE

TWELVE 7-INCH FLOUR TORTILLAS

CHOPPED TOMATOES

CHOPPED PICKLED JALAPEÑO PEPPERS

CHOPPED FRESH CILANTRO OR FLAT-
   LEAF PARSLEY

BAJA-STYLE TOMATO SALSA (PAGE 233;
   OPTIONAL)

1. Put the steak in a shallow glass or ceramic dish and add the marinade, turning the steak several times to coat. Cover and refrigerate for 4 to 8 hours, letting the meat come to room temperature before grilling.

2. Prepare a charcoal or gas grill: Lightly spray the grill rack with vegetable oil cooking spray. Light the coals or heating elements, and let them burn or heat until moderately hot to hot.

3. Lift the steak from the dish, letting the marinade drip back into the dish. Grill the meat for 8 minutes, brushing several times with the marinade during the first 5 minutes of grilling. (The oil in the marinade may cause flare-ups.) Turn and grill for 8 to 10 minutes longer for medium-rare, or until it is cooked to the desired degree of doneness. Let the meat rest for a few minutes.

4. Place the onion slices near the outside of the grill away from the most intense heat, brush with oil, and sprinkle with the pepper. Turn once or twice, brushing with more oil, and grill for 8 to 10 minutes, until the onions are lightly browned and tender. Wrap the tortillas in foil, place the packet on the outside edge of the grill, and let the tortillas warm while the steak and onions are cooking.

5. Slice the steak into strips and separate the onions into rings. Arrange the steak, onions, chopped tomatoes, and jalapeños in the tortillas and wrap into a sandwich. Garnish with cilantro and top with salsa, if desired.

We suggest top round for this steak salad, since it is tender enough and is a perfect steak for marinating. However, you can use a more expensive cut, too, such as shell, also known as New York strip, Kansas City strip, and strip loin. Or use sirloin tip, which is the bottom tip of the sirloin section. Sirloin tip is not quite as tender as other sirloin cuts but it has great flavor. For grilling, use sturdy, straight scallions—not any that are too slender or too bulbous.

Grilled Steak Salad with Grilled Mushrooms and Scallions *Serves 6*

HEAT =

STEAK AND VEGETABLES

2½ POUNDS TOP ROUND STEAK, ABOUT
   1½ INCHES THICK, TRIMMED

1¾ CUPS RED WINE VINEGAR
   MARINADE (PAGE 236)

VEGETABLE OIL COOKING SPRAY

2 LARGE PORTOBELLO MUSHROOMS
   (ABOUT ½ POUND), STEMMED

3 OR 4 SCALLIONS, TRIMMED

2 TO 3 TABLESPOONS OLIVE OIL

VINAIGRETTE

¼ CUP BALSAMIC VINEGAR

2 TEASPOONS DIJON MUSTARD

½ CUP OLIVE OIL

SALT AND FRESHLY GROUND BLACK
   PEPPER TO TASTE

1. Prepare the steak and vegetables: Put the steak in a shallow glass or ceramic dish and add the marinade, turning the steak several times to coat. Cover and refrigerate for 2 to 4 hours, letting the meat come to room temperature before grilling.

2. Prepare a charcoal or gas grill: Lightly spray the grill rack with vegetable oil cooking spray. Light the coals or heating elements, and let them burn or heat until moderately hot to hot.

3. Lift the steak from the dish, letting most of the marinade drip back into the dish. Grill the meat for 8 to 10 minutes, brushing several times with the marinade during the first 5 minutes of grilling. (The oil in the marinade may cause flare-ups.) Turn and grill for 8 to 10 minutes longer for medium-rare, or until it is cooked to the desired degree of doneness. Let cool.

4. While the steak grills, lay the mushrooms and scallions near the outside of the grill away from the most intense heat, brush with oil, and grill for 8 to 10 minutes, turning once or twice and brushing with more or, until the mushrooms are tender and the scallions are lightly browned and tender.

SALAD

1 HEAD BOSTON OR RED LEAF LETTUCE

1 BUNCH ARUGULA

2 RIPE TOMATOES, SLICED

½ CUP NIÇOISE OR KALAMATA OLIVES

½ CUP CRUMBLED FETA CHEESE

   (ABOUT 2 OUNCES)

5. Slice the steak and mushrooms into strips and transfer to a bowl. Cut the scallions into short lengths and transfer to the bowl.

6. To make the vinaigrette, whisk together the vinegar and mustard. Still whisking, slowly add the oil, whisking until emulsified. Season with salt and pepper. Pour half the vinaigrette over the warm steak and vegetables and toss gently to coat. Set aside for about 30 minutes to cool to room temperature. (If setting aside for any longer, cover, and refrigerate; bring to room temperature before serving.)

7. To make the salad, arrange the lettuce and arugula on a platter. Spoon the meat and vegetables over the lettuce. Garnish with the tomatoes and olives and sprinkle with the cheese. Pass the remaining vinaigrette on the side, whisking well before serving.

ender sirloin steak is terrific for cutting into kabobs and grilling, and when it's marinated with the flavors of Southeast Asia, it sings a happy song. You could also use the head and tail of filet mignon for these kabobs. When you're planning serving an elegant filet, cut the ends from it (which leaves you with the lovely chateaubrian), and freeze these pieces to use for kabobs.

Lemongrass is available in nearly every supermarket nowadays and really adds a pleasant, gentle flavor. If you can't locate it, add another tablespoon of lemon juice. We used frozen artichoke hearts, but canned artichoke hearts (sometimes called baby artichokes) work just as well. Just make sure they are not marinated but are packed whole in a simple brine.

Lemongrass Beef Sirloin Kabobs *Serves 6*

HEAT =

6 STALKS LEMONGRASS

1 TO 2 SERRANO CHILES OR OTHER HOT FRESH CHILE PEPPERS SUCH AS JALAPEÑOS, STEMMED, SEEDED, AND COARSELY CHOPPED

5 OR 6 SCALLIONS, WHITE AND GREEN PARTS, TRIMMED AND CHOPPED

½ CUP MIRIN (SEE NOTE)

¼ CUP SOY SAUCE

¼ CUP VEGETABLE OIL

2 TABLESPOONS FRESH LEMON JUICE

1 TABLESPOON GRATED LEMON ZEST

3 POUNDS SIRLOIN, TRIMMED AND CUT INTO THIRTY 1½-INCH CUBES

¾ POUND YELLOW SUMMER SQUASH, TRIMMED AND SLICED INTO ¾-INCH-THICK ROUNDS

1. Remove and discard the outer layer of each stalk of lemongrass. Trim and discard the root end and top of each stalk. This should leave about 6 inches of the tender, less fibrous lower bulb portion. Quarter each stalk lengthwise and chop.

2. In the bowl of a food processor fitted with the metal blade, combine the lemongrass, chile peppers, scallions, mirin, soy sauce, oil, lemon juice, and lemon zest. Pulse a few times, scrape down sides of bowl, and process for about 30 seconds to mix thoroughly.

3. Mix the meat with 1 cup of the marinade in a shallow glass or ceramic dish. In another dish, toss the squash and artichoke hearts with the remaining marinade. Cover both dishes and refrigerate for at least 2 hours, letting the meat come to room temperature before grilling.

4. Prepare a charcoal or gas grill: Lightly spray the grill rack with vegetable oil cooking spray. Light the coals or heating elements, and let them burn or heat until moderately hot to hot.

12 THAWED WHOLE FROZEN OR DRAINED
AND RINSED CANNED ARTICHOKE
HEARTS
VEGETABLE OIL COOKING SPRAY
SIX 12-INCH METAL SKEWERS

5. Lift the meat from the marinade but do not pat it dry. Thread it onto six 12-inch metal skewers, alternating with the artichoke hearts and squash and beginning and ending with a cube of meat. (Pierce the artichoke hearts through their centers.)

6. Grill for 10 to 12 minutes for medium-rare, or until the meat is cooked to the desired degree of doneness, turning the skewers several times during grilling until browned on all sides. Serve immediately.

note: Mirin is sweet rice wine with a very low alcohol content. It's sold in the Asian food aisle of most supermarkets as well as in specialty stores and Japanese markets.

ASK the BUTCHER

I see labels for natural, organic, and grass-fed beef. What do they mean?

You may see terms such as "natural," "organic," and "grass-fed" on the beef you buy in a few supermarkets and specialty shops. Ranchers and farmers are marketing to a niche clientele who want these products, which are generally more expensive and may or may not taste better than the beef otherwise available. Beef from these categories accounts for less than one-tenth of one percent of all American beef, although the number is growing.

Natural beef is from cattle raised without antibiotics or growth hormones but which may be fed grain on a feedlot. Organic beef, also antibiotic- and hormone-free, is fed from birth on feed determined to be certified organic according to USDA guidelines, and then it is processed at certified organic packing plants. Grass-fed beef is from cattle that spend their entire lives eating grasses rather than grain. The meat from these beasts tends to be leaner with a slightly different flavor from grain-fed beef.

For these kabobs, use boned sirloin or any other tender steak, such as shell steak or sirloin tip. Filet mignon or filet mignon tips would work well, too, particularly since this recipe does not call for lengthy marinating, which would be a waste with really good meat. Use thin-skinned potatoes and brush them gently when cleaning to avoid tearing the skins.

Sirloin Steak Kabobs with Rosemary-Brushed Potatoes and Red Peppers *Serves 6*

HEAT =

6 SMALL RED POTATOES (ABOUT
   1 POUND)

SALT TO TASTE

½ CUP OLIVE OIL

2 CLOVES GARLIC, CRUSHED

3 TABLESPOONS CHOPPED FRESH
   ROSEMARY

SALT AND FRESHLY GROUND BLACK
   PEPPER TO TASTE

VEGETABLE OIL COOKING SPRAY

2½ POUNDS SIRLOIN STEAK, TRIMMED
   AND CUT INTO TWENTY-FOUR
   1½-INCH CUBES

3 RED BELL PEPPERS (ABOUT 1½
   POUNDS), CUT INTO 18 CHUNKS

SIX 12-INCH METAL SKEWERS

1. Put the potatoes in a large saucepan and add enough water to cover by 2 to 3 inches. Lightly salt the water and bring to a boil over high heat. Reduce the heat and simmer briskly for about 15 minutes, until the potatoes are just fork-tender. Drain and cool to room temperature. Cut in half so there are 12 pieces. Handle the potatoes gently to prevent the skin from slipping off.

2. Combine the olive oil, garlic, and rosemary in a large bowl; season to taste with salt and pepper. Add the potatoes and stir gently to coat.

3. Prepare a charcoal or gas grill: Lightly spray the grill rack with vegetable oil cooking spray. Light the coals or heating elements, and let them burn or heat until moderately hot to hot.

4. Lift the potatoes from the dish. Transfer the marinade to a small saucepan and heat gently until warm and fragrant. Thread the potatoes, steak, and bell peppers onto skewers, beginning and ending with a potato and threading 4 pieces of meat and 3 chunks of peppers onto each. Grill for 10 to 12 minutes, turning several times and brushing with the warm marinade, until medium-rare, or until the meat is cooked to the desired degree of doneness, the potatoes are tender, and the peppers are slightly charred. Serve immediately.

Rib roast, also called prime rib, comes from the rib section of the forequarter and is a favorite for celebrations and holidays. The ribs encase wonderfully tender, juicy, and flavorful meat that is perfectly marbled and covered with a substantial layer of fat. Large rib roasts include the short ribs and can serve up to 16 people. Smaller ones, such as we suggest for grilling, are trimmed, with the short ribs removed, and are great for four to six people. For the grill, buy a three- or four-rib roast. All the roast needs is a little sliced garlic and salt and pepper. It has enough fat and so requires no olive oil. You will love how a rib roast tastes when grilled, served with the Horseradish Cream Sauce. When we grill a standing rib roast, we sometimes like to baste it with dark beer to deepen its flavor.

Grilled Standing Rib Roast
Serves 4 to 6

HEAT =

VEGETABLE OIL COOKING SPRAY
ONE 3½- TO 4-POUND STANDING RIB
    ROAST (3 OR 4 RIBS)
1 LARGE CLOVE GARLIC, THINLY CUT
    INTO WIDE SLICES
COARSE SALT AND FRESHLY GROUND
    BLACK PEPPER TO TASTE
HORSERADISH CREAM SAUCE (PAGE 223)

1. Prepare a charcoal or gas grill for indirect cooking (see page 7): Lightly spray the grill rack with vegetable oil cooking spray. Light the coals or heating elements, and let them burn or heat until moderately hot to hot.

2. Using a sharp knife, make small slits down the roast's meaty side. Insert the garlic in the slits. Sprinkle with salt and pepper.

3. Sear the meat over intense heat on the bone side and the narrow sides for 1 or 2 minutes per side. Sear the meaty top side for about 3 minutes. Turn the roast with tongs, if possible, to avoid piercing the meat so that none of the juices escape.

4. Transfer the roast, bone side down, to the cooler part of the grill. Cover the grill and cook for 1 hour and 20 minutes to 1 hour and 30 minutes for rare, or longer for more well-done meat. Add additional coals to the fire to maintain an even temperature during cooking. After 1 hour, insert an instant-read meat thermometer into the thickest part of the meat (not too close to a bone). When the thermometer registers 130° (for rare meat) to 140°F (for medium-rare meat), remove the roast from the grill and let rest for 5 to 10 minutes before carving. Do not overcook. Serve with the Horseradish Cream Sauce.

Brisket is the fatty, fibrous cut of meat behind the foreshank and below the chuck. The second cut of the brisket, toward the shoulder, is the cut most often preferred for corned beef and for grilling. Brisket needs precooking before grilling. Here, it is baked after first marinating in a dry rub. Following a stint on the grill, we serve it with the same barbecue sauce that flavors it during baking. For a smoky flavor, toss some soaked wood chips on the fire during grilling (see page 5).

Sweet 'n' Spicy Barbecued Brisket *Serves 6 to 8*

HEAT =

6 POUNDS BEEF BRISKET, TRIMMED

SWEET 'N' SPICY DRY RUB (PAGE 243)

2 TABLESPOONS CANOLA OIL

½ CUP FINELY CHOPPED ONIONS

1 CLOVE GARLIC, FINELY CHOPPED

1 TEASPOON CRUSHED RED PEPPER

1 TEASPOON DRIED MARJORAM

1 TEASPOON DRY MUSTARD

3 CUPS TOMATO PUREE

½ CUP ORANGE JUICE

½ CUP CIDER VINEGAR

¼ CUP FIRMLY PACKED LIGHT OR DARK
  BROWN SUGAR

1 TEASPOON SALT

VEGETABLE OIL COOKING SPRAY

1. Rub all sides of the brisket with the dry rub, transfer it to a shallow dish, and cover loosely. Set aside at room temperature for about 1 hour, or refrigerate for as long as 24 hours, letting the meat come to room temperature before grilling. Alternatively, put the brisket in a resealable plastic bag and refrigerate.

2. Heat the oil in a saucepan over medium heat. Add the onions and garlic and cook, stirring, for about 10 minutes, or until the onions soften and are translucent. Add the red pepper, marjoram, and mustard and cook, stirring, for 1 minute. Add the tomato puree, orange juice, vinegar, sugar, and salt and bring to a simmer, stirring to dissolve the sugar. Reduce the heat and simmer gently for about 30 minutes, or until slightly thickened.

3. Preheat the oven to 325°F.

4. Spread a thin layer of the sauce over the bottom of a roasting pan just large enough to hold the brisket. Put the brisket in the pan and spread a little more sauce over it. Cover the pan tightly with foil and bake for about 2 hours, or until tender.

5. Prepare a charcoal or gas grill: Lightly spray the grill rack with vegetable oil cooking spray. Light the coals or heating elements, and let them burn or heat until moderately hot.

6. Grill the brisket for about 20 minutes. Turn and cook for 20 minutes longer, or until the internal temperature is 190° to 200°F. Let the meat rest for about 15 minutes before slicing thinly across the grain.

7. Reheat the sauce over medium heat. Serve with the brisket.

Smoked brisket has got to be one of the best-kept secrets going, but as soon as you try this recipe, you will want to spread the word as loudly and happily as we do! Not only is the meat delicious right out of the smoker served with sides of baked beans, coleslaw, and cornbread, but the leftovers make amazing sandwiches. Brisket may not taste as smoky as some other smoked meats, but what you're after here is the texture. It's cooked low and slow so that it's as tender as can be.

Smoking the brisket is an all-day affair, which is one of the reasons we don't rub the meat with a dry rub a day ahead of time; the spices rubbed into the meat just before smoking do a great job. Our moppin' sauce is more fluid than traditional barbecue sauces, and when it's spooned over the meat during the last hour of smoking, its soft, fruity overtones provide a sweetness that balances the salty smokiness of the brisket. As with all smoked meats, take care to pat the brisket dry before you season and smoke it. During the last couple of hours, we wrap the meat in foil. When it's unwrapped, you'll find a lot of juice trapped in the foil. This liquid is too overpowering to use as a sauce, but you might like to reserve a little to use when you reheat leftover brisket. Brisket needs about 10 hours in the smoker, so plan wisely and then invite some friends over for a stupendous meal.

Smoked Brisket with Moppin' Sauce   *Serves 6 generously*

HEAT =

BRISKET

4 TO 5 POUNDS BEEF BRISKET,
   TRIMMED OF ALL BUT A
   ¼-INCH-THICK LAYER OF FAT
1 TABLESPOON FRESHLY GROUND BLACK
   PEPPER
1 TABLESPOON COARSE SALT
1 TABLESPOON SWEET PAPRIKA
1 TEASPOON CAYENNE
1 TEASPOON CRUSHED DRIED
   ROSEMARY
1 TEASPOON CRUSHED DRIED THYME

1. Let the brisket rest uncovered at room temperature for 30 to 45 minutes to come to room temperature and let its juices rise to the surface.

2. Meanwhile, in a small bowl, mix together the black pepper, salt, paprika, cayenne, rosemary, and thyme to make a dry rub.

3. Using paper towels, pat the meat dry. Coat the surface of the brisket with the dry rub.

4. Prepare and preheat the smoker according to the manufacturer's instructions. We used a mixture of hickory and apple wood for the brisket.

MOPPIN' SAUCE

1 TEASPOON WHOLE BLACK
   PEPPERCORNS

2 CUPS FRUITY RED WINE

$2/3$ CUP WATER

$2/3$ CUP WHOLE-CHERRY PRESERVES

6 TABLESPOONS KETCHUP

2 TABLESPOONS RED WINE VINEGAR

2 TEASPOONS WHOLE YELLOW MUSTARD
   SEEDS

$1/4$ TEASPOON COARSE SALT

$1/8$ TEASPOON GROUND ALLSPICE

5. Put the brisket on the smoker's rack, fat side up, and smoke for 4 hours at 225°F.

6. Meanwhile, make the moppin' sauce: Crush the peppercorns with a mortar and pestle or the side of a large knife.

7. Put the pepper along with the remaining sauce ingredients in a medium heavy-bottom saucepan. Stir well, bring to a simmer over medium-high heat, and cook for 15 to 20 minutes, until reduced to about $2½$ cups. The sauce will be syrupy and aromatic. Taste and adjust seasonings. Remove from the heat and set aside.

8. Using tongs or a spatula, transfer the brisket from the smoker's rack to a shallow pan. Do not use a fork or knife, which would pierce the meat and release juices. Wrap the meat in heavy-duty foil and seal well. Return to the smoker, seam side up, and smoke for 4 hours longer.

9. Unwrap the meat. Drain and discard all but a few tablespoons of the accumulated juices in the foil. (These reserved tablespoons can be used to moisten the brisket when you reheat any leftovers.)

10. Place the meat back on the foil. Spoon ½ cup of the moppin' sauce over the meat. Reseal the foil and return the package to the smoker. Smoke for 1 to 2 hours longer, until a fork can be poked easily through the meat and the internal temperature is 180°F. (Cut a thin slice off the meat to test for tenderness.) Discard the accumulated juices. Let the brisket rest about 10 minutes, thinly slice, and serve with the reheated moppin' sauce.

Brisket has to be precooked for several hours before it is grilled. Here, we parboil it and when it is tender, rub it with a dry rub, allow it to marinate in its own juices, and then finish it on the grill.

Grilled Peppery Beef Brisket   *Serves 6 to 8*

HEAT =

6 POUNDS BEEF BRISKET, TRIMMED

1 LARGE ONION, COARSELY CHOPPED OR
   SLICED

3 CLOVES GARLIC, CRUSHED

5 OR 6 WHOLE BLACK PEPPERCORNS

¼ CUP PEPPERY DRY RUB (PAGE 241)

VEGETABLE OIL COOKING SPRAY

MADISON AVENUE BARBECUE SAUCE
   (PAGE 221)

1. Combine the brisket, onion, garlic, and peppercorns in a stockpot or large saucepan. Add enough water to cover the meat by about 1 inch. Bring to a boil over high heat, reduce the heat to medium-low, and cook, covered, for 2 to 2½ hours, until the meat is tender when pierced with a fork. Check the meat for tenderness after 2 hours.

2. Lift the meat from the cooking liquid and discard the liquid. When the meat is cool enough to handle, pat dry with paper towels. Rub all sides of the brisket with the dry rub, transfer to a shallow dish, cover loosely, and set aside at room temperature for about 1 hour or refrigerate for as long as 24 hours, letting the meat come to room temperature before grilling. Alternatively, put the brisket in a resealable plastic bag and refrigerate.

3. Prepare a charcoal or gas grill: Lightly spray the grill rack with vegetable oil cooking spray. Light the coals or heating elements, and let them burn or heat until moderately hot.

4. Grill the brisket for about 20 minutes. Turn and cook for 20 minutes longer, or until the internal temperature is 190° to 200°F. Let the meat rest for about 15 minutes before slicing thinly across the grain. Serve with the barbecue sauce.

hese baked beans are a great favorite of Mark Lobel's. The recipe is adapted from one developed by Jeffrey Kohn, the chef/owner of Q Restaurant and Bar in Port Chester, New York. Jeffrey and his wife Jennifer opened the barbecue restaurant early in 2005 and like to call the authentic fare they serve "urban barbecue." If you prefer baked beans a little less sweet, decrease the brown sugar to ½ to ⅔ cup. To make this a substantial main course, double the amount of brisket. Jeff says most of his customers eat it as a side dish. Either way, it's a winner.

Hickory-Pit Smoked Baked Beans with Brisket   *Serves 6*

HEAT =

1½ QUARTS CANNED BACON AND
    BROWN SUGAR–FLAVORED BAKED
    BEANS (THREE 16-OUNCE CANS),
    SUCH AS BUSH'S ORIGINAL BAKED
    BEANS
¼ CUP DARK MOLASSES
¼ CUP KETCHUP
1 CUP PACKED LIGHT BROWN SUGAR
1½ TEASPOONS GARLIC POWDER
1½ TEASPOONS ONION POWDER
½ TEASPOON LIQUID SMOKE
    (OPTIONAL)
½ TEASPOON WORCESTERSHIRE SAUCE
½ TO ¾ POUND CHOPPED SMOKED
    BRISKET (PAGE 72, MAKE BRISKET
    ONLY, OR SAVE SAUCE FOR ANOTHER
    PURPOSE)

1. Prepare and preheat the smoker according to the manufacturer's instructions. We used hickory wood for the beans.

2. Mix together the baked beans, molasses, ketchup, brown sugar, garlic powder, onion powder, liquid smoke, if using, and Worcestershire sauce.

3. Spread in a 2-inch-deep foil or metal baking pan. Top with the brisket and mix the meat with the beans.

4. Put the pan on the smoker's rack and smoke for about 1 hour at 225°F, or until completely heated and the flavors blend. Serve.

Corned beef is brisket that has been cured in brine. Old-fashioned corned beef was quite salty, but nowadays the brine is less salty and usually contains no nitrites. Like brisket, corned beef must be parboiled for hours before it can be prepared for grilling. During grilling, watch for flare-ups, since the corned beef is fatty. Move the meat to a cooler part of the grill until the flames subside or while spritzing them with water. When you buy corned beef, it comes packed in Cryovac with explicit cooking instructions. Follow them or follow ours (Step 1); they are similar.

Grilled Glazed Corned Beef   *Serves 6*

HEAT =

ONE 4- TO 4½-POUND CORNED BEEF
   BRISKET, TRIMMED

1 TABLESPOON CANOLA OIL

1 TABLESPOON FROZEN ORANGE JUICE
   CONCENTRATE

1 TABLESPOON ORANGE-FLAVORED
   LIQUEUR, SUCH AS COINTREAU OR
   GRAND MARNIER

1 CLOVE GARLIC, FINELY CHOPPED

1½ TEASPOONS PACKED DARK BROWN
   SUGAR

½ TEASPOON GROUND GINGER

½ TEASPOON CHOPPED FRESH GINGER

½ TEASPOON GROUND CINNAMON

¼ TEASPOON DRY MUSTARD

VEGETABLE OIL COOKING SPRAY

1. Cook the corned beef according to the package instructions or by following this method: Combine the corned beef brisket and enough water to cover by 2 to 3 inches in a large stockpot. Add the spice pouch included with the beef (if the corned beef you buy does not have a spice pouch, add 2 or 3 black peppercorns to the water). Bring to a boil over high heat. Reduce the heat and simmer for 2½ to 3 hours, until the beef is tender when pierced with a fork. Lift the corned beef from the water, cool slightly, and pat dry.

2. Combine the remaining ingredients in a small bowl and stir well.

3. Put the corned beef in a shallow glass or ceramic dish and spoon the orange–brown sugar mixture over the meat, rubbing it into the beef on both sides. Cover and refrigerate for at least 4 hours or overnight, letting the meat come to room temperature before grilling. Alternatively, rub the mixture into the meat, put the meat in a resealable plastic bag, and refrigerate.

4. Prepare a charcoal or gas grill for indirect cooking (see page 7): Lightly spray the grill rack with vegetable oil cooking spray. Light the coals or heating elements, and let them burn or heat until hot.

5. Place the corned beef, fat side down, over the hottest part of the fire and sear for about 10 minutes to make defined grill marks. Transfer to the cooler part of the grill, fat side down, cover, and grill for 20 minutes. Turn the beef and grill for about 10 minutes, or until heated through and nicely browned and crusty.

This is a time-honored way of "grilling" short ribs, which are typically braised when cooked indoors. In this case, the ribs are parboiled before being finished on the grill. Meaty ribs are the best bet for grilling; ask the butcher to cut them into manageable lengths, if necessary.

Garlicky Grilled Short Ribs · Serves 6

HEAT =

6 TO 8 POUNDS MEATY SHORT RIBS, CUT INTO 4- TO 5½-INCH-LONG PIECES, TRIMMED

2 TEASPOONS SALT

1 CUP CANOLA OIL

1 CUP TOMATO PASTE

1 CUP DRY SHERRY

3 TABLESPOONS MINCED ONION

8 LARGE CLOVES GARLIC, MINCED

1½ CUPS LIGHTLY PACKED LIGHT OR DARK BROWN SUGAR

2 TABLESPOONS WORCESTERSHIRE SAUCE

1 TABLESPOON PLUS 1½ TEASPOONS HONEY

VEGETABLE OIL COOKING SPRAY

1. Put the ribs in a large stockpot. Add cold water to cover and the salt, and bring to a boil over high heat. Reduce the heat to medium-low, skim the foam, cover partially, and simmer for about 1½ hours, until fork tender. Drain and set aside in a shallow glass or ceramic dish until cool enough to handle.

2. Combine the oil, tomato paste, sherry, onion, garlic, brown sugar, Worcestershire sauce, and honey in a glass or ceramic bowl and whisk until mixed. Rub the mixture into the meat, cover, and set aside for no longer than 45 minutes at room temperature or for as long as 4 hours refrigerated, letting the meat come to room temperature before grilling.

3. Prepare a charcoal or gas grill: Lightly spray the grill rack with vegetable oil cooking spray. Light the coals or heating elements, and let them burn or heat until moderately hot to hot.

4. Lift the ribs from the dish. Transfer the marinade to a saucepan and cook over medium-high heat until boiling. Reduce the heat to medium and simmer briskly for 5 minutes. Cover and keep warm.

5. Put the ribs on the grill, meat side down, cover, and grill for about 10 minutes. Turn and grill for 8 to 10 minutes longer, until nicely browned. Cut between the ribs and serve with the marinade.

Also known as flanken, short ribs are cut from the ends of the rib roast and the plate, and are composed of layers of lean meat and fat with flat rib bones in between. They are one of the surprises of the grill—tasty and meaty and downright delicious when properly seasoned and cooked. We offer two different methods for grilling short ribs and invite you to try both before settling on one that suits you: They can be parboiled as on page 78 or, as here, baked and then held in the refrigerator until ready to grill. This makes planning easy.

Short Ribs with Quick Barbecue Sauce   *Serves 6 to 8*

HEAT =

3 TABLESPOONS OLIVE OIL

3 TABLESPOONS CIDER VINEGAR

1 TABLESPOON PLUS 1½ TEASPOONS
   DRIED OREGANO

1 TABLESPOON SWEET PAPRIKA

1 TABLESPOON FRESHLY GROUND BLACK
   PEPPER

1½ TEASPOONS SALT

6 TO 8 POUNDS MEATY SHORT RIBS,
   CUT INTO 4- TO 5½-INCH-LONG
   PIECES, TRIMMED

VEGETABLE OIL COOKING SPRAY

QUICK BARBECUE SAUCE (PAGE 222)

1. Combine the oil, vinegar, oregano, paprika, pepper, and salt in a small bowl and mix well. Put the ribs in a shallow glass or ceramic dish. Rub the paste over the ribs, working it into the meat. Cover and refrigerate for at least 3 hours or overnight, letting the meat come to room temperature before grilling. Alternatively, put the ribs in a resealable plastic bag and refrigerate.

2. Preheat the oven to 300°F. Lightly spray a roasting pan large enough to hold the ribs snugly with vegetable oil cooking spray.

3. Place the ribs in the pan in a single layer and cover the pan tightly with foil. Bake for 1½ to 2 hours, until the meat is tender enough to pierce easily with a knife.

4. Prepare a charcoal or gas grill: Lightly spray the grill rack with vegetable oil cooking spray. Light the coals or heating elements, and let them burn or heat until moderately hot to hot.

5. Heat the sauce in a small pan over medium heat. Brush the ribs generously with the sauce.

6. Put the ribs on the grill, meat side down, cover, and grill for about 10 minutes. Turn and grill for 8 to 10 minutes longer, until nicely browned. Cut between the ribs and serve with the remaining sauce.

We came up with these grilled mini meatballs cooked on bamboo skewers after seeing a photo of ground meat grilled on skewers that caught our fancy and imaginations—and made us hungry the instant we laid eyes on them. From there, it was an easy jump to meatball sandwiches, one of our all-time favorite weekend lunches.

This is a versatile recipe. You could change the flavor of the meatballs by adding different herbs, or substituting garlicky bread crumbs or grated cheese. Or flavor the sandwiches with a tangy relish, salsa, or even marinara sauce. Any way you make them, these sandwiches are great for a fun, casual meal.

Mini Meatball and Mushroom Sandwiches   *Serves 6*

HEAT =

TWELVE 10-INCH BAMBOO SKEWERS

MEATBALLS
½ POUND GROUND BEEF CHUCK
½ POUND GROUND VEAL
½ POUND GROUND PORK
3 TABLESPOONS MINCED SCALLIONS,
   GREEN PARTS ONLY
2 TABLESPOONS MINCED FLAT-LEAF
   PARSLEY
2 TABLESPOONS PLAIN DRY BREAD
   CRUMBS
2 TO 3 TABLESPOONS HALF-AND-HALF
   OR LIGHT CREAM
1 TEASPOON MINCED FRESH THYME
   LEAVES
½ TEASPOON CRUMBLED DRIED
   OREGANO
½ TEASPOON SALT

1. Soak the bamboo skewers in cold water to cover for 20 to 30 minutes.

2. Make the meatballs: Combine the beef, veal, pork, scallions, parsley, bread crumbs, 2 tablespoons of the half-and-half, the thyme, oregano, salt, and pepper in a large bowl. Mix well with your hands, adding the remaining tablespoon of half-and-half if needed. The mixture should hold together and not be soggy or crumbly, so that the meatballs will hold together on the skewers. Form into 24 packed meatballs, each weighing about an ounce and about the size of a walnut. Transfer the meatballs as they are formed to a baking sheet lined with parchment or waxed paper and refrigerate until ready to use.

3. Gently clean the mushrooms with a soft brush and remove and discard the stems. (Or reserve the stems for another use.)

4. Prepare a charcoal or gas grill: Lightly spray the grill rack with vegetable oil cooking spray. Light the coals or heating elements, and let them burn or heat until moderately hot.

½ TEASPOON FRESHLY GROUND BLACK
   PEPPER

FOR THE SANDWICHES

30 LARGE WHITE MUSHROOMS

VEGETABLE OIL COOKING SPRAY

⅓ CUP EXTRA VIRGIN OLIVE OIL

SIX 6-INCH HARD ROLLS, SPLIT

½ TO ¾ CUP HERBED MAYONNAISE
   (PAGE 250)

12 LEAVES BIBB LETTUCE, WASHED AND
   DRIED THOROUGHLY

2 BEEFSTEAK TOMATOES, CORED AND
   THINLY SLICED

GRATED ROMANO CHEESE, FOR GARNISH
   (OPTIONAL)

FRESHLY GROUND BLACK PEPPER
   (OPTIONAL)

MINCED CHIVES, FOR GARNISH
   (OPTIONAL)

5. Drain the bamboo skewers. Thread the mushrooms and meatballs on the skewers, using 2 skewers for each kabob to better hold the food securely. Start and end with the mushrooms. Brush the skewers with half the olive oil.

6. Grill the skewers for 3 to 4 minutes and then carefully turn, using a wide spatula to roll them over. Do not use tongs, which could break them. Cook for 4 to 5 minutes longer, turning once or twice more.

7. Brush the remaining oil over the insides of the rolls. Grill the rolls, oiled sides down, for 3 to 5 minutes, until lightly toasted.

8. Spread 1 to 2 tablespoons of mayonnaise on each toasted roll. Top with lettuce leaves and a few tomato slices. Slide the meatballs and mushrooms off skewers into the rolls, garnish with cheese, pepper, or chives, as desired, and serve.

For this recipe, use either rib or loin veal chops. Rib chops are cut from the rib roast and because butchers do not have as many requests for rib roasts of veal as they do for chops, they very often cut roasts into sizable, delicious chops. Loin veal chops have a large eye (meaty section), a tenderloin, and T-bone. Veal chops are among those cuts of meat that we feel benefit from a "less is more" treatment, and require neither a marinade nor much seasoning. We suggest serving these with a wine sauce to dress up the party.

Classic Grilled Veal Chops   *Serves 4*

HEAT =

FOUR 12-OUNCE RIB OR LOIN VEAL
   CHOPS, ABOUT 1½ INCHES THICK
OLIVE OIL
SALT AND FRESHLY GROUND BLACK
   PEPPER TO TASTE
FOUR TOOTHPICKS (SOAKED IN WATER
   FOR 10 MINUTES) OR SMALL METAL
   SKEWERS
VEGETABLE OIL COOKING SPRAY
MERLOT WINE SAUCE (PAGE 225;
   OPTIONAL)

1. Rub the chops with oil and season on both sides with salt and pepper. Secure the tails of the chops to the thicker section of meat with toothpicks or small metal skewers, if necessary.

2. Prepare a charcoal or gas grill: Lightly spray the grill rack with vegetable oil cooking spray. Light the coals or heating elements, and let them burn or heat until moderately hot.

3. Grill the chops for 8 to 10 minutes on each side until lightly browned for medium-rare, or until meat is cooked to the desired degree of doneness. Serve with the sauce, if desired.

For this recipe, buy top round of veal and ask the butcher to slice it across the grain and then flatten it for you so that it is about a quarter of an inch thick. You will note that we use double skewers to hold the meat and vegetables securely in place. This is not necessary for all brochettes but does make turning them easier. (Use this technique in any recipe calling for skewers.) In this instance, the veal is cut into thin strips and woven on the skewers, so two skewers are necessary.

Veal and Mushroom Brochettes with Fresh Sage   *Serves 6*

HEAT =

2 POUNDS VEAL TOP ROUND, TRIMMED
    AND POUNDED TO AN EVEN
    THICKNESS OF ABOUT $\frac{1}{4}$ INCH
1 POUND BROAD-CAPPED CREMINI
    MUSHROOMS, STEMMED (ABOUT 36
    MUSHROOMS)
$\frac{1}{4}$ CUP FINELY CHOPPED SCALLIONS,
    WHITE AND GREEN PARTS
$\frac{1}{4}$ CUP CHOPPED FRESH SAGE
2 TABLESPOONS GRATED LEMON ZEST
3 TABLESPOONS FRESH LEMON JUICE
2 TABLESPOONS OLIVE OIL
$\frac{1}{2}$ TEASPOON SALT
$\frac{1}{2}$ TEASPOON FRESHLY GROUND BLACK
    PEPPER
TWENTY-FOUR 12-INCH BAMBOO
    SKEWERS
VEGETABLE OIL COOKING SPRAY

1. Cut the veal into 24 strips about 4 inches long and 2 inches wide. Put in a shallow glass or ceramic dish. Add the mushrooms, scallions, sage, lemon zest, lemon juice, olive oil, salt, and pepper and toss gently to mix. Cover and refrigerate for at least 30 minutes and as long as 2 hours, letting the meat come to room temperature before grilling.

2. Soak the skewers in cold water to cover for at least 20 minutes. Drain just before using.

3. Prepare a charcoal or gas grill: Lightly spray the grill rack with vegetable oil cooking spray. Light the coals or heating elements, and let them burn or heat until moderately hot.

4. Thread the veal and mushrooms on the skewers, using 2 skewers at a time to secure them in place. Hold the skewers about $\frac{1}{2}$ inch apart and thread a mushroom on the skewers, pushing it so that it is about 2 inches from the bottom of the skewers. Weave a strip of veal onto the skewers, thread another mushroom on the skewers and another strip of veal. Finally, push a third mushroom onto the skewers. Repeat with the remaining skewers and veal and mushrooms so that each 2-skewer brochette holds 2 strips of veal and 3 mushrooms.

5. Grill the brochettes for 6 to 8 minutes, turning once or twice, until the veal is medium-rare. Serve immediately.

While we like to make these kabobs with boneless loin of veal, it's not always available, so top round of veal is our second choice. Look for veal that is as light in color as possible. It won't be white, but should be pink. The tropical fruits are lovely with the mild veal—and for a little punch, use a fiery curry paste rather than a mild one.

Curried Veal and Island Fruit Kabobs   *Serves 6*

HEAT =

½ CUP EXTRA VIRGIN OLIVE OIL

1 TABLESPOON GRATED ORANGE ZEST

¼ CUP FRESH ORANGE JUICE

1 TABLESPOON GRATED LEMON ZEST

2 TABLESPOONS FRESH LEMON JUICE

ONE 3-INCH PIECE FRESH GINGER,
   PEELED AND COARSELY GRATED
   (ABOUT 1 TABLESPOON)

2 TABLESPOONS YELLOW CURRY PASTE
   (SEE NOTE)

½ TEASPOON CRUSHED RED PEPPER

¼ TEASPOON GROUND CLOVES

3 POUNDS BONELESS LOIN VEAL OR TOP
   ROUND OF VEAL, CUT INTO ABOUT
   THIRTY 1½-INCH CUBES

3 FIRM, RIPE BANANAS, PEELED

2 RIPE MANGOES

VEGETABLE OIL COOKING SPRAY

TWELVE 12-INCH METAL SKEWERS

FRESH MINT LEAVES, FOR GARNISH
   (OPTIONAL)

1. Whisk together the oil, orange zest, orange juice, lemon zest, lemon juice, ginger, curry paste, red pepper, and cloves in a shallow glass or ceramic dish. Remove and set aside a quarter of the marinade.

2. Add the veal to the dish, tossing to coat. Cover and refrigerate for at least 2 hours and up to 6 hours, letting the meat come to room temperature before grilling.

3. Cut the bananas into 12 equal-sized chunks. Peel the mangoes and cut the flesh from the pit. Cut the mangoes into 12 equal-sized chunks, too, about the same size as the meat. The mangoes will be more difficult to cut than the bananas, but do your best. If you have more mango than you need, reserve it for another use (or eat it!). Put the fruit in another shallow glass or ceramic dish and toss gently with the reserved marinade. Cover and refrigerate.

4. Prepare a charcoal or gas grill: Lightly spray the grill rack with vegetable oil cooking spray. Light the coals or heating elements, and let them burn or heat until moderately hot to hot.

5. Lift the meat and fruit from the marinade but do not pat them dry. Thread the meat and fruit onto the skewers, beginning and ending with the meat. Handle the fruit carefully (skewer the bananas through the sides) and do not crowd the skewers.

6. Grill, covered, for 8 to 10 minutes, turning after 5 minutes and then several times until evenly browned. Serve garnished with fresh mint leaves, torn into the size you like, if desired.

note: Curry pastes are usually Thai or Indian and are sold in Asian, East Indian, and specialty markets as well as many supermarkets. They commonly are red, green, or yellow and can range from mild to very spicy. Refrigerate them after opening.

LAMB AND PORK

More and more, backyard cooks are turning to lamb and pork when deciding what to grill. Both are delicious when cooked over an open fire and both, being sweet-tasting meats, lend themselves to any number of marinades, rubs, sauces, and seasonings. Butterflied leg of lamb, marinated in a heady garlic-infused brew and then grilled, has become something of an American classic. Believe us, grilled pork tenderloin is not far behind in popularity.

At Lobel's, we sell only prime lamb and #1-grade pork. If possible, buy these top grades for the most tender and flavorful meat. Otherwise, buy the best you can find. Most important is to find a butcher you trust who can make suggestions.

Both lamb and pork are meats from young animals, rarely more than a year old and generally far younger. You may have heard the term "baby lamb," which means just that: very young lamb between four and six weeks old, never more than fifteen pounds, with very tender, pale-pink meat. Few butchers carry baby lamb and if they do, it is only in the spring, which is the season when lambs are born. It is possible to buy lamb younger even than baby lamb. This is called a "hothouse lamb" and is only one or two weeks old. These lambs have had nothing but mother's milk and their meat is so tender you can cut it with a fork. However, even butchers who can special-order baby lamb cannot always get hothouse lamb and we consider it rare.

Most lamb is six to eight months old and weighs about thirty-five pounds. The meat is pink, firm, and lean; the external fat is firm, white, and not too thick; and the bones are moist and healthfully red. Never buy lamb with dark red meat, yellowish fat, or pure white bones; these indicate older animals whose texture will be tough and flavor overly intense.

People have been eating pork longer than any other domesticated animal. This may explain why so many ancient dietary restrictions grew up around pork, but it may also explain why we have such an abiding fondness for this rich-tasting, sweet meat. Today, Americans eat an average of 50 pounds of pork a year, making it second only to beef in per-capita consumption, and a growing percentage is pork cooked on the grill. Pork is graded differently from beef, veal, and lamb. Instead of being labeled as prime, choice, or good, pork is graded as #1, #2, and #3. If your butcher sells #1-grade pork, you are in luck. The pork will have pinkish-gray, lean meat and the fat will be firm and white. The bones should have red running through them to indicate blood and a young animal. With the exception of suckling pigs, most hogs are about 6 months old and weigh just over 200 pounds. Avoid pork with deep red meat, a coarse texture, bright white bones, and fat that appears yellow.

When grilling lamb or pork, remember that the cooking times provided in our recipes are not exact. All grills cook a little differently, and some fires burn hotter than others. You will soon get to know your own grill and your own style and will be able to use our cooking times as guidelines. Test for doneness by looking at the meat (or by touch), and particularly with pork, use an instant-read thermometer to determine when the meat is done. Lamb can be served rare (140°F) or better done, but pork must be cooked thoroughly to 160°F. However, because meat continues to cook for a few minutes after it has been removed from the heat, take the pork off the grill when the thermometer registers 150° to 155°F. The pork's internal temperature will continue to rise to 160°F and the meat will not become overcooked or dry.

Smoked pork is fabulous and so we include recipes to celebrate it. From smoked ribs to smoked pork chops and bacon, the pork you take from the smoker will be moist and full of flavor.

Preparing Lamb and Pork for Grilling

When you get the meat home from the butcher or supermarket, immediately stow it in the coldest part of the refrigerator, which usually is the rear of the lowest shelf. Do not unwrap it; you do not want to unnecessarily expose it to the air, and keeping it wrapped in its original packaging is a good idea.

When you are ready to prepare the meat, take it from the refrigerator and let it come to room temperature, which means leaving it on the counter for 15 to 30 minutes. If it is a particularly hot, humid summer day, reduce the counter time by a few minutes. Pat the meat dry with paper towels and then marinate it, rub it with dry rub, or otherwise prepare it for the grill. We have not always included this important step in the recipe instructions, because it is universally appropriate for all recipes calling for beef, veal, poultry, lamb, or pork that will be grilled or smoked. If the meat is dry prior to cooking, it will brown nicely.

Buying Meat in Season

Very few shoppers think of meat as being seasonal and while it is not as true as it once was, some types of meat are better at different times of year. Because of old-time farming practices, fresh pork used to be most available in the late fall, while lamb was reserved for the spring. Such strictures are not as clear nowadays—with modern farming, all meats and poultry are quite good year round. Nevertheless, lamb is certainly at its best from mid-April through October. Pork is tastiest from May until early October. Venison is best from October through December. Pheasant taste better when bought in the autumn, although they are quite good all year. Beef, veal, chicken, duck, and quail are excellent all year long.

Buying Boned Leg of Lamb and Butterflied Leg of Lamb

Not all boned leg of lamb is "butterflied." Once the leg bone has been removed, the meat can either be rolled for roasting or butterflied for grilling. To ensure that you are buying a butterflied leg of lamb, ask the butcher specifically for it, and ask him to "butterfly it at both ends." One end is the top round end; the other end is the sirloin end. Both create a flap, which can then be flattened to even out and open up the meat. However, regardless of the skill of the butcher, all butterflied legs of lamb are imperfectly shaped by nature, which means that when grilling you have to tend to the meat carefully to ensure that it does not overcook.

Buying Lamb Chops

Nowadays lamb chops are considered a great treat and so it's important to know what you're buying to get the most for your money. Without question, we prefer loin or rib chops. The meat in both chops is tender and flavorful, and they grill beautifully. A two-inch-thick loin chop weighs about seven ounces and a one-and-one-half-inch-thick loin chop weighs about five ounces. The thicker the chop, the better the flavor, so we urge you to buy the thickest chops you can find. If you have a butcher, ask him to cut thick chops for you. You won't regret it. Loin chops sold by butchers sometimes have longer tail bones than those sold in supermarkets, which can affect the weight and consequently the price.

Loin chops are from the loin of the lamb. Rib chops are those chops that, when attached, make up the rack (as in "rack of lamb" or "rack roast"). Loin chops have a small T-bone that separates the tenderloin from the eye. Some butchers insert a kidney below the tenderloin and curve the tail around it, securing it with a skewer; this is very fancy and not too common in this day of impersonal butcher counters. When loin chops are boned, trimmed, and rolled they are called "noisettes." Rib chops, which can be used whenever loin chops are called for, do not have tenderloins but are just as flavorful.

Other lamb chops are from the shoulder, and include both the blade and the arm chops. Blade shoulder chops are cut from the beginning of the shoulder, right after the rack, and are more desirable than arm shoulder chops. Arm shoulder chops are from the lower part of the shoulder, near the shank, and have a small round bone. These chops are less tender than the loin and rib chops but have good lamb flavor. They are less expensive and take well to marinating.

Leg of lamb is a popular cut, one that most lamb lovers adore, and when the tip end of the shank is removed and the leg completely boned, the leg becomes a butterflied leg of lamb. Lay the meat out flat and you will note that although it is not uniformly even, its thickest parts are thin enough to grill nicely. You may choose to pound the thicker parts so that the entire piece of meat will cook more evenly. Here, we rub a simple lemony paste enhanced with cumin and garlic into the meat for a delectable crust once it's grilled.

Butterflied Leg of Lamb with Cumin and Garlic   *Serves 6*

HEAT =

2 TABLESPOONS FRESH LEMON JUICE

2 TABLESPOONS GROUND CUMIN

3 LARGE CLOVES GARLIC, MINCED

FRESHLY GROUND BLACK PEPPER TO

    TASTE

ONE 4- TO 5-POUND BUTTERFLIED LEG

    OF LAMB

VEGETABLE OIL COOKING SPRAY

1/3 CUP EXTRA VIRGIN OLIVE OIL

1 LARGE CLOVE GARLIC, CRUSHED

1. Combine the lemon juice, cumin, garlic, and pepper in a small bowl and stir into a paste.

2. Put the lamb in a shallow glass or ceramic dish and rub both sides with the garlic-cumin paste. Cover and refrigerate for 4 to 6 hours. About 30 minutes before grilling, remove the meat from the refrigerator and let it come to room temperature.

3. Prepare a charcoal or gas grill for indirect cooking (see page 7): Lightly spray the grill rack with vegetable oil cooking spray. Light the coals or heating elements, and let them burn or heat until hot.

4. Combine the oil and crushed garlic in a small dish for brushing on the meat.

5. Sear the lamb over the hot coals for about 5 minutes on each side, brushing with the olive oil and garlic mixture several times; continue brushing the lamb with olive oil and garlic during the first 20 minutes of grilling. Move the lamb to the cooler part of the grill, cover, and cook for about 10 minutes. Turn the meat, cover, and cook for 10 to 15 minutes longer for medium-rare meat (145° to 150°F), or until it is cooked to the desired degree of doneness. Let the lamb rest for about 10 minutes before slicing.

Butterflied leg of lamb is not a pretty sight when you bring it home. It's a lumpy piece of meat, often folded back on itself—one that frequently requires trimming and gentle flattening—but once you prepare and grill it, nothing beats it! It's one of our favorite grilled meats—tender, full flavored, and aromatic.

Butterflied Leg of Lamb with Garlicky Grilled Eggplant   *Serves 6*

HEAT =

LAMB
1 CUP DRY RED WINE

1/2 CUP OLIVE OIL

2 LARGE CLOVES GARLIC, CHOPPED

3 TABLESPOONS CHOPPED FRESH THYME

1 1/2 TEASPOONS FRESHLY CRACKED
   BLACK PEPPER

1 TEASPOON SALT

ONE 4- TO 5-POUND BUTTERFLIED LEG
   OF LAMB

FRESHLY GROUND BLACK PEPPER TO
   TASTE

1/3 CUP EXTRA VIRGIN OLIVE OIL

1 LARGE CLOVE GARLIC, CRUSHED

VEGETABLE OIL COOKING SPRAY

EGGPLANT
2 LARGE EGGPLANTS

COARSE SALT TO TASTE

1/2 CUP OLIVE OIL

3 CLOVES GARLIC, MINCED

1. To prepare the lamb, combine the wine, oil, garlic, thyme, cracked pepper, and salt in a glass or ceramic bowl and whisk well.

2. Put the lamb in a shallow glass or ceramic dish and pour the marinade over it, turning several times to coat. Cover and refrigerate for at least 6 hours and up to 24 hours. About 30 minutes before grilling, remove the meat from the refrigerator and let it come to room temperature.

3. To prepare the eggplant, about 1 hour before grilling, trim the eggplant and cut into 1/2-inch-thick slices. Sprinkle both sides of the slices generously with coarse salt, place them between sheets of paper towels, and set aside for about 30 minutes. Turn them once or twice. Rinse well under cool running water and pat dry. Set aside.

4. Combine the olive oil and minced garlic in a small bowl. Brush the eggplant generously on both sides and set aside in a shallow dish for about 30 minutes.

5. Prepare a charcoal or gas grill for indirect cooking (see page 7): Lightly spray the grill rack with vegetable oil cooking spray. Light the coals or heating elements, and let them burn or heat until hot.

6. Lift the lamb from the dish, pat dry, and season the lamb on both sides with freshly ground black pepper. Discard the marinade.

7. Combine the oil and crushed garlic in a small bowl for brushing on the meat.

8. Sear the lamb over the hot coals for about 5 minutes on each side, brushing with the olive oil and garlic mixture several times. Move the lamb to the cooler part of the grill, cover, and cook for about 10 minutes. Continue brushing the lamb with the remaining olive oil and garlic mixture during the first 20 minutes of grilling. Turn the meat over, cover, and cook for 10 to 15 minutes longer for medium-rare meat, or until it is cooked to the desired degree of doneness. An instant-read thermometer inserted in the thickest part of the meat should register 140°F for rare meat and 145° to 150°F for medium-rare. Let the lamb rest for about 10 minutes before slicing.

9. About 10 minutes before the lamb is done, cook the eggplant on the edge of the grill, away from the hottest part of the fire, for about 4 minutes. Turn and cook for about 5 minutes longer, or until tender. Serve with the lamb.

Lamb and yogurt is a match made in heaven, and when the yogurt is mixed with garlic, mint, and fresh thyme, the perfect combination just gets better. With flavorful marinades such as those we suggest with lamb, you won't miss gravy made from pan juices. Butterflied leg of lamb is an uneven piece of meat and so you will have to adjust the cooking time or pound sections of the lamb to promote even cooking.

Butterflied Leg of Lamb Marinated in Yogurt and Mint   *Serves 6*

HEAT =

1 CUP PLAIN YOGURT

2 TABLESPOONS FRESH LEMON JUICE

1 TABLESPOON OLIVE OIL

4 SCALLIONS, WHITE AND GREEN PARTS, FINELY CHOPPED

3 LARGE CLOVES GARLIC, MINCED, PLUS 1 LARGE CLOVE GARLIC

¼ CUP CHOPPED FRESH MINT

2 TABLESPOONS CHOPPED FRESH THYME

GRATED ZEST OF 1 LEMON

1 TABLESPOON FRESHLY CRACKED BLACK PEPPER

SALT TO TASTE

ONE 4- TO 5-POUND BUTTERFLIED LEG OF LAMB

VEGETABLE OIL COOKING SPRAY

⅓ CUP EXTRA VIRGIN OLIVE OIL

1 LARGE CLOVE GARLIC, CRUSHED

1. Combine the yogurt, lemon juice, olive oil, scallions, minced garlic, mint, thyme, lemon zest, pepper, and salt in a large bowl and stir to mix.

2. Rub the garlic clove over both sides of the lamb and put the lamb in a shallow glass or ceramic dish. Pour the marinade over the meat and turn it several times to coat. Cover and refrigerate for 4 to 6 hours. About 30 minutes before grilling, remove the meat from the refrigerator and let it come to room temperature.

3. Prepare a charcoal or gas grill for indirect cooking (see page 7): Lightly spray the grill rack with vegetable oil cooking spray. Light the coals or heating elements, and let them burn or heat until hot.

4. Lift the lamb from the dish, scrape off the excess marinade, and season both sides with salt and pepper. Discard the marinade.

5. Combine the oil and crushed garlic in a small bowl for brushing on the meat.

6. Sear the lamb over the hot coals for about 5 minutes on each side, brushing with the olive oil and garlic mixture several times; continue brushing the lamb with the remaining olive oil and garlic mixture during the first 20 minutes of grilling. Move the lamb to the cooler part of the grill, cover, and cook for about 10 minutes. Turn the meat over, cover, and cook for 10 to 15 minutes longer for medium-rare meat (145° to 150°F), or until it is cooked to the desired degree of doneness. Let the lamb rest for about 10 minutes before slicing.

Boneless top round of lamb is not a particularly common cut, but a good butcher will be able to order it for you. Because it usually has to be special ordered, it may come packaged in Cryovac. While we don't like the practice of using Cryovac in many cases, here it is fine. The meat will be great. If it's tied, we suggest removing the string so that the juices run more freely during grilling. In fact, we never like to tie meat. Why squeeze the moisture out during cooking? Two pounds of lamb is ample for these stacks of meat, summer eggplant, bell peppers, and cheese. If you can't find boneless top round of lamb, try this recipe with beef flank steak.

Roast Lamb with Grilled Summer Vegetables   *Serves 4 to 6*

HEAT =

SPICE BLEND

1 TABLESPOON YELLOW MUSTARD
   SEEDS

1 TABLESPOON FENNEL SEEDS

1 TEASPOON BLACK PEPPERCORNS

1 TEASPOON DRIED ROSEMARY LEAVES

¼ TEASPOON GROUND CUMIN

¼ TEASPOON GROUND ALLSPICE

½ CUP EXTRA VIRGIN OLIVE OIL

3 TABLESPOONS SHERRY VINEGAR

2 TEASPOONS COARSE SALT

LAMB

2 POUNDS BONELESS TOP ROUND LAMB
   ROAST

2 POUNDS EGGPLANT (2 TO 4
   EGGPLANTS, DEPENDING ON
   VARIETY), TRIMMED BUT NOT PEELED

1. To prepare the spice blend, spread the mustard seeds, fennel seeds, peppercorns, rosemary leaves, and cumin in a small, dry skillet and toast over medium heat for 3 to 4 minutes, until aromatic, stirring or shaking the pan occasionally. Remove from the heat, stir in the allspice, and set aside for about 5 minutes to cool.

2. Transfer the spices to a spice grinder, coffee grinder, or mortar and pestle and grind until lightly ground with some good texture still remaining. In a spice grinder this will take 10 to 15 seconds.

3. Whisk together the olive oil, vinegar, and salt in a small bowl until the salt dissolves. Add the ground spices and stir well.

4. To prepare the lamb, put the meat in a shallow glass or ceramic dish. Coat it with about ⅓ cup of the spice blend, rubbing it into the meat. Cover and refrigerate for at least 1 hour and up to 2 hours, letting the meat come to room temperature before grilling.

5. Slice the eggplant on a slight diagonal into ½-inch-thick slices. Put them and the bell peppers in a large resealable plastic bag and add the remaining spice blend. Seal the bag, shake to coat the vegetables evenly, and set aside until ready to use. Slice the mozzarella into ¼-inch-thick slices and cover until ready to use.

4 RED BELL PEPPERS, HALVED
  LENGTHWISE, SEEDED, AND
  STEMMED
ONE 1-POUND WHOLE PIECE FRESH
  MOZZARELLA
VEGETABLE OIL COOKING SPRAY
1 BUNCH FRESH BASIL, LEAVES ONLY,
  LEFT WHOLE
FRESH ROSEMARY SPRIGS, FOR
  GARNISH (OPTIONAL)

6. Prepare a charcoal or gas grill: Lightly spray the grill rack with vegetable oil cooking spray. Light the coals or heating elements, and let them burn or heat until moderately hot.

7. Grill the lamb for about 15 minutes until grill marks appear on one side. Turn and grill, covered, for 25 to 30 minutes longer, until an instant-read thermometer registers 140°F for medium-rare, or until it is cooked to the desired degree of doneness. (If using flank steak, grill 7 minutes per side for medium-rare.)

8. Let the meat rest, loosely tented with foil, for about 5 minutes before serving.

9. About 20 minutes before the meat is done, put the vegetables on the grill (start the vegetables 5 minutes before adding the flank steak, if using). Turn once or twice until browned and cooked through. If they are done before the lamb is, move the vegetables to the cooler side of the grill to keep them warm.

10. Slice the meat thinly across the grain and put on a serving platter. Top with half the eggplant slices, spreading them to cover the meat. Top these with the slices of mozzarella, the basil leaves, the red bell peppers, and finally the rest of the eggplant. The mozzarella will soften, sandwiched as it is by the warm meat and vegetables.

11. Garnish the platter with fresh rosemary sprigs, if desired, and serve.

Lamb chops are small, juicy, utterly irresistible treasures. Loin chops are deliciously tender, with a small T-bone that separates the tenderloin from the eye. Rib chops match loin chops in flavor and tenderness. These are the chops from a rack of lamb and while they have no tenderloin, they are tasty. If you choose to grill them, watch them carefully as they may take a little less time to cook.

Mint-Brushed Lamb Chops   *Serves 6*

HEAT =

½ CUP CIDER VINEGAR

2 TEASPOONS SUGAR

½ CUP COARSELY CHOPPED FRESH
   MINT

12 LOIN LAMB CHOPS, EACH ABOUT
   2 INCHES THICK

VEGETABLE OIL COOKING SPRAY

FRESHLY GROUND BLACK PEPPER TO
   TASTE

1. Combine the vinegar and sugar in a small bowl and stir until the sugar dissolves. Transfer to a blender and add the mint. Blend until the mint is finely chopped. Brush on both sides of the chops and set aside at room temperature for about 10 minutes. Reserve some of the mixture to brush on the chops during grilling.

2. Prepare a charcoal or gas grill: Lightly spray the grill rack with vegetable oil cooking spray. Light the coals or heating elements, and let them burn or heat until moderately hot to hot.

3. Grill the chops for 6 to 8 minutes on each side until medium-rare, or they are cooked to the desired degree of doneness. Baste with the vinegar mixture several times during grilling. Watch for flare-ups. If they occur, move the chops to a cooler part of the grill and extinguish the flames with a spritz of water. Then move the chops back to the hot fire. Season with pepper just before serving.

Rosemary is perhaps the herb that best brings out the flavor of lamb, and while we usually prefer fresh rosemary, for this recipe, we like the dried herb because of its intensity. We call for loin chops for this and a number of other recipes in the book. You could also use rib chops, which make up a rack of lamb. They have no tenderloin but their meat is succulent and tasty. The rack roast can be cut into single, double, or triple chops. When the fat is trimmed and the end of the bone is left bare so that the meat resembles a small circle attached to the bone, the chops are called "French rib lamb chops"—and sometimes a paper frill is slipped over the bone to disguise it. However, when we grill chops, we leave the frilly decorations inside the house! You can grill any size lamb chop you like, although watch it carefully if it's thicker or thinner than we suggest here.

Grilled Loin Lamb Chops with Rosemary   *Serves 6*

HEAT =

½ CUP OLIVE OIL

¼ CUP RED WINE VINEGAR

2 TABLESPOONS DRIED ROSEMARY

2 CLOVES GARLIC, MINCED

12 LOIN LAMB CHOPS, EACH ABOUT 1½
   INCHES THICK

VEGETABLE OIL COOKING SPRAY

SALT AND FRESHLY GROUND BLACK
   PEPPER TO TASTE

1. Combine the olive oil, vinegar, rosemary, and garlic in a small bowl. Put the chops in one layer in a shallow glass or ceramic dish and add the marinade, turning the chops several times to coat. Cover and refrigerate for 4 hours or overnight, letting the meat come to room temperature before grilling.

2. Prepare a charcoal or gas grill: Lightly spray the grill rack with vegetable oil cooking spray. Light the coals or heating elements, and let them burn or heat until moderately hot to hot.

3. Grill the chops for about 6 to 8 minutes on each side for medium-rare, or until they are cooked to the desired degree of doneness. Season with salt and pepper and serve.

For this recipe we use loin lamb chops for their tenderness and sweet flavor. However, you could substitute rib chops or even shoulder lamb chops, which, while not as tender, are less expensive and quite flavorful.

Lamb Chops with Grilled Stuffed Mushrooms   *Serves 4*

HEAT =

LAMB CHOPS

2 CLOVES GARLIC, CRUSHED

¼ CUP PLUS 2 TABLESPOONS FINELY
  GRATED ONION (SEE NOTE)

1½ TEASPOONS FRESHLY GROUND
  BLACK PEPPER

1 TEASPOON CHOPPED FRESH
  ROSEMARY

1 TEASPOON CHOPPED FRESH THYME

½ TEASPOON SALT

8 LOIN LAMB CHOPS, EACH ABOUT
  1½ INCHES THICK

¼ CUP OLIVE OIL

¼ CUP DRY RED WINE

VEGETABLE OIL COOKING SPRAY

1. To prepare the chops, combine the garlic, onion, pepper, rosemary, thyme, and salt in a small bowl and stir into a paste. Rub the paste into both sides of the chops. Put the chops in a large, shallow glass or ceramic dish, pour the oil and wine over them, turning the chops to coat. Cover and refrigerate at least 2 hours or overnight, letting the meat come to room temperature before grilling.

2. Prepare a charcoal or gas grill: Lightly spray the grill rack with vegetable oil cooking spray. Light the coals or heating elements, and let them burn or heat until moderately hot to hot.

3. To prepare the mushrooms, combine the feta, cream cheese, parsley, thyme, and marjoram in a small bowl, season with pepper, and mix well.

4. Remove the stems from the mushrooms, leaving a cavity in the cap. Rub the caps inside and out with oil and sprinkle lightly with salt. Put the mushrooms on the grill, cavity side down, and grill for 2 or 3 minutes, until lightly browned and softened. Transfer the mushrooms to a pan, cavity side up, and spoon an equal amount of the cheese filling in each.

5. Lift the chops from the dish and let the marinade drip back into the dish. Grill the chops for 6 to 8 minutes on each side for medium-rare, or until they are cooked to the desired degree of doneness.

MUSHROOMS

¾ CUP CRUMBLED FETA CHEESE (3½
   TO 4 OUNCES)

¼ CUP CREAM CHEESE, SOFTENED

2 TABLESPOONS CHOPPED FLAT-LEAF
   PARSLEY

½ TEASPOON CHOPPED FRESH THYME

½ TEASPOON CRUSHED DRIED
   MARJORAM

FRESHLY GROUND BLACK PEPPER TO
   TASTE

TWENTY-FOUR 2-INCH-DIAMETER WHITE
   OR CREMINI MUSHROOMS

OLIVE OIL

SALT TO TASTE

6. Just before turning the chops, put the mushrooms filled side up on the edge of the grill, away from the hottest part of the fire, and cook for 5 to 6 minutes, until the cheese begins to melt. Remove the mushrooms and the chops from the grill and serve them together.

note: To grate the onion, rub the cut portion of the onion along a handheld cheese grater or grate the onion in a food processor.

In butcher-shop terminology, lambs don't have front legs. There are back legs and there are shoulders. Shoulder meat is not as tender as leg and loin and rib meat, and therefore is less expensive. Blade lamb chops are cut from the top of the shoulder, right after the rack, and arm lamb chops are cut from lower in the shoulder, near the shank. Arm chops have a small round bone near their centers. Both are great on the grill, particularly if flavored boldly, as these are with mustard and cumin.

Mustard-Glazed Shoulder Lamb Chops *Serves 6*

HEAT =

VEGETABLE OIL COOKING SPRAY

¼ CUP DIJON MUSTARD

¼ CUP RED WINE VINEGAR

1 TABLESPOON GROUND CUMIN

FRESHLY GROUND BLACK PEPPER TO
    TASTE

12 SHOULDER LAMB CHOPS, EACH
    ABOUT 1 INCH THICK

1. Prepare a charcoal or gas grill: Lightly spray the grill rack with vegetable oil cooking spray. Light the coals or heating elements, and let them burn or heat until moderately hot to hot.

2. Combine the mustard, vinegar, cumin, and a pinch of pepper in a small bowl. Brush on the chops and marinate at room temperature for 10 to 20 minutes.

3. Grill the chops for 5 to 6 minutes on each side for medium-rare, or until they are cooked to the desired degree of doneness. Season with pepper just before serving.

A rack is a connected series of rib chops. The butcher usually cracks the bones so that the rack is easy to separate into chops after cooking. For some reason, home cooks regard racks of lamb as too fancy to grill—which couldn't be farther from the truth. A rack lends itself to grilling as readily as do separate chops—and it looks magnificent when lifted from the grill, perfectly browned and just a little crusty.

Simple Grilled Rack of Lamb   *Serves 4 to 6*

HEAT =

2 RACKS OF LAMB (8 CHOPS EACH,
    EACH RACK ABOUT 1 1/2 POUNDS),
    TRIMMED BY THE BUTCHER
1/4 CUP OLIVE OIL
1 TABLESPOON CHOPPED FRESH
    ROSEMARY
FRESHLY GROUND BLACK PEPPER TO
    TASTE
VEGETABLE OIL COOKING SPRAY

1. Trim the lamb of silver skin and fat, if necessary, and rub both sides of the rack with olive oil. Sprinkle with rosemary and pepper, rubbing them into the meatiest parts of the racks.

2. Prepare a charcoal or gas grill: Lightly spray the grill rack with vegetable oil cooking spray. Light the coals or heating elements, and let them burn or heat until moderately hot to hot.

3. Grill the racks, meat side down, for 4 to 5 minutes, until the temperature of the meatiest part reaches 100°F. Move the racks to the edge of the grill, away from the hottest part of the fire, and cook, covered, for 10 to 15 minutes longer, until the temperature reaches 140°F for rare meat. Remove the racks from the grill and let them rest for about 5 minutes before cutting between the ribs into individual chops.

Because we like grilled rack of lamb so much, we are constantly on the lookout for new ways to season it. This recipe relies on the meat's classic flavor partners: rosemary, garlic, and mustard; the result is out of this world. Try this in the springtime when really good lamb is young and readily available. Of course, this is good anytime!

Crusted Rack of Lamb   *Serves 4 to 6*

HEAT =

2 RACKS OF LAMB (8 CHOPS EACH,
   EACH RACK ABOUT 1 1/2 POUNDS),
   TRIMMED BY THE BUTCHER
1/4 CUP PLUS 2 TABLESPOONS OLIVE OIL
3/4 CUP PANKO OR OTHER DRY BREAD
   CRUMBS (SEE NOTE)
3 TABLESPOONS MINCED FRESH
   ROSEMARY
3 TABLESPOONS COUNTRY-STYLE DIJON
   MUSTARD
2 LARGE CLOVES GARLIC, MINCED
2 TABLESPOONS BALSAMIC VINEGAR
1 TEASPOON COARSE SALT
1/2 TEASPOON FRESHLY GROUND BLACK
   PEPPER
VEGETABLE OIL COOKING SPRAY

1. Rub the lamb all over with 1/4 cup of the olive oil and set aside.

2. In a small bowl, mix together the panko, rosemary, mustard, garlic, the remaining 2 tablespoons of olive oil, the vinegar, salt, and pepper. Blend thoroughly to make about 1 cup of paste.

3. Spread the paste over the meaty side of each rack. This will form a crust so make sure to coat the racks evenly, spreading it over the meaty portions but not covering the bones. Set aside, loosely covered with foil, while the grill heats.

4. Prepare a charcoal or gas grill: Lightly spray the grill rack with vegetable oil cooking spray. Light the coals or heating elements, and let them burn or heat until moderately hot.

5. Lay the racks on the grill, crust side down, and cook for 3 to 4 minutes, until aromatic and grill marks form on the crust. Using tongs or a wide spatula, carefully turn the racks over. If a little of the crust slides off, lift it off the grill and push it back in place.

6. Cover the grill and cook for 15 to 20 minutes longer, depending on the thickness of the meat, until an instant-read thermometer inserted in a meaty portion of a rack registers 140ºF for medium-rare, or until the meat is cooked to the desired degree of doneness. Move the meat around on the grill to ensure even cooking but don't turn it again. Let the racks rest for 5 minutes before cutting between the ribs into individual chops for serving.

note: Panko bread crumbs, easy to find in many supermarkets and Asian stores, are Japanese-style bread crumbs that cling well and produce a light, crispy crust.

We like to rub rack of lamb with a heady mixture of blue cheese, rosemary, and garlic before grilling it. The resulting meat is boldly flavored and absolutely delicious.

Rack of Lamb Rubbed with Blue Cheese *Serves 4 to 6*

HEAT =

2 RACKS OF LAMB (8 CHOPS EACH,
   EACH RACK ABOUT 1¹⁄₂ POUNDS),
   TRIMMED BY THE BUTCHER
¹⁄₄ CUP PLUS 2 TABLESPOONS OLIVE OIL
2 HEAPING TABLESPOONS CRUMBLED
   BLUE CHEESE
2 TABLESPOONS MUSTARD SEEDS
4 TEASPOONS MASHED GARLIC
2 TEASPOONS CHOPPED FRESH
   ROSEMARY
FRESHLY GROUND BLACK PEPPER
   TO TASTE
VEGETABLE OIL COOKING SPRAY

1. Trim the lamb of silver skin and fat, if necessary. Combine the oil, blue cheese, mustard seeds, garlic, and rosemary in a small bowl, season with pepper, and stir to make a paste. Spread the paste on the racks, rubbing it into the meatiest parts of the racks.

2. Prepare a charcoal or gas grill: Lightly spray the grill rack with vegetable oil cooking spray. Light the coals or heating elements, and let them burn or heat until moderately hot to hot.

3. Grill the racks, meat side down, for 4 to 5 minutes, until the temperature of the meatiest part reaches 100°F. Move the racks to the edge of the grill, away from the most intense heat and grill, covered, for 10 to 15 minutes longer, turning once, until the temperature reaches 140°F for medium-rare meat. Lift the racks from the grill and let them rest for about 5 minutes before cutting between the ribs into individual chops.

S ome butchers cut meat for kabobs from nearly any part of the lamb, but we feel that the best meat for skewered, grilled lamb comes from the leg. If the butcher hasn't done so, trim the meat well to ensure that no tough membranes remain.

Lamb Kabobs Marinated in Red Wine   *Serves 6*

HEAT =

1 CUP DRY RED WINE

1/4 CUP OLIVE OIL

2 OR 3 SCALLIONS, WHITE AND GREEN
PARTS, CHOPPED

2 LARGE CLOVES GARLIC, MINCED

2 TABLESPOONS CHOPPED FLAT-LEAF
PARSLEY

1 TABLESPOON CHOPPED FRESH
ROSEMARY

SALT AND FRESHLY CRACKED BLACK
PEPPER TO TASTE

3 POUNDS BONELESS LEG OF LAMB,
TRIMMED AND CUT INTO 1 1/2-INCH
CUBES

VEGETABLE OIL COOKING SPRAY

1 SMALL ONION, CUT INTO 6 WEDGES

12 LARGE WHITE MUSHROOMS (ABOUT
1/2 POUND), STEMMED

12 CHERRY TOMATOES

SIX 12-INCH METAL SKEWERS

1. Combine the wine, oil, scallions, garlic, parsley, and rosemary in a large, shallow glass or ceramic dish; season to taste with salt and pepper. Add the lamb, toss to coat, cover, and refrigerate for at least 4 hours or overnight, letting the meat come to room temperature before grilling.

2. Prepare a charcoal or gas grill: Lightly spray the grill rack with vegetable oil cooking spray. Light the coals or heating elements, and let them burn or heat until moderately hot to hot.

3. Thread the lamb, onion wedges, mushrooms, and tomatoes onto each skewer, beginning and ending with meat. Grill for 8 to 10 minutes, turning several times with tongs and brushing 2 or 3 times with the marinade during the first few minutes of grilling. Cook until the lamb is medium-rare and the vegetables are tender. Serve immediately.

The front section of the hindsaddle of the lamb is the sirloin, which is the thickest part of the leg. The rear section of hindsaddle is the shank. A whole leg of lamb includes both the sirloin and the shank. The two sections can be separated into a sirloin leg of lamb and a shank leg of lamb. Meat for kabobs can come from either section, with the sirloin obviously being a little more tender.

Lamb Kabobs with Garam Masala and Yogurt Marinade *Serves 6*

HEAT =

1 CUP PLAIN YOGURT

1/4 CUP FRESH LEMON JUICE

2 CLOVES GARLIC, MINCED OR CRUSHED

2 TABLESPOONS MINCED FRESH GINGER

1 TABLESPOON GARAM MASALA (PAGE 244; SEE NOTE)

2 TEASPOONS SUGAR

1 TEASPOON GROUND CUMIN

1 TEASPOON SALT

1/4 TEASPOON CAYENNE

3 POUNDS BONELESS LEG OF LAMB, TRIMMED AND CUT INTO 1 1/2-INCH CUBES

VEGETABLE OIL COOKING SPRAY

SIX 12-INCH METAL SKEWERS

1. Combine the yogurt, lemon juice, garlic, ginger, garam masala, sugar, cumin, salt, and cayenne in a large glass or ceramic bowl. Add the lamb, toss to coat, cover, and refrigerate for at least 4 hours or overnight, letting the meat come to room temperature before grilling.

2. Prepare a charcoal or gas grill: Lightly spray the grill rack with vegetable oil cooking spray. Light the coals or heating elements, and let them burn or heat until moderately hot to hot.

3. Thread 4 or 5 pieces of lamb on six skewers. Discard the marinade. Grill for 8 to 10 minutes, turning several times with tongs, until the lamb is medium-rare. Serve immediately.

note: Garam masala is sold in Indian markets and specialty food stores. We have a recipe for making your own on page 244 and while it may seem like a lot of trouble, it keeps for months.

When you cut meat into cubes for kabobs, make sure you cut them into good-sized cubes, at least 1½ inches thick. These are large enough to hold up to grilling and not to fall through the grill rack if one slips off the skewer. For sturdy kabobs that are easy to turn, lay two skewers next to each other and thread the meat and vegetables on both. That way, the food cannot twist on the skewers. You will need twice the number of skewers called for in the recipe.

South India-Style Lamb Kabobs   *Serves 6*

HEAT =

¾ CUP CANOLA OIL

2 CLOVES GARLIC, MINCED

2 TABLESPOONS GRATED FRESH GINGER

1 TABLESPOON GROUND CORIANDER

2 TEASPOONS GROUND CUMIN

PINCH OF GROUND CINNAMON

PINCH OF GROUND CARDAMOM

3 POUNDS BONELESS LEG OF LAMB,
    TRIMMED AND CUT INTO 1½-INCH
    CUBES

SALT AND FRESHLY GROUND BLACK
    PEPPER TO TASTE

VEGETABLE OIL COOKING SPRAY

1 SMALL ONION, CUT INTO 6 WEDGES

1 LARGE GREEN BELL PEPPER, CUT INTO
    1½-INCH CHUNKS

1 LARGE RED BELL PEPPER, CUT INTO
    1½-INCH CHUNKS

SIX 12-INCH METAL SKEWERS

1. Combine the oil, garlic, ginger, coriander, cumin, cinnamon, and cardamom in a large, shallow glass or ceramic dish. Sprinkle the lamb generously with salt and pepper and add the lamb to the marinade. Toss to coat, cover, and refrigerate for at least 2 hours and as long as 6 hours, letting the meat come to room temperature before grilling.

2. Prepare a charcoal or gas grill: Lightly spray the grill rack with vegetable oil cooking spray. Light the coals or heating elements, and let them burn or heat until moderately hot to hot.

3. Thread the lamb, onion wedges, and bell peppers onto each skewer, beginning and ending with the meat. Grill for 8 to 10 minutes, turning several times with tongs and brushing 2 or 3 times with any excess marinade during the first few minutes of grilling. Cook until the lamb is medium-rare and the vegetables are tender. Serve immediately.

The best lamb steaks are cut from the leg, where the meat is finely textured and full of good lamb flavor. It makes sense, when buying a whole leg of lamb, to ask the butcher to cut a few steaks from the sirloin end to use for grilling. Any good butcher will cut lamb steaks for you if you ask. Because these steaks are quite large, they are cut relatively thin. These steaks are also called "leg lamb chops."

Lamb Steaks with Lemon and Parsley
Serves 6

HEAT =

6 LAMB STEAKS, EACH 1¼ INCHES
   THICK, CUT FROM THE LEG (2½ TO 3
   POUNDS TOTAL)
FRESHLY CRACKED BLACK PEPPER TO
   TASTE
3 TABLESPOONS OLIVE OIL
GRATED ZEST OF 1 LEMON
JUICE OF 2 LEMONS
3 TABLESPOONS CHOPPED FLAT-LEAF
   PARSLEY
VEGETABLE OIL COOKING SPRAY

1. Rub both sides of the lamb steaks with cracked pepper and put them in a large, shallow glass or ceramic dish.

2. Combine the oil, lemon zest, lemon juice, and parsley in a small bowl, stirring well, and add to the lamb, turning the steaks several times to coat. Cover and refrigerate for at least 4 hours and as long as 12 hours, letting the meat come to room temperature before grilling.

3. Prepare a charcoal or gas grill: Lightly spray the grill rack with vegetable oil cooking spray. Light the coals or heating elements, and let them burn or heat until moderately hot to hot.

4. Lift the steaks from the dish, reserving the marinade. Grill the steaks for 10 to 12 minutes for medium-rare, or until they are cooked to the desired degree of doneness, turning several times with tongs and brushing 2 or 3 times with the marinade during the first few minutes of cooking.

Pull up a chair and dig in! Few offerings off the grill beat spareribs for plain, old-fashioned "good eats." The spareribs are the breast and rib bones from the lower part of the center section of the hog, with tender, lean meat tucked between the bones. Cooking times can vary wildly when cooking ribs—some are meatier than others—so keep a close watch to keep them from burning or drying out.

Western-Style Grilled Spareribs   *Serves 6*

HEAT =

5 TO 6 POUNDS SPARERIBS (TWO
2½- TO 3-POUND RACKS)
½ CUP PEPPERY DRY RUB (PAGE 241)
VEGETABLE OIL COOKING SPRAY
MADISON AVENUE BARBECUE SAUCE
(PAGE 221)

1. Trim the spareribs of silver skin and fat, if necessary, and rub both sides of the ribs with the dry rub, working it into the meat. Put the ribs in a large, shallow glass or ceramic dish, cover, and set aside at room temperature for no longer than 30 minutes, or refrigerate for up to 24 hours, letting the meat come to room temperature before grilling. Alternatively, enclose the ribs in a resealable plastic bag and refrigerate. Let spareribs come to room temperature before grilling.

2. Prepare a charcoal or gas grill for indirect cooking (see page 7): Lightly spray the grill rack with vegetable oil cooking spray. Light the coals or heating elements, and let them burn or heat until hot.

3. Set the ribs, meat side down, over the hottest part of the fire and sear for about 10 minutes, until there are defined grill marks on the meat. Transfer the ribs to the cooler part of the grill, cover, and cook for about 1½ hours, turning the ribs every 15 to 20 minutes. If using a charcoal grill, add fresh coals to maintain the heat at medium; if using a gas grill, turn the heat to medium on the burner away from the meat and turn off the burner under the meat. Cut the ribs between the bones and serve with sauce on the side.

A full slab of spareribs has thirteen ribs, but a rack, which indicates human manipulation, can have any number up to twelve, depending on how the butcher or chef prepares it. Most full slabs weigh from three to three and one-half pounds, so when you want enough ribs to feed at least six hungry people, you will have to buy at least two slabs or twelve-rib racks.

Southeast Asian-Flavored Spareribs   *Serves 6*

HEAT =

5 TO 6 POUNDS SPARERIBS (TWO 2½- TO 3-POUND RACKS)

1 CUP ASIAN-STYLE LEMONGRASS PASTE (PAGE 246)

VEGETABLE OIL COOKING SPRAY

1. Trim the spareribs of silver skin and fat, if necessary, and rub both sides of the ribs with the paste, working it into the meat. Put the ribs in a large, shallow glass or ceramic dish, cover, and set aside at room temperature for no longer than 30 minutes, or refrigerate for up to 24 hours, letting the meat come to room temperature before grilling. Alternatively, enclose the ribs in a resealable plastic bag and refrigerate. Let spareribs come to room temperature before grilling.

2. Prepare a charcoal or gas grill for indirect cooking (see page 7): Lightly spray the grill rack with vegetable oil cooking spray. Light the coals or heating elements, and let them burn or heat until hot.

3. Set the ribs, meat side down, over the hottest part of the fire and sear for about 10 minutes, until there are defined grill marks on the meat. Transfer the ribs to the cooler part of the grill, cover, and cook for about 1½ hours, turning the ribs every 15 to 20 minutes. If using a charcoal grill, add fresh coals to maintain the heat at medium; if using a gas grill, turn the heat to medium on the burner away from the meat and turn off the burner under the meat. Cut the ribs between the bones and serve.

Country-style ribs—cut from the blade end of the loin, with no fewer than three and no more than six ribs in a rack—are much meatier than spareribs. You can make this recipe with spareribs. Whichever ribs you select, leave your indoor table manners behind and bring a good appetite to the feast.

Sweet Heat Country-Style Pork Ribs *Serves 6 to 8*

HEAT =

2 VERY RIPE PAPAYAS, PEELED, SEEDED,
   AND COARSELY CHOPPED
½ CUP DRY WHITE WINE
¼ CUP FRESH LIME JUICE
3 TABLESPOONS GRATED FRESH GINGER
2 TABLESPOONS SOY SAUCE
2 TEASPOONS CHINESE FIVE-SPICE
   POWDER
2 TEASPOONS HOT HUNGARIAN PAPRIKA
5 TO 6 POUNDS COUNTRY-STYLE PORK
   RIBS
VEGETABLE OIL COOKING SPRAY

1. Combine the papaya flesh, wine, lime juice, ginger, soy sauce, five-spice powder, and paprika in a food processor and pulse 4 or 5 times, until smooth.

2. Put the ribs in a shallow glass or ceramic dish large enough to hold them in a single layer and add the marinade, turning the ribs several times to coat. Cover and refrigerate for 4 hours, letting the meat come to room temperature before grilling.

3. Prepare a charcoal or gas grill for indirect cooking (see page 7): Lightly spray the grill rack with vegetable oil cooking spray. Light the coals or heating elements, and let them burn or heat until hot.

4. Lift the ribs from the dish and scrape most of the marinade from them. Discard the marinade. Set the ribs, meat side down, over the hottest part of the fire and sear for about 10 minutes, until there are defined grill marks on the meat. Transfer the ribs to the cooler part of the grill, cover, and cook for about 1½ hours, turning the ribs every 15 to 20 minutes, until a meat thermometer inserted in the meatiest part of the ribs registers 160°F. If using a charcoal grill, add fresh coals to maintain the heat at medium; if using a gas grill, turn the heat to medium on the burner away from the meat and turn off the burner under the meat. Cut the ribs between the bones and serve.

Ribs just don't get much better than these: they're fall-off-the-bone tender and tantalizingly succulent. We rub them first with our dry rub and then, once they're smoked, serve them with our legendary barbecue sauce and a side of slaw or potato salad. We smoke these with mesquite for its mildness, but slightly more pungent hickory would be great, too. Both baby-back and St. Louis–style ribs are shorter than spareribs, usually cut to about 3 inches. Succulent baby-back ribs are from the back of the pork loin, while St. Louis–style are meaty belly ribs. Both are out of this world.

As-Good-As-They-Get Smoked Baby-Back Ribs   *Serves 6*

HEAT =

½ CUP PACKED LIGHT OR DARK BROWN
   SUGAR

¼ CUP COARSE SALT

2 TABLESPOONS COARSELY GROUND
   BLACK PEPPER

2 TABLESPOONS SWEET PAPRIKA

2 TABLESPOONS CRUMBLED DRIED
   OREGANO

2 TEASPOONS CAYENNE

2 TEASPOONS GROUND CINNAMON

1 TEASPOON GROUND ALLSPICE

THREE 2½- TO 3-POUND RACKS BABY-
   BACK OR ST. LOUIS–STYLE RIBS

MADISON AVENUE BARBECUE SAUCE
   (PAGE 221)

1. In a small bowl, whisk together the brown sugar, salt, pepper, paprika, oregano, cayenne, cinnamon, and allspice.

2. Rub each rack with about ⅓ cup of the rub, working it quite well into the meaty part of the ribs. Reserve the remaining rub to use later. Wrap each rack in plastic wrap, stack them in a shallow pan, and refrigerate for at least 12 hours and up to 24 hours.

3. Prepare and preheat the smoker according to the manufacturer's instructions.

4. Unwrap each rack of ribs and rinse the seasoning mixture off them with cool running water. Pat the meat dry with paper towels and lay on a work surface. Coat both sides of the racks with the reserved rub, about 1 tablespoon per rack.

5. Put the racks on the shelf of the smoker and smoke for 2 hours at 200ºF. Remove from the smoker and wrap each rack separately in heavy-duty aluminum foil. Return to the smoker, seam side down, and smoke for 2 hours longer. Maintain the heat at 200ºF.

6. Carefully remove one rack of ribs from the smoker and open the foil packet. Test for tenderness: Twist a rib bone to determine if its moves freely. The meat should not be tough or chewy. If the ribs are not done, reseal and smoke for 30 minutes longer or until the ribs are cooked to the desired degree of doneness.

7. Discard the juices accumulated in the foil; they will be salty and bitter. Cut each rack into ribs and serve with barbecue sauce on the side.

ASK THE BUTCHER

What are the best meats for smoking?

As a rule, choose cuts of meat that hold up to long cooking, such as beef brisket, thick pork chops, and pork roasts. Chicken and turkey are great in the smoker, as is any game. (We love the duck breasts on page 205!) Because we have had the best success with relatively lean cuts of meat in the smoker, we did not smoke lamb, which is high in fat, for this book. We prefer the sweet-tasting meat as it comes off the grill: rich, juicy, and tantalizing. Many smoking enthusiasts like smoked lamb, however, and so if you want to try, smoke a lean cut such as the shoulder.

The slender tenderloin is cut from the front part of the center loin pork roast. We suggest grilling three loins for six people, which is generous. Once you taste this tender, sweet meat, you will be happy there is enough for seconds.

Pork Tenderloin Rubbed with Mustard and Bourbon *Serves 6*

HEAT =

¾ CUP SPICY BROWN MUSTARD

¼ CUP PLUS 2 TABLESPOONS BOURBON

3 TABLESPOONS OLIVE OIL

3 CLOVES GARLIC, MINCED

¼ CUP PLUS 2 TABLESPOONS CHOPPED
FRESH THYME

3 TABLESPOONS CHOPPED FLAT-LEAF
PARSLEY

FRESHLY GROUND BLACK PEPPER TO
TASTE

3 PORK TENDERLOINS, EACH ¾ TO 1
POUND, TRIMMED

VEGETABLE OIL COOKING SPRAY

1. Combine the mustard, bourbon, oil, garlic, thyme, parsley, and pepper in a bowl, stirring well. Rub into the tenderloins, covering the meat on all sides.

2. Put the tenderloins in a shallow glass or ceramic dish, cover, and set aside at room temperature for no longer than 30 minutes, or refrigerate for as long as 4 hours. If they have been refrigerated, let the tenderloins stand at room temperature for about 15 minutes before grilling.

3. Prepare a charcoal or gas grill: Lightly spray the grill rack with vegetable oil cooking spray. Light the coals or heating elements, and let them burn or heat until moderately hot to hot.

4. Grill the tenderloins for 12 to 14 minutes, turning with tongs once or twice, until cooked through and the internal temperature reaches 150° to 155°F. Let the pork rest for about 10 minutes before slicing; the temperature will rise to 160°F during the resting period. Slice thinly and serve.

One of the best ways to cook pork is on the grill. The succulent tenderloin especially shines when marinated with a full-bodied marinade and then grilled. Because you want to cook pork fully, use a reliable meat thermometer so that it will be perfect—but not overcooked.

Pork Tenderloin Marinated in Apple Cider   *Serves 6*

HEAT =

1 CUP APPLE CIDER OR APPLE JUICE

2 TO 3 TABLESPOONS RAISINS

2 TABLESPOONS PACKED DARK OR LIGHT
   BROWN SUGAR

$\frac{1}{4}$ TEASPOON GROUND CLOVES

1 TEASPOON GROUND CINNAMON

$\frac{1}{4}$ TEASPOON GROUND MACE

$\frac{1}{4}$ TEASPOON GROUND CARDAMOM

FRESHLY GROUND BLACK PEPPER TO
   TASTE

3 PORK TENDERLOINS, EACH $\frac{3}{4}$ TO 1
   POUND, TRIMMED

VEGETABLE OIL COOKING SPRAY

1. Combine the cider, raisins, brown sugar, cloves, cinnamon, mace, cardamom, and pepper in a small saucepan and bring to a boil over high heat. Reduce the heat to medium and cook, stirring, for 4 or 5 minutes, until the flavors blend and the raisins plump slightly. Remove from the heat and let cool slightly.

2. Put the tenderloins in a shallow glass or ceramic dish and pour the marinade over them. Cover and set aside at room temperature for no longer than 30 minutes, or refrigerate for as long as 4 hours. If they have been refrigerated, let the tenderloins stand at room temperature for about 15 minutes before grilling.

3. Prepare a charcoal or gas grill: Lightly spray the grill rack with vegetable oil cooking spray. Light the coals or heating elements, and let them burn or heat until moderately hot to hot.

4. Lift the tenderloins from the dish, reserving the marinade. Grill the tenderloins for 14 to 17 minutes, turning with tongs once or twice and brushing with the marinade during the first 10 minutes of cooking. Grill the tenderloins until cooked through and the internal temperature reaches 150° to 155°F. Let the pork rest for about 10 minutes before slicing; the temperature will rise to 160°F during the resting period. Slice thinly and serve.

ork tenderloin is easily available at all markets, generally packed in Cryovac and already trimmed. Still, we recommend you ask the butcher to remove it from the packaging for you and trim the fat and silver skin a little more completely. You don't want all the fat removed but it's a good idea to get rid of the silver skin. You can do this at home, too. With a sharp knife, it's pretty easy to slice away the thin, silvery membrane.

Pork tenderloins benefit from bold flavors and these get a threefold kick from eye-watering wasabi, pungent ginger, and fiery chili oil. Cool, crunchy slaw is the perfect complement.

Wasabi-Lime Pork Tenderloin with Asian Slaw   *Serves 6*

HEAT =

1/4 CUP TAMARI SOY SAUCE

3 TABLESPOONS FRESH LIME JUICE

2 TABLESPOONS WASABI POWDER (SEE
NOTE)

1/4 CUP VEGETABLE OIL

2 TABLESPOONS HONEY

6 SCALLIONS, WHITE AND GREEN PARTS,
CHOPPED

2 TABLESPOONS THINLY SLICED FRESH
GINGER (FROM ONE 2-INCH-LONG
PIECE)

1/2 TEASPOON CHILI OIL

GRATED ZEST OF 1 LIME

2 PORK TENDERLOINS, EACH ABOUT 1
POUND, TRIMMED

VEGETABLE OIL COOKING SPRAY

1/2 CUP FRESH CILANTRO LEAVES, FOR
GARNISH

ASIAN SLAW (PAGE 252)

1. Stir together the tamari, lime juice, and wasabi powder in a small bowl until the powder dissolves. Mix in the oil, honey, scallions, ginger, chili oil, and lime zest.

2. Place the pork tenderloins in a shallow glass or ceramic dish and pour the marinade over them. Turn to coat the meat evenly. Cover and set aside at room temperature for 30 minutes, or refrigerate for at least 1 hour and up to 4 hours, letting the meat come to room temperature before grilling.

3. Prepare a charcoal or gas grill: Lightly spray the grill rack with vegetable oil cooking spray. Light the coals or heating elements, and let them burn or heat until moderately hot to hot.

4. If the tenderloins were refrigerated, let them sit at room temperature for about 15 minutes before grilling. Lift the tenderloins from the dish and let the excess marinade drip back into the dish.

5. Grill the tenderloins, covered, for 14 to 17 minutes, turning with tongs once or twice, until cooked through and the internal temperature reaches 150° to 155°F. Let the pork rest for about 10 minutes before slicing; the temperature will rise to about 160°F. Slice thinly, garnish with cilantro, and serve with the Asian Slaw.

note: Green wasabi powder is sold in most supermarkets and Asian markets. It may be used as powder, as it is here, or, for other uses, reconstituted by mixing it with water.

Butterflying a pork tenderloin is a simple task. Cut along the length of the tenderloin, nearly but not quite splitting the meat in two separate pieces. Lay it open like a book and proceed with the recipe. The tenderloins are then stuffed and rolled back to their original shape. This is an impressive way to serve grilled pork when you are in the mood only for a little fussing but with a big payoff.

Barbecued Rolled-and-Stuffed Pork with Parsley and Cilantro *Serves 6*

HEAT =

1⅓ CUPS QUICK BARBECUE SAUCE
   (PAGE 222)

2 TABLESPOONS SWEET 'N' SPICY DRY
   RUB (PAGE 243)

⅓ CUP ROUGHLY CHOPPED FLAT-LEAF
   PARSLEY

⅓ CUP ROUGHLY CHOPPED FRESH
   CILANTRO LEAVES

2 PORK TENDERLOINS, EACH ABOUT
   1 POUND, TRIMMED OF FAT AND
   BUTTERFLIED

32 STURDY 4-INCH BAMBOO SKEWERS,
   SOAKED FOR AT LEAST 30 MINUTES

3 TABLESPOONS EXTRA VIRGIN
   OLIVE OIL

VEGETABLE OIL COOKING SPRAY

1. In a small bowl, mix together 2 tablespoons of the barbecue sauce and the dry rub. Reserve the remaining barbecue sauce to serve with the grilled pork.

2. In another bowl, toss together the parsley and cilantro.

3. Lay the meat on a work surface and open the tenderloins like a book with the cut side up.

4. Spread the pork with a thin layer of the spiced sauce. Sprinkle with the herbs. Fold each tenderloin back up into its original shape. Slice each tenderloin into 8 rounds, each about 1½ inches thick.

5. Pierce each of the rolls through the side with 1 skewer. Pierce again with a second skewer at a 90-degree angle to the first. (If the skewers used are too long, snip them so that they are easy to work with.) Brush the surface of the skewered rolls with the olive oil and then set aside, covered, for about 30 minutes. If you won't be cooking them immediately, refrigerate the rolls for up to 4 hours and let them return to room temperature before grilling.

6. Prepare a charcoal or gas grill: Lightly spray the grill rack with vegetable oil cooking spray. Light the coals or heating elements, and let them burn or heat until moderately hot.

7. Lay the pork rolls on the grill, cut surface down, and cook for 8 to 10 minutes, turning 2 or 3 times, until browned and an instant-read thermometer reaches 150° to 155°F.

8. Put the meat on a serving platter and brush with some of the reserved barbecue sauce. Let the rolls rest for 3 to 5 minutes and then serve with the barbecue sauce on the side.

A boneless pork loin roast is the center loin roast with the ribs and T-bones removed. It may contain the tenderloin, although usually this has been cut out of the loin. If you have the option, remove the tenderloin and freeze it for up to a month for later grilling.

It's important to use a meat thermometer to determine when pork is cooked. Take the meat from the grill when the thermometer registers 150° to 155°F and then let it rest for a few minutes. The temperature will rise to 160°F during resting. This avoids the possibility of overcooking.

Honey-Orange Pork Loin Roast *Serves 6 to 8*

HEAT =

½ CUP FRESH ORANGE JUICE

2 TABLESPOONS FROZEN ORANGE JUICE
   CONCENTRATE

2 TABLESPOONS HONEY

1 TABLESPOON SOY SAUCE

1 TABLESPOON OLIVE OIL

1 TEASPOON MINCED GARLIC

1 TEASPOON MINCED FRESH GINGER

½ TEASPOON CHINESE FIVE-SPICE
   POWDER

1 TEASPOON ASIAN CHILI PASTE

2 TO 3 DROPS HOT CHILI OIL

ONE 4- TO 4½-POUND BONELESS PORK
   LOIN ROAST, TRIMMED

VEGETABLE OIL COOKING SPRAY

MINTED SUMMER FRUIT SALSA (PAGE
   231) OR BAJA-STYLE TOMATO SALSA
   (PAGE 233), OPTIONAL

1. Combine the orange juice, juice concentrate, honey, soy sauce, oil, garlic, ginger, five-spice powder, chili paste, and chili oil in a bowl, stirring well.

2. Put the roast in a shallow glass or ceramic dish and pour the marinade over it. Turn to coat. Cover and refrigerate for at least 2 hours and as long as 12 hours, letting the meat come to room temperature before grilling.

3. Prepare a charcoal or gas grill for indirect cooking (see page 7): Lightly spray the grill rack with vegetable oil cooking spray. Light the coals or heating elements, and let them burn or heat until moderately hot.

4. Lift the roast from the dish, reserving the marinade and brushing it on the roast 2 or 3 times during the first 30 minutes of cooking. Grill over indirect heat with the grill covered for about 1 hour and 10 minutes, or until a meat thermometer inserted in the center of the roast registers 150° to 155°F. Remove the roast from the grill and let it rest for about 10 minutes before slicing. Serve with salsa, if desired.

Loin pork chops are cut from the front of the center loin and have a tasty nugget of tenderloin nestled next to the T-bone. They are juicy and delicious—a favorite for grilling. You could substitute rib pork chops, which are equally tasty but don't have the tenderloin. Beware of this spice rub: It is not for the faint of heart. The salsa cools it down a little, but not completely! If the rub is to your liking, try it on pork loin or spareribs, too.

Southwest-Style Pork Chops with Ancho Chile Powder   *Serves 4*

HEAT =

3 TABLESPOONS ANCHO CHILE POWDER
(SEE NOTES)

1 TABLESPOON TOASTED CUMIN SEEDS,
CRUSHED (SEE NOTES)

1 TEASPOON TOASTED CORIANDER
SEEDS, CRUSHED (SEE NOTES)

1 TEASPOON DRY MUSTARD

SALT AND FRESHLY GROUND BLACK
PEPPER TO TASTE

4 LOIN PORK CHOPS, EACH ABOUT
1½ INCHES THICK

VEGETABLE OIL COOKING SPRAY

BAJA-STYLE TOMATO SALSA (PAGE 233)

1. Combine the chile powder, cumin seeds, coriander seeds, and dry mustard in a small bowl. Season with salt and pepper, stirring well.

2. Rub the mixture into the meatiest parts of the pork chops and put the chops in a large, shallow glass or ceramic dish. Cover and set aside at room temperature for about 30 minutes, or refrigerate for as long as 8 hours, letting the meat come to room temperature before grilling.

3. Prepare a charcoal or gas grill: Lightly spray the grill rack with vegetable oil cooking spray. Light the coals or heating elements, and let them burn or heat until moderately hot.

4. Grill the chops for 8 to 10 minutes on each side, until a meat thermometer inserted in the center of the meatiest sections registers 150° to 155°F. Let the chops rest for a few minutes before serving. Serve with the salsa.

notes: Ancho chile powder is made from ground ancho chiles, which are mildly hot. The powder is generally available in Hispanic and specialty markets. If you cannot find it, substitute any chili powder.

To toast coriander seeds, spread them in a small dry skillet and cook over medium-high heat for about 60 seconds or until fragrant. Shake the pan during toasting to prevent burning. Crush the seeds with the back of a skillet.

Pork chops, when cut nice and thick, lend themselves to grilling like no other chop. A lamb chop or veal chop can be ruined if overcooked, but a pork chop tolerates a little more abuse. Although care should be taken never to overcook it, it will not turn from rare and juicy to gray and tough in a blink as red meat does. We especially like blending pork with Asian spices and flavorings.

Asian-Marinated Pork Chops with Sesame Seeds
Serves 4

HEAT =

½ CUP SOY SAUCE

¼ CUP MINCED SCALLIONS, WHITE AND GREEN PARTS

2 TABLESPOONS PLUS 1½ TEASPOONS PACKED LIGHT OR DARK BROWN SUGAR

2 TABLESPOONS TOASTED SESAME SEEDS (SEE NOTE)

1 TABLESPOON MINCED FRESH GINGER

1 TABLESPOON RICE WINE VINEGAR

½ TEASPOON ASIAN CHILI PASTE

4 LOIN PORK CHOPS, EACH ABOUT 1½ INCHES THICK

VEGETABLE OIL COOKING SPRAY

1. Combine the soy sauce, scallions, sugar, sesame seeds, ginger, vinegar, and chili paste in a small bowl, stirring well.

2. Put the pork chops in a shallow glass or ceramic dish and pour the marinade over them. Turn to coat. Cover and set aside at room temperature for about 30 minutes, or refrigerate for as long as 8 hours, letting the meat come to room temperature before grilling.

3. Prepare a charcoal or gas grill: Lightly spray the grill rack with vegetable oil cooking spray. Light the coals or heating elements, and let them burn or heat until moderately hot.

4. Lift the chops from the dish, reserving the marinade. Grill for about 10 minutes on each side, turning several times with tongs and brushing 2 or 3 times with the marinade during the first 10 or 15 minutes of cooking. Grill until a meat thermometer inserted in the center of the meatiest sections registers 150° to 155°F. Let the chops rest for a few minutes before serving.

note: To toast sesame seeds, spread them in a small, dry skillet and cook over medium-high heat for about 60 seconds or until fragrant. Shake the pan during toasting to prevent burning. Crush the seeds with the back of a skillet.

A sweet meat such as pork marries well with sweet ingredients like the maple syrup found in this marinade. Although we recommend loin chops, rib pork chops work equally well here. You could also marinate blade pork chops, which are cut from the blade roast and are larger and more robust than other pork chops. Grill blade chops a little longer than loin chops.

Maple-Flavored Pork Chops *Serves 6*

HEAT =

6 LOIN PORK CHOPS, EACH ABOUT
   1½ INCHES THICK
FRESHLY GROUND BLACK PEPPER TO
   TASTE
VEGETABLE OIL COOKING SPRAY
1½ CUPS MAPLE SYRUP MARINADE
   (PAGE 240)

1. Trim the pork chops, if necessary, and rub pepper into both sides of the meat. Put the chops in a large, shallow glass or ceramic dish and pour the marinade over the meat, turning several times to coat. Cover and refrigerate for at least 4 hours or overnight, letting the meat come to room temperature before grilling.

2. Prepare a charcoal or gas grill: Lightly spray the grill rack with vegetable oil cooking spray. Light the coals or heating elements, and let them burn or heat until moderately hot.

3. Lift the chops from the dish, reserving the marinade. Grill for about 10 minutes on each side, turning several times with tongs and brushing 2 or 3 times with the marinade during the first 10 or 15 minutes of cooking. Grill until a meat thermometer inserted in the center of the meatiest sections registers 150° to 155°F. Let the chops rest for a few minutes before serving.

Pork is not as juicy as some meats, but when cooked in foil packets after being soaked in a robust brine for hours, it is surprisingly moist. Try this with any style of pork chops—loin, rib, blade, or sirloin—although we make it with loin chops most often. We refer to these chops as "farmhouse-style," because curing pork in brine is an old-fashioned method. Here, we use the brine for moisture only—not curing.

Grilled Farmhouse-Style Pork Chops

Serves 6

HEAT =

2 CUPS APPLE CIDER

½ CUP FIRMLY PACKED LIGHT OR DARK BROWN SUGAR

½ CUP LIGHTLY PACKED FRESH THYME SPRIGS

3 TABLESPOONS SALT

2 TABLESPOONS COARSELY CHOPPED FRESH HOT CHILE OR ¼ TEASPOON CRUSHED RED PEPPER

12 WHOLE ALLSPICE BERRIES

2 BAY LEAVES

ONE 2-INCH STICK CINNAMON

1 TEASPOON BLACK PEPPERCORNS

6 LOIN PORK CHOPS, EACH ABOUT 1½ INCHES THICK

VEGETABLE OIL COOKING SPRAY

1. In a nonreactive saucepan, combine the cider, sugar, thyme, salt, chile, allspice, bay leaves, cinnamon, and peppercorns and bring to a boil over high heat. Reduce the heat to low and cook for about 20 minutes, or until the flavors blend. Set aside to cool completely.

2. Put the pork chops in a glass or ceramic dish just large enough so that when the brine is added, it will cover the meat. Add the brine, tucking the spices and herbs around the meat. Cover and refrigerate for 12 hours, letting the meat come to room temperature before grilling.

3. Drain the brine from the meat, reserving the herbs and spices.

4. On a work surface, layer 2 or 3 sheets of heavy-duty foil large enough to wrap 2 or 3 chops and lightly spray the top sheet with vegetable oil cooking spray. Place 2 or 3 chops close together and scatter with some of the reserved herbs and spices. Fold the foil over to cover the chops; double wrap the package with more foil. Repeat for the remaining chops.

5. Prepare a charcoal or gas grill for indirect cooking (see page 7): Lightly spray the grill rack with vegetable oil cooking spray. Light the coals or heating elements, and let them burn or heat until moderately hot.

6. Put the foil packages on the grill, seam side up, away from the heat. Cover and cook for 35 to 40 minutes, adding fresh coals as necessary to keep the heat constantly at a moderate to moderately hot temperature. Using insulated mitts, open the packages occasionally to make sure the meat is gently simmering in its own juices and not cooking too fast. Halfway through cooking, rotate the packages with a spatula so that the side nearest the most intense heat is turned away from it.

7. Remove from the grill and unwrap the packages carefully, taking care not to get burned by the escaping steam. Lift the chops from the packages with tongs, brushing off the herbs and spices. Place the chops on the grill over the most intense heat and cook for 2 to 3 minutes on each side, until browned and crisp around the edges. An instant-read thermometer inserted in the center of the meatiest section of a chop should register 150° to 155°F. Let the chops rest for a few minutes before serving.

Pork marries happily with fennel, the flavor of which is echoed by the sambuca liqueur. Easy and straightforward, this is one of our favorite recipes for grilled pork chops.

Pork Chops with Fennel and Garlic   *Serves 6*

HEAT =

6 RIB OR LOIN PORK CHOPS, EACH
    ABOUT 1$\frac{1}{2}$ INCHES THICK

18 SLIVERS GARLIC (FROM 3 CLOVES)
    PLUS ONE WHOLE CLOVE

ABOUT 3 SPRIGS ROSEMARY, CUT INTO
    18 ONE-INCH PIECES, AVOIDING ANY
    TOUGH STALKS

2 LARGE BULBS FENNEL

$\frac{1}{2}$ CUP EXTRA VIRGIN OLIVE OIL

$\frac{2}{3}$ CUP DRY WHITE WINE

$\frac{1}{3}$ CUP ANISE-FLAVORED LIQUEUR,
    SUCH AS SAMBUCA

1 TEASPOON COARSE SALT

1$\frac{1}{2}$ TEASPOONS FRESHLY GROUND
    BLACK PEPPER

VEGETABLE OIL COOKING SPRAY

1. With the tip of a sharp paring knife, make three 2-inch-deep slits through the fatty side of each chop into the meat. Push a sliver of garlic and a small sprig of rosemary into each slit. (It's fine if a little hangs out.) Transfer to a shallow glass or ceramic dish that will hold the pork chops in a single layer.

2. Trim the fennel and reserve the fronds for garnish. Slice the fennel bulbs lengthwise into 5 or 6 slices and transfer to another shallow glass or ceramic dish. Drizzle with 2 tablespoons of the olive oil.

3. In a small bowl, whisk together the wine, liqueur, remaining olive oil, salt, and pepper. Crush the remaining garlic clove and add to the marinade along with any leftover rosemary stems.

4. Pour ¼ cup of the marinade over the fennel slices. Pour the remaining marinade over the pork chops and turn to coat evenly. Cover and let rest at room temperature 30 minutes or refrigerate for at least 1 hour and up to 4 hours, letting the meat come to room temperature before grilling.

5. Prepare a charcoal or gas grill: Lightly spray the grill rack with vegetable oil cooking spray. Light the coals or heating elements, and let them burn or heat until moderately hot to hot.

6. Lift the chops from the marinade but do not pat them dry. Put the chops on the hottest part of the grill. Lay the fennel slices around the cooler edge of the grill.

7. Cover and grill for about 10 minutes. Turn the chops and fennel and grill, uncovered, for 8 to 10 minutes longer, until the fennel is browned, tender, and well marked. Remove the fennel from the grill and set aside, covered, to keep warm.

8. Grill the chops for 3 to 4 minutes longer, until an instant-read thermometer inserted in the center of the meatiest sections registers 150° to 155°F. Let rest a few minutes (the temperature will rise to about 160°F). Scatter reserved fennel fronds over the pork chops and serve with the fennel slices.

The most commonly grilled pork chops are loin and rib chops, both tender and delicious. Sirloin pork chops are cut from sirloin roast, which is in front of the butt and has wonderfully tender meat and a small round bone. You could use sirloin pork chops for any of these recipes, although they are harder to find in supermarkets and butcher shops than the other cuts.

Loin Pork Chops in Honey-Orange Marinade   *Serves 6*

HEAT =

JUICE OF 4 ORANGES

3 TABLESPOONS OLIVE OIL

3 TABLESPOONS HONEY

3 TABLESPOONS SNIPPED FRESH CHIVES

1 LARGE CLOVE GARLIC, CRUSHED

1 TEASPOON FRESHLY GROUND BLACK
   PEPPER, OR TO TASTE

SALT TO TASTE

6 LOIN PORK CHOPS, EACH ABOUT
   1 1/2 INCHES THICK

VEGETABLE OIL COOKING SPRAY

1.   Combine the orange juice, oil, honey, chives, garlic, and pepper in a small bowl. Season with salt, stirring well.

2.   Trim the pork chops of excess fat, if necessary, and put in a large, shallow glass or ceramic dish. Pour the marinade over the chops, turning them several times to coat. Cover and refrigerate for at least 4 hours or overnight, letting the meat come to room temperature before grilling. Turn the chops several times during marinating.

3.   Prepare a charcoal or gas grill: Lightly spray the grill rack with vegetable oil cooking spray. Light the coals or heating elements, and let them burn or heat until moderately hot.

4.   Lift the chops from the dish, reserving the marinade. Grill for about 10 minutes on each side, turning several times with tongs and brushing 2 or 3 times with the marinade during the first 10 or 15 minutes of cooking. Grill until a meat thermometer inserted in the center of the meatiest sections registers 150° to 155°F. Let the chops rest for a few minutes before serving.

While both rib and loin pork chops do well in the smoker, we prefer rib chops only because they tend to have a little more marbling and therefore a little more flavor. The apple cider–based brine, sweetened with maple sugar, punches up their flavor and guarantees their moistness. Smoking is such low and slow cooking, you really can't overcook these chops, so if you follow our instructions they will be luscious and tender. We like to smoke these with apple wood, but any fruit wood, such as cherry or pear, would work well. Serve these with our tangy dried fruit sauce or another fruit side dish such as applesauce.

Smoked Pork Chops Brined in Apple Cider   *Serves 6*

HEAT =

PORK

1½ QUARTS FRESH APPLE CIDER

2 CUPS WATER

⅓ CUP APPLE CIDER VINEGAR

½ CUP COARSE SALT

½ CUP GRANULATED MAPLE SUGAR

2 TABLESPOONS FRESH GROUND BLACK
   PEPPER

1 TABLESPOON CHINESE FIVE-SPICE
   POWDER

2 CINNAMON STICKS, EACH ABOUT 3
   INCHES LONG

6 RIB OR LOIN PORK LOIN CHOPS, EACH
   ABOUT 1½ INCHES THICK

1. Prepare the pork: Combine the cider, water, vinegar, coarse salt, maple sugar, pepper, five-spice powder, and cinnamon sticks in a large pot. Stir over medium heat for 5 to 8 minutes, until the sugar and salt dissolve and the brine is aromatic. Do not boil. Remove from the heat and set aside to cool completely. (If not using right away, refrigerate for up to 24 hours.)

2. Lay the chops in a glass or ceramic dish just large enough so that they will be completely submerged in the brine. Pour the cooled brine over the chops, cover, and refrigerate for at least 12 hours and up to 24 hours.

3. When ready to smoke them, lift the chops from the brine and pat dry with paper towels. Discard the brine.

4. Prepare and preheat the smoker according to the manufacturer's instructions.

5. Put the chops on the smoker's rack and smoke at 225°F for 2 to 2½ hours, until their internal temperature registers 160°F.

SAUCE

1 TABLESPOON VEGETABLE OIL

2 SHALLOTS, MINCED

2 CUPS FRESH APPLE CIDER

$\frac{1}{4}$ CUP BALSAMIC VINEGAR

$\frac{1}{2}$ CUP DRIED CRANBERRIES OR GOLDEN
   RAISINS

SALT AND FRESHLY GROUND BLACK
   PEPPER

6. Meanwhile, make the sauce: Warm the oil in a saucepan over medium heat. Add the shallots and cook for 2 to 3 minutes, until translucent but not brown.

7. Add the cider, vinegar, and cranberries, bring to a simmer, and cook for 10 to 15 minutes, until the sauce is reduced by about half. You should have about 1½ cups. Season to taste with salt and pepper. Do not strain.

8. Serve the chops with about a tablespoon of sauce spooned over each one. Pass the remaining sauce on the side.

For kabobs, we think the loin meat is best to use, although you can substitute the ham butt, if necessary. The butt is the most desirable part of the ham, which is cut from the leg, and often is labeled "fresh ham" in supermarkets and some butcher shops. Do not confuse it with Boston shoulder (or Boston butt), which is cut from the upper half of the shoulder—while its meat is tender, it is not as good for kabobs as the other two cuts of pork.

Pork and fruit are an obvious pairing.

Grilled Curried Pork Kabobs with Pears   *Serves 6*

HEAT =

2½ POUNDS TRIMMED BONELESS PORK
LOIN OR BUTT, CUT INTO ABOUT
THIRTY 1½-INCH CUBES

6 TABLESPOONS CURRY PASTE RUB
(PAGE 247)

4 FIRM, RIPE PEARS, SUCH AS
BARTLETT OR BOSC, HALVED
LENGTHWISE AND CORED

VEGETABLE OIL COOKING SPRAY

1 RED BELL PEPPER, CUT INTO 12
CHUNKS, EACH ABOUT 1½ INCHES
SQUARE

1 RED ONION, CUT INTO 12 WEDGES

SIX 12-INCH METAL SKEWERS

OLIVE OIL

1. Put the pork in a shallow glass or ceramic dish and, using your fingers, rub 4 tablespoons curry paste into the meat. Cover and set aside at room temperature for about 30 minutes or refrigerate for as long as 4 hours, letting the meat come to room temperature before grilling.

2. Rub the remaining 2 tablespoons of the curry paste on the cut side of the pears. Cover and refrigerate until ready to grill.

3. Prepare a charcoal or gas grill: Lightly spray the grill rack with vegetable oil cooking spray. Light the coals or heating elements, and let them burn or heat until moderately hot.

4. Thread the pork, bell peppers, and onions onto skewers, beginning and ending with the meat. Brush or drizzle the meat, vegetables, and the halved pears lightly with olive oil. Place the skewers and pears on the grill, beginning cut side up, and cook, covered, for 12 to 15 minutes, turning frequently with tongs until the the meat is cooked through, and looks white and opaque when cut with a small knife. The pears will brown. If the pears seem to be cooking more quickly than the meat, move the pears to the edge of the grill.

While the grapes are good with the pork, for a more traditional kabob you could substitute chunks of fresh pineapple. Be sure to use tenderloin or ham butt (not Boston butt) for these kabobs so that they cook relatively quickly and evenly.

Pork and Grape Kabobs with Sweet-Sour Sauce   *Serves 4*

HEAT =

SAUCE

¼ CUP SUGAR

½ CUP CIDER VINEGAR

1 CUP FRESH ORANGE JUICE

2 TABLESPOONS FRESH LIME JUICE

1 SERRANO CHILE, STEMMED, SEEDED, AND CHOPPED

1 TABLESPOON CHOPPED FRESH LEMONGRASS

1. To prepare the sauce, combine the sugar and vinegar in a nonreactive saucepan and simmer over medium heat, stirring often, for 5 to 6 minutes, until reduced in volume by half. Add the orange juice, lime juice, chile, and lemongrass and cook about 10 minutes longer, until the sauce is slightly syrupy. The sauce can be served warm or at room temperature.

2. To prepare the kabobs, put the pork in a shallow glass or ceramic dish and add the onion, chile, lemongrass, pepper, and turmeric. Using your hands, rub the seasonings into the meat. Add the orange juice, lime juice, soy sauce, and oil and mix well, coating the meat. Cover and refrigerate for at least 4 hours and as long as 12 hours, letting the meat come to room temperature before grilling.

3. Prepare a charcoal or gas grill: Lightly spray the grill rack with vegetable oil cooking spray. Light the coals or heating elements, and let them burn or heat until moderately hot.

KABOBS

2½ POUNDS TRIMMED BONELESS PORK
    LOIN OR BUTT, CUT INTO 1½-INCH
    CUBES

½ CUP FINELY CHOPPED ONION

1 SERRANO CHILE, STEMMED, SEEDED,
    AND CHOPPED

1 TABLESPOON FINELY CHOPPED FRESH
    LEMONGRASS

1 TEASPOON FRESHLY GROUND BLACK
    PEPPER

¼ TEASPOON GROUND TURMERIC

¾ CUP FRESH ORANGE JUICE

3 TABLESPOONS FRESH LIME JUICE

3 TABLESPOONS SOY SAUCE

3 TABLESPOONS CANOLA OIL

VEGETABLE OIL COOKING SPRAY

32 TO 40 LARGE RED SEEDLESS GRAPES

FOUR 12-INCH METAL SKEWERS

4. Thread the pork and grapes onto the skewers, beginning and ending with the meat. Grill for 15 to 20 minutes, turning several times with tongs, until the meat is cooked through, and looks white and opaque when cut with a small knife. Serve with the sauce, reheated, if desired.

ASK THE BUTCHER

What are these new meat cuts I've heard about—Wagyu beef and Kurobuta pork?

Wagyu beef is the breed of cattle that sometimes is referred to as Kobe beef, named for the region of Japan where the famed beef cattle were first raised and are still carefully tended. The resulting meat is extremely tender and heavily marbled; in Japan, it's such a luxury item that small portions are served—but even a few bites satisfy. In this country, the term is loosely used to describe beef from Wagyu cattle that may or may not be raised quite as intensely. Nonetheless, good Wagyu beef is always well marbled. Instead of being designated as choice or prime, the meat is graded according to a number, with 1 being the least desirable and 12 being the most.

Kurobuta pork is as rich and delicious as Wagyu beef. Although it's associated with Japan (where it is popular), the meat is from purebred Berkshire hogs, a breed that originated in England. The pork is well marbled with fat and has amazingly deep flavor.

Both Wagyu and Kurobuta are well worth trying, although they may be hard to find. You can order them from our website, www.lobels.com.

We cook these pork kabobs long and slow over a relatively moderate fire in an effort to approximate the true flavor of Jamaican jerk pork. Buy pork loin or butt with visible fat for this recipe so that it can withstand the long cooking time.

Jerk Pork Kabobs   *Serves 6 to 8*

HEAT =

2½ POUNDS TRIMMED BONELESS PORK
    LOIN OR BUTT, CUT INTO 1½-INCH
    CUBES
¾ CUP JERK SEASONING (PAGE 245)
VEGETABLE OIL COOKING SPRAY
SIX TO EIGHT 12-INCH METAL SKEWERS

1. Put the pork in a shallow glass or ceramic dish and, using your fingers, rub the seasoning into the meat. Cover and refrigerate for at least 4 hours or overnight, letting the meat come to room temperature before grilling.

2. Prepare a charcoal or gas grill for indirect cooking (see page 7): Lightly spray the grill rack with vegetable oil cooking spray. Light the coals or heating elements, and let them burn or heat until moderately hot.

3. Thread the pork onto six to eight skewers and grill over the hottest part of the fire for about 10 minutes, turning often, until lightly browned. Move the skewers to the cooler part of the grill, cover, and cook for 25 to 30 minutes longer, turning several times, until the pork is very tender.

Everyone loves pulled pork sandwiches—when you smoke the meat yourself and then serve it doused with our tangy barbecue sauce on top of generously large, soft rolls, nothing beats it! You'll probably have to order the pork butt from the butcher. It's the most desirable part of the shoulder, cut so that it's three to four inches thick. Once it's smoked, the bone is easy to dislodge, and then the fun begins. This meat is so tender, tradition says it can be pulled apart. Use your hands, a fork, a knife, or a combination of all three. We like pulling it in front of everyone. A real crowd pleaser!

Pulled Smoked Pork on Soft Rolls   *Serves 6*

HEAT =

PORK

5 TO 7 POUNDS PORK BUTT

10 TO 12 SLIVERS GARLIC (2 OR 3 LARGE CLOVES)

2 TABLESPOONS PACKED DARK OR LIGHT BROWN SUGAR

2 TABLESPOONS SWEET PAPRIKA

1 TABLESPOON COARSE SALT

1 TABLESPOON FRESHLY GROUND BLACK PEPPER

1 TEASPOON CAYENNE OR HOT HUNGARIAN PAPRIKA

1/4 TEASPOON GROUND CINNAMON

SAUCE

2 TABLESPOONS VEGETABLE OIL

1/2 CUP FINELY DICED ONION

1/4 CUP FINELY DICED GREEN BELL PEPPER

1. To prepare the pork, trim all but a thin layer of fat from the meat. With the tip of a sharp knife, poke 10 to12 holes into the fatty side of the meat and insert the garlic slivers.

2. In a small bowl, mix together the brown sugar, sweet paprika, salt, pepper, cayenne, and cinnamon. Rub this into the meat to coat it thoroughly. Transfer the meat to a shallow glass or ceramic dish, cover tightly, and refrigerate for at least 12 hours and up to 24 hours.

3. Prepare and preheat the smoker according to the manufacturer's instructions. We used mesquite wood.

4. When the smoker is ready, pat the meat dry with paper towels, wiping off most of the seasoning. Put the meat, fat side up, on the smoker's rack, and smoke for 5 hours at 225°F.

5. Take the meat from the smoker and wrap it in heavy-duty foil. Return it to the smoker, seam side up, and smoke for 3 hours longer or until the internal temperature is 185° to 190°F. At this point, the meat will be extremely tender and moist and can be easily pulled apart or shredded. A reliable test for doneness is to poke the side of the meat with a dinner fork and twist. If the fork turns a full 360 degrees, the meat is ready.

1 OR MORE JALAPEÑOS, SEEDED AND
  DICED
1 TABLESPOON CHILI POWDER
$\frac{1}{2}$ TEASPOON DRIED THYME
$\frac{1}{2}$ TEASPOON COARSE SALT
$\frac{1}{4}$ TEASPOON FRESHLY GROUND BLACK
  PEPPER
1 CUP KETCHUP
1 CUP TOMATO SAUCE
$\frac{1}{2}$ CUP BREWED BLACK COFFEE
$\frac{1}{3}$ CUP APPLE CIDER VINEGAR
$\frac{1}{4}$ CUP WATER
3 TABLESPOONS MOLASSES
1 TABLESPOON WORCESTERSHIRE
  SAUCE
1 TEASPOON BROWN MUSTARD
SMALL WEDGE OF LEMON
6 SOFT ROLLS, SUCH AS KAISER OR
  POTATO ROLLS

6. Meanwhile, prepare the barbecue sauce: In a nonreactive saucepan, heat the oil over medium heat. Add the onions, bell peppers, and jalapeño and cook for 2 to 3 minutes, stirring, until softened.

7. In a small bowl, stir together the chili powder, thyme, salt, and pepper. Add to the saucepan and stir for about 1 minute, until the vegetables are coated with the spices. Stir in the ketchup and tomato sauce and cook for 1 to 2 minutes, until hot and bubbling.

8. In another small bowl, whisk together the coffee, vinegar, water, molasses, Worcestershire sauce, and mustard. Add to the saucepan, squeeze the lemon wedge into the sauce, and reduce the heat to low. Simmer gently for about 20 minutes, until the flavors blend. Stir often. Cover and set aside until ready to reheat gently and serve. You will have about 3 cups of sauce.

9. Unwrap the meat and let it cool just enough so that you can pull it apart with a fork and your hands. If you prefer, you can shred or chop it with a knife. Toss the pulled pork with some of the sauce and then pile meat onto the rolls. Spoon on more sauce and serve.

We toyed with the idea of curing and smoking raw pork belly to make our own bacon, but decided instead to work with already-smoked bacon. Smoking it heightens its flavor and enhanced our already keen appreciation of bacon. It's hard to believe that bacon could get any better, but it did. After a while in the smoker, it acquired an earthy smokiness that we just loved.

You'll want to skip the thin strips of packaged, supermarket bacon and find a butcher or market that sells slab bacon. Ask to have it cut about ¼ inch thick (at a setting 6 or 8 on a commercial slicing machine). This thick-cut bacon will emerge from the smoker richly flavored and ready to be finished in a frying pan. It's so good we urge you to smoke two pounds, although the potato salad only calls for one. Freeze the other pound for another day. You won't be sorry.

In this recipe, we rub the bacon with coarse ground black pepper before smoking it, but try granulated maple sugar if you like sweet-cured bacon, or the Spicy Dry Rub on page 242 for a little fire.

Apple Wood Double-Smoked Bacon with Warm German-Style Potato Salad
Serves 6; about 9 cups of potato salad

HEAT =

1 OR 2 POUNDS THICK-SLICED BACON
(¼-INCH-THICK SLICES)

1½ TO 2 TEASPOONS COARSELY
GROUND BLACK PEPPER PER POUND
OF BACON

3 POUNDS RED POTATOES, PEELED AND
CUT INTO LARGE CHUNKS

1 CUP THINLY SLICED CELERY (2 TO 3
STALKS)

¾ CUP MINCED SHALLOTS OR RED
ONION

1 TABLESPOON SUGAR

1 TEASPOON COARSE SALT, IF NEEDED

1 TEASPOON FRESHLY GROUND BLACK
PEPPER

1. Work with each pound of bacon separately. If smoking hand-sliced or custom-ordered bacon, lay the bacon strips on a work surface so that they overlap slightly with a ¼-inch strip exposed for each slice (similar to how they are packaged). Sprinkle the coarsely ground pepper over the bacon and rub it into the meat to distribute it evenly.

2. Prepare and preheat the smoker according to the manufacturer's instructions to 225°F. We use apple wood.

3. When smoke curls from the smoker, lay a pound of the bacon on the rack and reduce the temperature to 150°F. Smoke the bacon for 45 minutes. Transfer the bacon to a rack to cool for about 30 minutes. When cool, proceed with this recipe (or use the bacon in another recipe), or wrap the bacon tightly in plastic wrap and refrigerate for up to 3 days or freeze for up to 1 month. (The bacon will not be fully cooked at this point. Before you use it, cook it further to the desired degree of doneness.)

½ TEASPOON PAPRIKA

½ CUP APPLE CIDER VINEGAR

⅓ CUP WATER

½ CUP FINELY DICED DILL PICKLE

½ CUP MINCED FLAT-LEAF PARSLEY

4. Prepare and smoke the other pound of bacon and reserve for another use.

5. To make the potato salad: Boil the potatoes in a pot of lightly salted water for 12 to 15 minutes, until tender when pierced with the tip of sharp knife. Do not overcook. Drain the potatoes, cut into ½-inch-thick slices, transfer to a bowl, cover, and keep warm.

6. Cut the bacon into ¼-inch dice and sauté in a large skillet over medium-low heat for 10 to 15 minutes, until the bacon is crispy and browned. (You may need to do this in two batches.) Spoon off and reserve ⅓ cup of the bacon drippings. Drain the bacon on paper towels. You will have about 2¼ to 2½ cups cooked bacon "bits."

7. Return the reserved bacon drippings to the skillet. Add the celery and shallots and sauté over medium-low heat for 2 to 3 minutes, until soft. Add the sugar, salt, pepper, and paprika, stirring to coat the vegetables. Add the vinegar and water and stir for 1 to 2 minutes to heat thoroughly. Stir in the pickles and parsley, and all but ½ cup of the bacon bits. Stir to blend.

8. Pour the mixture over the warm potatoes and toss gently with a spatula to coat with the dressing. Taste and adjust the seasonings. Serve garnished with the reserved bacon bits.

A pig roast is the ultimate outdoor party, and if you have a large enough grill, you might want to try one. The meat is indescribably tender and tasty, and needs no sauce or salsa. It tastes great served with classic summer side dishes such as coleslaw and potato salad.

You will need a grill that is at least 26 to 30 inches long. (A standard round Weber kettle grill is too small.) Buy the largest disposable foil turkey pan; even so, you may have to bend the sides outward to fit the pig inside. A small pig, such as the one we grill for this recipe, is hard to find. Much more common are larger pigs, weighing about twenty-five pounds. These are too large for a grill—they are cooked in pits. You will have to order a small pig well in advance, and may have to locate a specialty butcher. Be sure the butcher has cleaned and dressed the pig for you, which means it should be free of hair and its eyes should be removed, leaving behind only clean cavities. The intestines and other organs should be cleaned from the beast, and the belly should be split. The pig will have its head, tail, and feet still intact. Very likely, the pig will be frozen when you get it. Let it thaw for about 24 hours in the refrigerator before marinating it. Wrap the snout, ears, tail, and feet in foil to prevent burning—even so, do not be surprised if the tail and feet break off during cooking.

For this recipe, we prepared a typical Italian-style marinade. You can substitute rosemary or tarragon for the thyme, or devise a spicier, Southwestern-style marinade. If you want to add authenticity to the recipe, toss some soaked oak wood chips on the coals to impart a little flavor. Keep the fire relatively cool, and if your grill is not fitted with an external thermometer, use an oven thermometer to determine its temperature, which should be about 325°F. Gas grills are far easier to control when grilling a pig, but you can have great success with a charcoal fire, too.

A small, 15-pound pig needs only 10 minutes to the pound to cook because the meat-to-bone ratio is relatively low. However, if you attempt to pit-roast a larger pig, the time will go up to at least 20 minutes a pound. But that is for another book!

Grilled Suckling Pig   *Serves 10 to 14*

HEAT =

1 CUP OLIVE OIL

JUICE OF 3 LEMONS

3 CLOVES GARLIC, CHOPPED

2 TABLESPOONS CHOPPED FRESH THYME

1. Combine the olive oil, lemon juice, garlic, thyme, parsley, and fennel seeds in a bowl. Season generously with pepper, stirring well.

2. Using your hands, rub the pig with the marinade, inside and out, working it into the meat. Transfer the pig to a large plastic bag such as a garbage bag (make sure it's free of chemicals or

2 TABLESPOONS CHOPPED FLAT-LEAF
   PARSLEY
1 TEASPOON CRUSHED FENNEL SEEDS
FRESHLY GROUND BLACK PEPPER TO
   TASTE
ONE 15-POUND SUCKLING PIG, CLEANED
   AND DRESSED
VEGETABLE OIL COOKING SPRAY
ABOUT 3 CUPS WHITE WINE
ABOUT 3 CUPS CHICKEN BROTH

deodorizers) or an XXL resealable plastic bag. Pour any remaining marinade over the pig, and seal the bag. Put this bag inside another bag (the first bag will be greasy) and fold closed. Refrigerate for at least 8 hours, or overnight. Let the pig come to room temperature at least 1 hour before grilling.

3. Prepare a charcoal or gas grill for indirect grilling (see page 7): Lightly spray the grill rack with vegetable oil cooking spray. Light the coals or heating elements, and let them burn or heat until moderately hot. During grilling, the internal temperature of the grill should be maintained at 325°F.

4. Wrap the pig's tail, feet, ears, and snout with foil to prevent burning. Put a metal roasting rack in the foil turkey pan. Set the pig on its back on the rack. Pour enough wine and broth into the pan to a depth of 1 to 2 inches, and set the pan over the cooler part of the grill.

5. Grill the pig in the pan, with the grill covered, for 2½ to 3 hours (10 minutes to the pound). Baste the pig every 15 or 20 minutes with the pan drippings, and turn it several times for even browning. Add more wine, broth, or water (or a mixture of all three) to the pan as necessary. The pig should begin and end grilling on its back. The pig is done when the internal temperature of the thickest section, the rump, reaches 150°F. The thickest part will reach 160°F during resting.

6. Let the pig rest for at least 30 minutes before serving. Transfer the pig to a large cutting board. Remove the head and legs. Slice the meat from the legs, as you would from a turkey drumstick. Peel the skin from the body, using your fingers and a sharp knife. Remove the thick layer of fat just beneath the skin. Carve the meat from the bones, slicing it diagonally, working forward toward the head end. When you have cut as much meat as possible this way, tear the rib cage apart into ribs and slice what meat there is from the ribs. Serve immediately.

POULTRY

Grilled chicken is just about as popular as grilled burgers or steaks in America's backyards—and in many households it is a far more familiar sight on the grill than red meat. Chicken and turkey, both well suited for the grill (as are other birds), are widely available and relatively inexpensive. The mildness of the meat means they can take on both subtle and bold flavorings in the guises of marinades, rubs, and pastes. Smoked chicken and turkey is fantastic, too, and can be eaten right out of the smoker or held for a day or two for "leftover preparations" such as salads and sandwiches. Plus, as we all know, poultry—and white meat in particular—is especially heart- and health-friendly. Who can (or wants to) argue with such merits? Not us. We love grilled poultry!

We wish everyone would buy poultry from reputable butchers, who usually have the best birds. However, most folks rely on supermarkets for chicken and other poultry, not only because these all-purpose markets are their only choice, but also because they are convenient. If they shop at a butcher at all, most home cooks reserve the trip for more expensive meats, which is too bad. As with all meat and poultry purchases, establishing a relationship with your butcher can make a big difference in quality and service.

When buying poultry, buy Grade A, which is roughly equivalent to prime meat (but Grades B and C poultry are rarely available to retail consumers, so don't spend much time worrying about this). For chicken, look for even coloring that is neither bright yellow nor dead white. The chicken should be slightly yellow, which is a sure sign that the bird was fed corn. The birds should be plump, with well-developed breasts and rounded thighs, both of which indicate firm meat and a good inner coating of fat. Avoid chickens that appear scrawny or dried up.

It's always a good idea to buy whole chickens and cut them up yourself, because the less the chicken has been handled, the better, and this will save money. We know that convenience and time often preclude this. If you try it a few times, though, you will find it's far easier than you think—and you'll find yourself gravitating to whole chickens more and more often. When you buy packaged chicken, avoid any where you can see puddles of water, which could mean that the bird has been frozen, thawed, and refrozen—a process that will leave the meat chewy and dry.

Turkeys should be pale colored; some even have a bluish cast, which is perfectly acceptable. Their breasts should be plump and nicely formed, and the thighs rounded. Buy only fresh turkeys; frozen birds are tasteless and dry. Rock Cornish game hens, the third type of poultry we address in this chapter, should be plump and pale colored.

Many chefs recommend buying free-range chickens and other poultry. At the very least, the consumer is regularly advised to buy "minimally processed" chicken. We don't disagree with this advice, but we are not sure either term means much. Free-range poultry should refer to birds that are raised in natural surroundings where they can peck and scratch in the dirt for organically grown feed under the shining sun. Minimally processed, on the other hand, should refer to birds that are not overmedicated when alive or treated with unnecessary chemicals after slaughter. However, neither term is universally trustworthy. Instead, we suggest buying chickens and other poultry that at the very least have labels reading "no antibiotics administered," "no animal byproducts in feed," or both. If your butcher stands behind his free-range poultry, which ideally means he knows the farmers who supply him, then buy these birds, despite their higher cost. They will be tastier, more tender, and less fatty than others. You can also find organically grown poultry, which means it's been raised on organic feed and processed in a plant certified as USDA organic.

In recent years, pasture-raised chickens, turkeys, and other fowl have entered the market, too. You are most likely to find pasture-raised poultry at farmers' markets, greenmarkets, and specialty butchers. The term refers to birds raised in the open (a pasture) in pens the farmer can move around a fairly large area. These birds are usually also fed supplemental grain, but the theory is that they eat naturally growing vegetation and dig up grubs and insects so that their diet is rich and varied. They also move around more than even some free-range chickens, so their meat is less fatty, firmer, and more full-flavored. While we applaud this method of raising chickens and other poultry, we suggest that the buyer beware of the authenticity of the claims. Again: Get to know the butcher so that you can verify the source of the poultry.

Grilling can be kind to poultry, whether it's chicken, Rock Cornish game hens, turkey, duck, quail, or pheasant. (We deal with the game birds in the following chapter.) The birds pick up just enough of the charred flavor to be deliciously appealing, and they mark nicely with seared lines when laid on a hot grill rack. But without proper tending, the kindness goes south and the poultry runs the risk of burning and drying out near the surface while staying uncooked at the bone. To avoid this, turn the birds during grilling: Stand at the grill and use long-handled tongs to turn the poultry pieces often. This will encourage even cooking without burning. Even whole chickens roasted on the grill should be turned several times. Whole turkeys, however, do not require turning.

As with all grilling, use our cooking times as guides—not absolutes. Every grill and every fire burns somewhat differently and therefore the poultry may cook faster or slower than the recipe indicates. Get to know your own grill and your grilling style, and you will soon understand how it cooks.

In addition, rely on a meat thermometer—nothing is less appetizing than undercooked poultry and, frankly, it is not safe to eat. Dark meat in both chicken and turkey should be cooked to an internal temperature of 180° to 185°F, and white meat to 170°F. When using a thermometer, insert it in the thickest section of meat and don't let it touch the bone.

This is also good advice for smoked chickens and turkey. Get to know your smoker, start with the recommended amount of wood, and use an instant-read thermometer to determine that the birds are thoroughly cooked. When exposed to more smoke than recommended, chicken especially can turn an unappetizing gray.

Preparing Poultry for Grilling

Poultry should be cooked soon after purchase and should never be left at room temperature longer than necessary. Do not unwrap it, but store it in its original packaging in the coldest part of the refrigerator, which usually is the rear of the lowest shelf.

When you are ready to prepare the poultry, take it from the refrigerator and let it come to room temperature, which means leaving it on the counter for about 30 minutes. If it is a particularly hot, humid summer day, reduce this time by up to 10 minutes. Pat the chicken or turkey dry with paper towels and then marinate it, rub it with dry rub, or otherwise prepare it for the grill or smoker. We have not included the important step of patting the meat dry in the recipe instructions, because it is universally appropriate for all recipes calling for beef, veal, poultry, lamb, or pork. As soon as the chicken or other poultry is seasoned, return it to the refrigerator if you are not ready to cook it.

Although we have recipes for whole chicken, we also have recipes that call for chickens cut into eight pieces. These pieces represent the breast halves, thighs, legs, and wings. Most chicken producers pack chicken cut into these pieces, but it is not difficult to cut whole chickens into these parts; discard the back or use it for making stock. And of course, you can ask the butcher to cut the chicken for you. When you are smoking, we suggest you smoke the backbone with the chicken and then use it in soups and bean dishes to add indescribable flavor.

Raw poultry runs the risk of carrying harmful bacteria, regardless of the brand, quality, or source. When working with the raw birds, exercise sensible caution. Wash all work surfaces with warm, soapy water; keep other foods away from the birds and their juices to avoid cross contamination; and be sure to wash your hands and cooking tools before you move on to your next culinary task. Cooking poultry renders it not only harmless but also healthful and delicious.

Boneless or Bone-In Chicken on the Grill

Recipes for bone-in chicken parts can be made with boneless, skinless chicken breasts, and vice versa. For a recipe that serves six, you will need two whole chickens (each weighing about three pounds) cut into eight pieces. For the same recipe, you will need two to two and one-quarter pounds of boneless, skinless chicken breast meat, although it's more important to have at least six boneless chicken breast halves for easy serving.

To convert a recipe for boneless, skinless chicken breasts to bone-in chicken parts, grill the chicken for 40 to 45 minutes all together, beginning with the legs and thighs, which will need about 15 minutes on the grill before the white-meat breasts are laid on the grill. To prevent burning, start the chicken with the skin side up and while the chicken parts should be turned frequently during grilling, they should spend more time with the skin side up than down. The chicken is done when the juices run clear when the thickest sections of the meat are pierced with a fork or sharp knife. You can also insert a meat thermometer into the dark meat to make sure it registers 180°F, or into the white meat for 170°F. Be sure the thermometer does not touch the bone.

To convert a recipe for bone-in chicken to one for boneless breasts, cook the breasts for 12 to 16 minutes, turning them several times, until they are cooked through.

How to Guarantee Juicy and Moist Boneless, Skinless Chicken Breasts

Although we do not insist that you take this extra step (you won't find it in the recipes), we have found that boneless, skinless chicken breasts remain moister and juicier if you precook them before marinating and grilling. To do so, bring an inch or so of water to a boil in a deep skillet and poach the chicken breasts for 1 minute—this will not cook them through but will give them a head start. Remove them from the water, cool for a few minutes, and then marinate them or otherwise prepare them for grilling. Even when refrigerated for several hours after poaching, the chicken breasts will be plumper and juicier than otherwise.

If you come across boneless chicken breasts with the skin on, buy them. The skin adds great flavor and moisture. Begin grilling with the skin side up to prevent burning. The skin will crisp when you turn the breasts.

When roasting a whole chicken on the grill, begin with a plump bird. You can also grill-roast capons, which are fat, compact male birds that are castrated at an early age to promote plumpness, tenderness, and sweet flavor.

Mahogany-Glazed Chicken   *Serves 6 to 8*

HEAT =

1½ CUPS DARK BEER (SEE NOTE)
½ CUP WORCESTERSHIRE SAUCE
1 YELLOW ONION, SLICED VERY THIN
1 TABLESPOON DIJON MUSTARD
1 TABLESPOON SALT
2 TEASPOONS SWEET PAPRIKA
TWO 3- TO 3½-POUND CHICKENS
VEGETABLE OIL COOKING SPRAY
1 TABLESPOON MOLASSES

1. Combine the beer, Worcestershire sauce, onion, mustard, salt, and paprika in a small bowl, stirring well.

2. Put the chickens, breast side down, in a shallow glass or ceramic dish and pour the marinade over them. Cover and refrigerate for 4 hours or overnight, letting the chicken come to room temperature before grilling.

3. Prepare a charcoal or gas grill for indirect cooking (see page 7): Lightly spray the grill rack with vegetable oil cooking spray. Light the coals or heating elements, and let them burn or heat until moderately hot.

4. Lift the chickens from the dish. Transfer the marinade to a small saucepan. Place the chickens over the cooler part of the grill, cover, and roast for 1 hour and 20 minutes to 1 hour and 30 minutes, turning with tongs at least 3 or 4 times during grilling to brown on all sides. Cook until the juices run clear when the thigh is pierced with a fork or sharp knife, or an instant-read thermometer inserted in the thickest part of the thigh (don't touch the bone) registers 180°F. Add fresh coals to the fire as necessary to maintain a moderate, constant heat. If using a gas grill, adjust the burner farthest from the chicken to medium.

5. Meanwhile, bring the marinade to a boil over medium-high heat. Reduce the heat and simmer for about 20 minutes, until reduced to about 1 cup. Add the molasses, stir, and cook for 5 minutes longer. Remove ¼ cup of the marinade to a small bowl and set aside the rest.

6. During the final 5 minutes of grilling, brush the chickens with the ¼ cup of marinade, turning the chicken to crisp the skin on all sides. Let the chickens sit for at least 10 minutes for the juices to collect. Serve the remaining marinade with the chicken.

note: When cooking with beer, it can be either dark or light, flat or not, chilled or at room temperature.

With a whole chicken, it's important to turn the bird on the grill several times to promote even cooking and browning. Resting time is extremely important for whole chickens cooked on the grill, as it gives the juices time to settle.

Roast Chicken with Lemon and Rosemary   *Serves 6 to 8*

HEAT =

2 SMALL ONIONS

4 SPRIGS FRESH ROSEMARY (2 SHOULD
   BE ABOUT 4 INCHES LONG, WITH
   THICK, WOODY STEMS; THE OTHERS
   MAY BE SMALLER)

2 SMALL LEMONS

2 TABLESPOONS RICE WINE VINEGAR

¼ CUP DIJON MUSTARD

2 TEASPOONS SALT

1 TEASPOON FRESHLY GROUND BLACK
   PEPPER

TWO 3- TO 3½-POUND CHICKENS

VEGETABLE OIL COOKING SPRAY

1.   Thinly slice 1½ onions. Cut the remaining half onion into 2 wedges. Strip the leaves from the 2 smaller sprigs of rosemary; set the longer sprigs aside. Coarsely chop the rosemary leaves. Grate the zest from 1 lemon and juice the lemon. Cut the other lemon in half; juice one half and cut the other half into 2 wedges. Insert the woody sprigs of rosemary through the onion and lemon wedges, piercing them first with a small, sharp knife, if necessary.

2.   Combine the sliced onion, chopped rosemary leaves, lemon zest, combined lemon juice, vinegar, mustard, salt, and pepper in a small glass or ceramic bowl. Mix well.

3.   Rub the marinade over the chickens and inside the cavities. Insert a rosemary skewer in each cavity. Put the chickens in a shallow pan, cover, and refrigerate for at least 2 hours or overnight, letting the chicken come to room temperature before grilling.

4.   Prepare a charcoal or gas grill for indirect cooking (see page 7): Lightly spray the grill rack with vegetable oil cooking spray. Light the coals or heating elements, and let them burn or heat until moderately hot.

5. Place the chickens over the cooler part of the grill, breast side up to start, cover, and roast for 1 hour and 20 minutes to 1 hour and 30 minutes, turning with tongs at least 3 or 4 times during grilling to brown on all sides. Cook until the juices run clear when the thigh is pierced with a fork or sharp knife, or an instant-read thermometer inserted in the thickest part of the thigh (don't touch the bone) registers 180°F. Add fresh coals to the fire as necessary to maintain a moderate, constant heat. If using a gas grill, adjust the burner farthest from the chicken to medium. Let the chicken sit for at least 10 minutes for the juices to collect. Remove the onion and lemon from the cavities before serving.

This roasted chicken is for garlic lovers only. The creamy garlic sauce that accompanies the chicken is strong—a little bit goes a long way, which is why the recipe yields only about half a cup. Making small incisions in the garlic cloves before roasting promotes more thorough cooking so that their flavor is milder.

Ten-Clove Garlic-Roasted Chicken   *Serves 4*

HEAT =

VEGETABLE OIL COOKING SPRAY

10 CLOVES GARLIC, PEELED

3 TABLESPOONS SNIPPED FRESH CHIVES

ONE 3- TO 3$\frac{1}{2}$-POUND CHICKEN

OLIVE OIL

FRESHLY GROUND BLACK PEPPER TO
   TASTE

$\frac{1}{4}$ CUP HALF-AND-HALF

3 TABLESPOONS SOUR CREAM OR PLAIN
   YOGURT

2 TEASPOONS CHOPPED FLAT-LEAF
   PARSLEY OR CHIVES

SALT TO TASTE

1.   Prepare a charcoal or gas grill for indirect cooking (see page 7): Lightly spray the grill rack with vegetable oil cooking spray. Light the coals or heating elements, and let them burn or heat until moderately hot.

2.   Using a small sharp knife, cut an X halfway through each garlic clove, cutting from one end to the middle of the clove. Rub the outside of the chicken with 1 garlic clove. Insert all the garlic cloves and the chives in the cavity of the chicken. Rub the chicken with oil and pepper. Truss with kitchen twine.

3.   Place the chicken over the cooler part of the grill, breast side up to start, cover, and roast for 1 hour and 20 minutes to 1 hour and 30 minutes, turning with tongs 3 or 4 times to brown on all sides. Cook until the juices run clear when the thigh is pierced with a fork or sharp knife, or an instant-read thermometer inserted in the thickest part of the thigh (don't touch the bone) registers 180°F. Add fresh coals to the fire as necessary to maintain a moderate heat. If using a gas grill, turn the burner away from the chicken to medium. Let the roast chicken sit for about 10 minutes for the juices to collect.

4.   Remove the garlic from the chicken's cavity and transfer half of the cloves to a blender. Discard the remaining cloves. Add the half-and-half and sour cream and process until quite smooth. Scrape the sauce into a small bowl, stir in the parsley and season to taste with salt. Serve with the chicken.

Butterflying a chicken enables you to lay the chicken flat on the grill. Ask the butcher to butterfly the chicken for you, or do it yourself: cut out the backbone by cutting from end to end on either side of it; then flip the chicken breast side up and press the bird flat by pushing against it with the palm of your hand (this action breaks the breast bone).

Southeast Asian Ginger-Lemongrass Chicken *Serves 4*

HEAT =

½ CUP PEANUT OIL

JUICE OF 2 LEMONS

1 CUP CHOPPED FRESH CILANTRO

1 CUP CHOPPED SCALLIONS, WHITE AND
   GREEN PARTS (7 OR 8 SCALLIONS)

2 CLOVES GARLIC, CHOPPED

2 TABLESPOONS CHOPPED FRESH
   GINGER

4 OR 5 STALKS LEMONGRASS, CHOPPED

GRATED ZEST OF 1 LEMON

TWO 2½- TO 3-POUND CHICKENS,
   BUTTERFLIED

VEGETABLE OIL COOKING SPRAY

1. Combine the oil, lemon juice, cilantro, scallions, garlic, ginger, lemongrass, and lemon zest in a bowl.

2. Using a small knife, loosen the chicken skin. Put the chickens in a shallow glass or ceramic dish and pour the marinade over them. Using a spoon or your fingers, push some cilantro, scallions, garlic, ginger, and lemongrass underneath the loosened skin. Turn to coat, cover, and refrigerate for 4 to 6 hours, letting the chicken come to room temperature before grilling.

3. Prepare a charcoal or gas grill: Lightly spray the grill rack with vegetable oil cooking spray. Light the coals or heating elements, and let them burn or heat until moderately hot.

4. Grill the chicken for 30 to 40 minutes, skin side up to start, and turning several times. Cook until the juices run clear when the thigh meat is pierced with a fork or sharp knife, or an instant-read thermometer inserted in the thickest part of the thigh registers 180°F. Don't let the thermometer touch the bone. Serve immediately.

Split chicken is cut right though the middle so that each half is composed of a breast, a thigh, and a leg and is very easy to grill. Lay the halves skin side down over the hot fire and then, using tongs, turn them several times as they cook so that they pick up attractive grill marks. We grill relatively small chickens and expect a half chicken to be one serving, but you might prefer to cut the grilled chicken into breasts and dark meat for smaller portions.

Tuscan-Flavored Split Chicken   *Serves 6*

HEAT =

THREE 2- TO 2½-POUND CHICKENS,
   SPLIT
⅔ CUP OLIVE OIL
1 SMALL LEMON, THINLY SLICED
½ CUP FRESH LEMON JUICE
⅓ CUP PACKED, COARSELY CHOPPED
   FRESH OREGANO LEAVES
2 TABLESPOONS GRATED LEMON ZEST
2 TABLESPOONS ROUGHLY CHOPPED
   FRESH ROSEMARY LEAVES
2 TEASPOONS SALT
2 TEASPOONS CRUSHED RED PEPPER
½ TEASPOON FRESH GROUND BLACK
   PEPPER
VEGETABLE OIL COOKING SPRAY
LEMON SLICES, FOR GARNISH
ROSEMARY SPRIGS, FOR GARNISH

1. Divide the chicken halves between two large, resealable plastic bags or shallow glass or ceramic dishes.

2. In a medium bowl, stir together the olive oil, lemon slices, lemon juice, oregano, lemon zest, rosemary, salt, red pepper, and pepper. Rub the marinade into the chicken and under the skin. Seal the bags closed or cover the dishes and refrigerate for at least 4 hours and up to 6 hours, letting the chicken come to room temperature before grilling.

3. Prepare a charcoal or gas grill: Lightly spray the grill rack with vegetable oil cooking spray. Light the coals or heating elements, and let them burn or heat until moderately hot.

4. Lift the chicken from the dish, allowing the herbs to cling to the meat. Discard the marinade and lemon slices.

5. Grill the chicken halves, skin side down to start, and turning several times, for 30 to 40 minutes, until the juices run clear and an instant-read thermometer registers 180°F in the thickest part of the thigh.

6. Serve garnished with the fresh lemon slices and rosemary sprigs.

This recipe is as simple as it is classic for a backyard supper. With some good sharp mustard, Italian seasoning, and dried herbs you can put together a redolent, easy marinade perfect for chicken. Because so many home cooks buy chicken parts, we developed a number of recipes for chickens cut into eight pieces: two breast halves, two thighs, two legs, and two wings. If you prefer, buy the chicken already cut up, or ask the butcher to cut chickens for you. But we suggest you buy whole chickens, which are less expensive than parts, and cut them yourself. It's not hard with a sharp chef's knife. After you've tackled a few chickens, you will be a pro!

Lobel's Herbed Grilled Chicken
Serves 6 to 8

HEAT =

1 CUP CANOLA OIL

2 TABLESPOONS DRIED ITALIAN
   SEASONING

1 TEASPOON DRIED BASIL

1 TEASPOON DRIED OREGANO

2 LARGE CLOVES GARLIC, MINCED

6 TABLESPOONS PREPARED MUSTARD
   (WE LIKE COUNTRY-STYLE DIJON)

TWO 3- TO 3½-POUND CHICKENS, EACH
   CUT INTO 8 PIECES

SALT TO TASTE

VEGETABLE OIL COOKING SPRAY

1. Combine the oil, Italian seasoning, basil, oregano, garlic, and mustard in a small bowl, whisking until smooth.

2. Sprinkle the chicken with salt and put the pieces in a large, shallow glass or ceramic dish. Pour the marinade over the chicken and toss to coat. Cover and refrigerate for at least 1 hour and as long as 6 hours, letting the chicken come to room temperature before grilling.

3. Prepare a charcoal or gas grill: Lightly spray the grill rack with vegetable oil cooking spray. Light the coals or heating elements, and let them burn or heat until moderately hot.

4. Lift the chicken from the dish, reserving the marinade. Grill the legs and thighs, skin side up to start, for about 15 minutes, turning frequently with tongs and brushing several times with the marinade. Place the breasts and wings on the grill, skin side up. Cook all the chicken for 25 to 30 minutes longer, turning often and brushing several times with marinade during the first 10 minutes of cooking. The chicken is done when the juices run clear when the thickest sections are pierced with a fork or sharp knife, or when an instant-read thermometer inserted into the thickest part of the thigh registers 180°F and into the thickest part of the breast (not touching the bone) registers 170°F. Serve immediately.

The chickens in markets are labeled as broilers, fryers, roasters, and broiler-fryers. Unfortunately, these monikers can be inconsistent. As a rule, fryers and broilers are smaller than roasters and broiler-fryers. For these recipes we recommend the slightly larger roasters (at times also called pullets), which have more meat than broiler-fryers. However, broiler-fryers are acceptable choices, too.

Fired-Up Chipotle Chicken   *Serves 6 to 8*

HEAT =

4 CLOVES GARLIC

3 CHIPOTLE CHILES IN ADOBO SAUCE
   (SEE NOTE)

¼ CUP RED WINE VINEGAR

2 TEASPOONS SALT

JUICE OF 1 LEMON

GRATED ZEST OF 1 LEMON

TWO 3- TO 3½-POUND CHICKENS, EACH
   CUT INTO 8 PIECES

VEGETABLE OIL COOKING SPRAY

1. Combine the garlic, chiles, vinegar, salt, lemon juice, and lemon zest in a food processor and pulse 4 or 5 times to make a paste.

2. Put the chicken pieces in a shallow glass or ceramic dish and rub the paste thoroughly into the meat. Cover and refrigerate for at least 3 hours or overnight, letting the chicken come to room temperature before grilling.

3. Prepare a charcoal or gas grill: Lightly spray the grill rack with vegetable oil cooking spray. Light the coals or heating elements, and let them burn or heat until moderately hot.

4. Lift the chicken from the dish, reserving the marinade. Grill the legs and thighs, skin side up to start, for about 15 minutes, turning frequently with tongs and brushing several times with the marinade. Place the breasts and wings on the grill, skin side up. Cook all the chicken for 25 to 30 minutes longer, turning often and brushing several times with marinade during the first 10 minutes of cooking. The chicken is done when the juices run clear when the thickest sections are pierced with a fork or sharp knife, or when an instant-read thermometer inserted into the thickest part of the thigh registers 180°F and into the thickest part of the breast registers 170°F. Don't let the thermometer touch the bone. Serve immediately.

note: When rubbing the chicken with the paste, wear plastic gloves to protect your hands. If you have no gloves, wash your hands as soon as you are finished.

Be sure to rub the spice mixture well into the meat. As it sits, the dry rub will coax the natural juices to the surface of the meat and the chicken will marinate. This technique works for other meats, too, such as pork and beef.

Spicy-Rubbed Chicken   *Serves 6 to 8*

HEAT =

TWO 3- TO 3½-POUND CHICKENS, EACH
   CUT INTO 8 PIECES
3 TABLESPOONS SPICY DRY RUB
   (PAGE 242)
VEGETABLE OIL COOKING SPRAY
MADISON AVENUE BARBECUE SAUCE
   (PAGE 221)

1. Put the chicken pieces in a shallow glass or ceramic dish and rub the seasoning thoroughly into the meat. Cover and refrigerate for 6 to 8 hours, letting the chicken come to room temperature before grilling.

2. Prepare a charcoal or gas grill: Lightly spray the grill rack with vegetable oil cooking spray. Light the coals or heating elements, and let them burn or heat until moderately hot.

3. Grill the legs and thighs, skin side up to start, for about 15 minutes, turning frequently with tongs. Place the breasts and wings on the grill, skin side up. Cook all the chicken for 25 to 30 minutes longer, turning often. The chicken is done when the juices run clear when the thickest sections are pierced with a fork or sharp knife, or when an instant-read thermometer inserted into the thickest part of the thigh registers 180°F and into the thickest part of the breast registers 170°F. Don't let the thermometer touch the bone. Serve immediately with the barbecue sauce.

Never buy chicken parts that are bruised or discolored, but instead look for even, yellowish coloration and plump breasts and thighs. This marinade, redolent with the flavors of Asia, blends beautifully with the chicken, although it would taste good, too, with pork.

Gingery Chicken   *Serves 6 to 8*

HEAT =

½ CUP SOY SAUCE

¼ CUP RICE WINE VINEGAR

3 TABLESPOONS FRESH LEMON JUICE

1 TABLESPOON HONEY

1 TABLESPOON PLUS 1½ TEASPOONS
   CHOPPED FRESH GINGER

1 CLOVE GARLIC, CHOPPED

½ TEASPOON CRUSHED RED PEPPER

SALT AND FRESHLY GROUND BLACK
   PEPPER TO TASTE

TWO 3- TO 3½-POUND CHICKENS, EACH
   CUT INTO EIGHT PIECES

VEGETABLE OIL COOKING SPRAY

1. Combine the soy sauce, vinegar, lemon juice, honey, ginger, garlic, and red pepper in a nonreactive saucepan. Season with salt and pepper. Bring to a boil, remove from the heat, and let cool.

2. Transfer the marinade to a shallow glass or ceramic dish and add the chicken pieces. Turn several times to coat. Cover and refrigerate for 4 to 6 hours, letting the chicken come to room temperature before grilling.

3. Prepare a charcoal or gas grill: Lightly spray the grill rack with vegetable oil cooking spray. Light the coals or heating elements, and let them burn or heat until moderately hot.

4. Lift the chicken from the dish, reserving the marinade. Grill the legs and thighs, skin side up to start, for about 15 minutes, turning frequently with tongs and brushing several times with the marinade. Place the breasts and wings on the grill, skin side up. Cook all the chicken for 25 to 30 minutes longer, turning often and brushing several times with marinade during the first 10 minutes of cooking. The chicken is done when the juices run clear when the thickest sections are pierced with a fork or sharp knife, or when an instant-read thermometer inserted into the thickest part of the thigh registers 180°F and into the thickest part of the breast registers 170°F. Don't let the thermometer touch the bone. Serve immediately.

In this recipe, we skin the chicken and then rub the spice mixture deep into the meat. This method flavors the meat more intensely than if it were protected by the chicken skin. The cool chutney offsets the curry flavor.

Curried Chicken with Mango-Curry Chutney   *Serves 6*

HEAT =

TWO 3- TO 3½-POUND CHICKENS, EACH
  CUT INTO EIGHT PIECES AND
  SKINNED
¾ CUP CURRY PASTE RUB (PAGE 247)
1 TABLESPOON CANOLA OR
  SAFFLOWER OIL
3 TABLESPOONS CHOPPED ONIONS
1 SMALL SERRANO CHILE, STEMMED,
  SEEDED, AND CHOPPED
1 MANGO, CUT LENGTHWISE IN HALF,
  PITTED, AND CUBED
2 TABLESPOONS FRESH ORANGE JUICE
1 TEASPOON CIDER VINEGAR
FRESHLY GROUND BLACK PEPPER TO
  TASTE
2 TABLESPOONS CHOPPED FRESH
  CILANTRO
VEGETABLE OIL COOKING SPRAY

1. Put the chicken pieces in a shallow glass or ceramic dish and rub all but 1 tablespoon of the curry rub thoroughly into the meat. Cover and refrigerate for at least 30 minutes and as long as 4 hours, letting the chicken come to room temperature before grilling.

2. Heat the oil in a small skillet over medium heat. Add the onions and cook for 3 or 4 minutes, until the onions begin to soften. Add the chile and cook for about 30 seconds, just until fragrant. Add the mango, orange juice, vinegar, and the remaining tablespoon of curry rub and cook, stirring occasionally, for 5 to 7 minutes, until the mango softens but still retains its shape. Season with pepper to taste and stir in the cilantro. Cook for about 1 minute longer and transfer to a bowl. Cover and refrigerate until chilled. (The chutney will keep for up to 3 days.)

3. Prepare a charcoal or gas grill: Lightly spray the grill rack with vegetable oil cooking spray. Light the coals or heating elements, and let them burn or heat until moderately hot.

4. Grill the legs and thighs, skin side up to start, for about 15 minutes, turning frequently with tongs. Place the breasts and wings on the grill, skin side up to start. Cook all the chicken for 25 to 30 minutes longer, turning often. The chicken is done when the juices run clear when the thickest sections are pierced with a fork or sharp knife, or when an instant-read thermometer inserted into the thickest part of the thigh registers 180°F and into the thickest part of the breast registers 170°F. Don't let the thermometer touch the bone. Serve immediately with the chutney.

Teriyaki chicken is a backyard classic. This marinade is great on chicken, but also good with beef or pork.

Teriyaki Chicken   *Serves 6*

HEAT =

TWO 3- TO 3½-POUND CHICKENS, EACH
CUT INTO 8 PIECES
2 CUPS TERIYAKI MARINADE (PAGE 239)
VEGETABLE OIL COOKING SPRAY

1. Put the chicken in a shallow glass or ceramic dish and pour the marinade over the chicken pieces, turning the chicken to coat. Cover and refrigerate for at least 2 hours and as long as 24 hours, letting the chicken come to room temperature before grilling.

2. Prepare a charcoal or gas grill: Lightly spray the grill rack with vegetable oil cooking spray. Light the coals or heating elements, and let them burn or heat until moderately hot.

3. Lift the chicken from the dish, reserving the marinade. Grill the legs and thighs, skin side up to start, for about 15 minutes, turning frequently with tongs and brushing several times with the marinade. Place the breasts and wings on the grill, skin side up. Cook all the chicken for 25 to 30 minutes longer, turning often and brushing several times with marinade during the first 10 minutes of cooking. The chicken is done when the juices run clear when the thickest sections are pierced with a fork or sharp knife, or when an instant-read thermometer inserted into the thickest part of the thigh registers 180°F and into the thickest part of the breast registers 170°F. Don't let the thermometer touch the bone. Serve immediately.

$\mathbf{Y}$ou could easily make the argument that smoked chicken is the most versatile of smoked meats. Not only is it delicious right out of the smoker slathered with barbecue sauce or another favorite condiment, but when it's chilled it makes amazing chicken salad, sandwiches, and wraps. Slice it and toss it with green salads or make a smoked chicken Caesar salad. Yum! Before you smoke it, rinse off the rub and pat the meat dry with paper towels. It will be plenty flavorful.

Smoked Chile-Garlic Chicken Breasts *Serves 6*

HEAT =

6 BONE-IN, SKIN-ON CHICKEN BREAST
    HALVES (4½ TO 5 POUNDS TOTAL)
⅓ CUP SPICY DRY RUB (PAGE 242)
3 LARGE CLOVES GARLIC CLOVES,
    CRUSHED

1. Divide the chicken between two large, resealable plastic bags or shallow glass or ceramic dishes.

2. Mix the rub with the garlic and then add this mixture to the chicken, tossing the chicken breasts to coat. Seal the bags or cover the bowls with plastic wrap and refrigerate for at least 4 hours and up to 8 hours.

3. Prepare and preheat the smoker according to the manufacturer's instructions. We used mesquite wood but hickory would be good, too.

4. Rinse the chicken and pat dry with paper towels. Discard the rub. Leave the skin on the chicken, spreading and reshaping it over each breast.

5. Lay the chicken breast on the smoker's rack, skin side up, and smoke for 1½ hours at 200°F, or until an instant-read thermometer registers 170°F.

6. Remove and discard the chicken skin before serving the chicken.

The mild, sweet flavor of chicken makes it a natural to pair with fruit, particularly when the chicken has been soaked in a slightly sweet marinade. Try this with pork, too.

Grilled Chicken Breasts and Apple Rings with Maple Syrup Marinade

Serves 6

HEAT =

6 BONE-IN, SKIN-ON CHICKEN BREAST
    HALVES
1½ CUPS MAPLE SYRUP MARINADE
    (PAGE 240)
VEGETABLE OIL COOKING SPRAY
3 LARGE FIRM APPLES, SUCH AS
    CORTLAND OR GRANNY SMITH,
    CORED, PEELED, AND CUT INTO
    1-INCH-THICK RINGS
CANOLA OIL FOR BRUSHING

1. Put the chicken breasts in a shallow glass or ceramic dish. Pour 1¼ cups of the marinade over the chicken, turning to coat. Cover and refrigerate for at least 4 hours and as long as 24 hours, letting the chicken come to room temperature before grilling. Refrigerate the remaining ¼ cup of marinade.

2. Prepare a charcoal or gas grill: Lightly spray the grill rack with vegetable oil cooking spray. Light the coals or heating elements, and let them burn or heat until moderately hot.

3. Put the apple rings on a plate or baking sheet and brush on both sides with the reserved ¼ cup of marinade. Set aside at room temperature to marinate while grilling the chicken.

4. Lift the chicken from the dish, reserving the marinade. Grill the chicken breasts, skin side down to start, for 25 to 30 minutes, turning frequently with tongs and brushing several times with any remaining marinade during the first 10 minutes of cooking. During the last 10 minutes of grilling, place the apples rings on the outer edge of the grill. Brush with some oil and grill for about 5 minutes. Turn, brush with some more oil, and grill for about 5 minutes longer, or until lightly browned on both sides and tender.

5. The chicken is done when the juices run clear when the thickest sections are pierced with a fork, or when an instant-read thermometer inserted into the thickest part of the breast registers 170°F (don't touch the bone). Serve immediately with the apple slices.

Our recipes for boneless, skinless chicken breasts call for the amount to be determined by the number of breasts, rather than by weight. As a rule, six cutlets or breast halves (three whole breasts) weigh 2 to 2½ pounds. Although you can find breasts weighing less or more, they will generally fall into this range.

Lemon-Thyme Grilled Chicken Breasts   *Serves 6*

HEAT =

JUICE OF 3 LEMONS

¼ CUP LOOSELY PACKED CHOPPED
   FRESH THYME

1 LARGE CLOVE GARLIC, CRUSHED

FRESHLY GROUND BLACK PEPPER TO
   TASTE

3 BONELESS, SKINLESS CHICKEN
   BREASTS, TRIMMED AND HALVED

VEGETABLE OIL COOKING SPRAY

1. Combine the lemon juice, thyme, garlic, and a generous amount of pepper in a bowl, stirring well. Put the chicken breasts in a shallow glass or ceramic dish and pour the marinade over them, turning to coat. Cover and refrigerate for at least 1 hour and as long as 6 hours, letting the chicken come to room temperature before grilling.

2. Prepare a charcoal or gas grill: Lightly spray the grill rack with vegetable oil cooking spray. Light the coals or heating elements, and let them burn or heat until moderately hot.

3. Lift the chicken from the dish. Discard the marinade. Grill the chicken breasts for 12 to 16 minutes, turning several times with tongs, until cooked through and the juices run clear when the breast meat is pierced with a small, sharp knife. Serve immediately.

Many home cooks find buying boneless, skinless breasts easier than boning the chicken breasts themselves. Today, these are so popular they generally are fresh and tender, but beware of chicken that looks discolored or, under the plastic wrapping, is sitting in small puddles of water, which indicates freezing and thawing and refreezing. This treatment renders the chicken tough and rubbery.

Citrus-Marinated Grilled Chicken Breasts *Serves 6*

HEAT =

3 BONELESS, SKINLESS CHICKEN
   BREASTS, TRIMMED AND HALVED
SALT TO TASTE
1¼ CUPS FRESH ORANGE JUICE
3 TABLESPOONS FRESH LEMON JUICE
2 TEASPOONS GROUND GINGER
1¼ TEASPOONS DRIED THYME
2 TABLESPOONS SOY SAUCE
4 TABLESPOONS PLAIN DRY BREAD
   CRUMBS
VEGETABLE OIL COOKING SPRAY

1. Sprinkle the chicken breasts lightly on both sides with salt and put the chicken in a shallow glass or ceramic bowl.

2. Combine the orange juice, lemon juice, ginger, thyme, soy sauce, and bread crumbs in a small bowl, stirring to make a thin paste. Pour the paste over the chicken and rub it into the chicken. Cover and refrigerate for no longer than 6 hours, letting the chicken come to room temperature before grilling.

3. Prepare a charcoal or gas grill: Lightly spray the grill rack with vegetable oil cooking spray. Light the coals or heating elements, and let them burn or heat until moderately hot.

4. Put the chicken on the grill and cook for 12 to 16 minutes, turning several times with tongs, until cooked through and the juices run clear when the breast meat is pierced with a small, sharp knife and the crumbs are browned. Serve immediately.

If you plan to grill a number of boneless, skinless chicken breasts, you will save money (if not time) by buying whole chicken breasts and boning and skinning them yourself. Remember that a chicken has only one breast and so what most people think of as a "chicken breast" is actually one half of a breast.

Grilled Chicken with Black Pepper and Goat Cheese   *Serves 6*

HEAT =

3 WHOLE BONELESS, SKINLESS CHICKEN
   BREASTS, TRIMMED AND HALVED
¼ CUP OLIVE OIL
FRESHLY GROUND BLACK PEPPER TO
   TASTE
6 OUNCES SOFT GOAT CHEESE
3 TABLESPOONS SNIPPED CHIVES
SALT TO TASTE
VEGETABLE OIL COOKING SPRAY
1 SMALL HEAD BOSTON LETTUCE

1. Put the chicken breasts in a shallow glass or ceramic dish. Rub the chicken with olive oil and pepper. Cover and refrigerate for at least 30 minutes and for as long as 6 hours, letting the chicken come to room temperature before grilling.

2. Combine the goat cheese and chives in a small bowl. Season with salt and pepper, blending well.

3. Prepare a charcoal or gas grill: Lightly spray the grill rack with vegetable oil cooking spray. Light the coals or heating elements, and let them burn or heat until moderately hot to hot.

4. Grill the chicken for about 5 minutes. Turn the breasts over and spread about 1 tablespoon of the goat cheese mixture in a thin coat on each breast half. Cook for 7 to 11 minutes longer, without turning the chicken, until the chicken is cooked through and the juices run clear when the breast meat is pierced with a small, sharp knife. About 1 minute before the chicken is done, use tongs to turn the breasts so that the cheese side faces the fire and the cheese bonds to the meat. Serve immediately on a bed of lettuce, with the remaining goat cheese–chive mixture on the side.

Boneless, skinless chicken breast halves lend themselves nicely to stuffing and rolling—and cook beautifully on the grill. Flatten them with a gentle hand to preserve their tenderness.

Grilled Chicken Breast Rolls with Olivada and Rosemary *Serves 4*

HEAT =

2 BONELESS, SKINLESS CHICKEN
   BREASTS, TRIMMED AND HALVED
1 TEASPOON FINELY CHOPPED FRESH
   ROSEMARY
¼ TEASPOON SALT
FRESHLY GROUND BLACK PEPPER TO
   TASTE
2 TABLESPOONS FRESH LEMON JUICE
2 TABLESPOONS OLIVE OIL
WOODEN TOOTHPICKS OR SMALL METAL
   SKEWERS
VEGETABLE OIL COOKING SPRAY
3 TABLESPOONS CHOPPED FLAT-LEAF
   PARSLEY
4 TEASPOONS OLIVADA (SEE NOTE)

1. Cover the chicken breasts with waxed paper or plastic wrap and, using a meat mallet or small heavy skillet, gently flatten the breasts to an even thickness of about ¼ inch.

2. Season the chicken breasts with the rosemary, salt, and pepper and put the breasts in a shallow glass or ceramic dish. Add the lemon juice and oil, turning to coat evenly. Cover and refrigerate for 2 to 4 hours, letting the chicken come to room temperature before grilling. Meanwhile, soak the toothpicks in cold water for 30 minutes, if using to fasten the breasts closed.

3. Prepare a charcoal or gas grill: Lightly spray the grill rack with vegetable oil cooking spray. Light the coals or heating elements, and let them burn or heat until moderately hot to hot.

4. Lift the breasts from the dish. Discard the marinade. Place the breasts on a work surface and sprinkle evenly with parsley. Spread 1 teaspoon of olivada on each breast. Roll the breasts up jelly-roll style to make neat rolls. Fasten with the toothpicks.

5. Grill the rolls for 14 to 18 minutes, turning frequently with tongs, until the chicken is lightly browned, feels springy when touched, and the meat is cooked through and the juices run clear when the breast meat is pierced with a small, sharp knife. Remove the toothpicks and serve immediately.

note: Olivada is a paste made mainly from niçoise olives, olive oil, and seasonings, and is sold in specialty stores.

We have long believed that some of our customers overlook the best-tasting part of the chicken: the legs and thighs. These constitute the dark meat portions of the bird—by definition the more flavorful parts. Plus, these are more economical than the breasts. What do you have to lose? Buy the whole leg, with the thigh attached, and cut them in half. Wiggle the leg at the joint so that you know where to cut. Believe us: this is very easy. Here, we soak these parts in a mildly seasoned buttermilk marinade for chicken with good, old-fashioned flavor.

Buttermilk-Soaked Chicken Legs and Thighs *Serves 6 to 8*

HEAT =

4 WHOLE CHICKEN LEGS, LEGS AND
    THIGHS SEPARATED (4½ TO 5
    POUNDS)

3 CUPS BUTTERMILK

2 LARGE SHALLOTS, THINLY SLICED

3 LARGE CLOVES GARLIC, CRUSHED

3 TABLESPOONS ROUGHLY CHOPPED
    FRESH THYME

2 TEASPOONS CAYENNE

2 TEASPOONS CELERY SEED

1 TEASPOON SALT

½ TEASPOON FRESHLY GROUND BLACK
    PEPPER

VEGETABLE OIL COOKING SPRAY

1. Rinse and pat dry the chicken legs and thighs. Divide them between two large resealable plastic bags or shallow glass or ceramic dishes.

2. Whisk together the remaining ingredients. Divide the marinade between the bags or dishes. Seal the bags or cover the dishes with plastic wrap and refrigerate for at least 2 hours and up to 4 hours, letting the chicken come to room temperature before grilling.

3. Prepare a charcoal or gas grill: Lightly spray the grill rack with vegetable oil cooking spray. Light the coals or heating elements, and let them burn or heat until moderately hot.

4. Lift the chicken from the dish, allowing the excess marinade to drip off. Discard the marinade.

5. Grill the chicken legs and thighs for 40 to 45 minutes, turning often with tongs. The chicken is done when the juices run clear when pierced with a fork or sharp knife, or when an instant-read thermometer registers 180°F inserted in the thickest part of the thighs. Don't let the thermometer touch the bone. Serve immediately.

Although you could use this marinade on a whole chicken with both white and dark meat, it is pungent enough to stand up to dark meat alone. Look for plump thighs with no drying or wrinkling on the skin.

Curried Chicken Thighs   *Serves 6*

HEAT =

½ CUP FRESH ORANGE JUICE

3 TABLESPOONS MILD OR HOT INDIAN
   CURRY PASTE, DEPENDING ON
   PREFERENCE (SEE NOTE)

2 TABLESPOONS HONEY MUSTARD

2 TEASPOONS SALT

½ TEASPOON GROUND ALLSPICE

½ TEASPOON FRESHLY GROUND BLACK
   PEPPER

4½ TO 5 POUNDS CHICKEN THIGHS
   (ABOUT 12 PIECES)

VEGETABLE OIL COOKING SPRAY

1. Combine the orange juice, curry paste, mustard, salt, allspice, and pepper in a glass or ceramic bowl, stirring well to dissolve the paste and salt completely.

2. Trim the chicken of excess fat and skin, but do not remove most of the skin. Put the thighs in a shallow glass or ceramic dish and rub the paste into the meat, being sure to coat well and to rub some paste under the chicken skin. Cover and refrigerate for at least 2 hours or overnight, letting the chicken come to room temperature before grilling.

3. Prepare a charcoal or gas grill: Lightly spray the grill rack with vegetable oil cooking spray. Light the coals or heating elements, and let them burn or heat until moderately hot.

4. Grill the chicken thighs for 40 to 45 minutes, starting skin side down and turning frequently with tongs. The chicken is done when the juices run clear when pierced with a fork or sharp knife, or when an instant-read thermometer registers 180°F when inserted in the thickest part of the thighs. Don't let the thermometer touch the bone. Serve immediately.

note: Indian curry paste is sold in small tubs in Asian markets as well as in some supermarkets and specialty food stores. Select hot or mild paste, depending on personal preference.

Everyone seems to love chicken wings—they're easy to eat with your fingers, are inexpensive, and can be served as a snack or as part of the main meal.

Grilled Chicken Wings with Lime Vinaigrette   *Serves 6*

HEAT =

VEGETABLE OIL COOKING SPRAY

20 TO 25 CHICKEN WINGS

1 TABLESPOON CAYENNE

SALT AND FRESHLY GROUND BLACK
    PEPPER TO TASTE

¾ CUP OLIVE OIL

6 TABLESPOONS FRESH LIME JUICE

4 CLOVES GARLIC, CHOPPED

¾ CUP CHOPPED FLAT-LEAF PARSLEY

1. Prepare a charcoal or gas grill: Lightly spray the grill rack with vegetable oil cooking spray. Light the coals or heating elements, and let them burn or heat until moderately hot.

2. Prepare the wings by cutting through the joint to make 2 pieces. Snip off and discard the tips (or reserve them to use in stock). Spread the wings on a baking pan and sprinkle with cayenne, and salt and pepper. Turn and season the other side of the wings. Rub the seasoning evenly into the wings.

3. Combine the olive oil, lime juice, garlic, and parsley in a small glass or ceramic bowl. Season with salt and pepper, stirring well. Set aside.

4. Grill the wings for 25 to 30 minutes, turning 3 or 4 times with tongs, until cooked through. Remove the wings from the grill and transfer to a shallow dish. Whisk the vinaigrette and pour over the wings, tossing to coat. Serve immediately.

When preparing chicken wings for the grill, we suggest snipping off the tips. The wings look better—and no one eats the tips anyway.

Peppery Chicken Wings   *Serves 6*

HEAT =

20 TO 25 CHICKEN WINGS

3 TABLESPOONS PEPPERY DRY RUB

(PAGE 241)

VEGETABLE OIL COOKING SPRAY

1. Prepare the wings by cutting through the joint to make 2 pieces. Snip off and discard the tips (or reserve them to use in stock). Spread the wings on a baking pan and sprinkle with half the dry rub. Turn and season the other side of the wings. Rub the seasoning evenly into the wings. Cover and refrigerate for at least 1 hour or overnight, letting the chicken come to room temperature before grilling.

2. Prepare a charcoal or gas grill: Lightly spray the grill rack with vegetable oil cooking spray. Light the coals or heating elements, and let them burn or heat until moderately hot.

3. Grill the wings for 25 to 30 minutes, turning 3 or 4 times with tongs, until cooked through. Serve immediately.

Try this sweet-and-sour glaze on other chicken parts, but we find it especially tasty on tiny wings to serve with ice cold beer or soda for a casual backyard gathering.

Glazed Sweet-and-Sour Chicken Wings   *Serves 6*

HEAT =

20 TO 25 CHICKEN WINGS

¾ CUP HOISIN SAUCE

3 TABLESPOONS SOY SAUCE

¼ CUP KETCHUP

¼ CUP RICE WINE VINEGAR

¼ CUP FRESH LIME JUICE

2 TABLESPOONS PACKED LIGHT OR DARK
   BROWN SUGAR

1 TABLESPOON CHOPPED GARLIC

1 TABLESPOON CHOPPED FRESH GINGER

½ TEASPOON ASIAN CHILI PASTE

VEGETABLE OIL COOKING SPRAY

1. Prepare the wings by cutting through the joint to make 2 pieces. Snip off and discard the tips (or reserve them to use in stock). Put the wings in a shallow glass or ceramic dish.

2. Combine the remaining ingredients in a small bowl and whisk well. Brush liberally on the chicken wings, turning them to coat both sides. Cover and refrigerate for at least 1 hour or overnight, letting the chicken come to room temperature before grilling.

3. Prepare a charcoal or gas grill: Lightly spray the grill rack with vegetable oil cooking spray. Light the coals or heating elements, and let them burn or heat until moderately hot.

4. Grill the wings for 25 to 30 minutes, turning 3 or 4 times with tongs and brushing with any remaining glaze during the first 10 minutes of grilling, until cooked through. Serve immediately.

Kabobs are favorites on the grill and for chicken kabobs, we recommend white meat, cut from boneless, skinless breasts.

Honey-Mustard Chicken Kabobs   *Serves 6*

HEAT =

6 TABLESPOONS HONEY

1/4 CUP DIJON MUSTARD

3 TABLESPOONS FRESH LEMON JUICE

1 TABLESPOON CHOPPED FRESH THYME

SALT AND FRESHLY GROUND BLACK
   PEPPER TO TASTE

2 TO 2 1/4 POUNDS BONELESS, SKINLESS
   CHICKEN BREASTS, CUT INTO ABOUT
   THIRTY 1 1/2-INCH CHUNKS

VEGETABLE OIL COOKING SPRAY

1 LARGE GREEN BELL PEPPER, CUT INTO
   TWELVE 1 1/2-INCH CHUNKS

1 LARGE RED BELL PEPPER, CUT INTO
   TWELVE 1 1/2-INCH CHUNKS

3 LARGE PORTOBELLO MUSHROOMS,
   TRIMMED AND QUARTERED

SIX 12-INCH METAL SKEWERS

1. Combine the honey, mustard, lemon juice, and thyme in a shallow glass or ceramic dish. Season with salt and pepper, stirring well. Add the chicken, tossing to coat. Cover and refrigerate for at least 3 hours and as long as 6 hours, letting the chicken come to room temperature before grilling.

2. Prepare a charcoal or gas grill: Lightly spray the grill rack with vegetable oil cooking spray. Light the coals or heating elements, and let them burn or heat until moderately hot to hot.

3. Lift the chicken from the dish. Thread the chicken, bell peppers, and mushrooms on skewers, beginning and ending with peppers. Drizzle a little of the remaining marinade over the skewers and discard the rest. Grill, covered, for 10 to 12 minutes, turning often with tongs, until the chicken is cooked through and the juices run clear when the meat is pierced with a small, sharp knife, the bell peppers are charred, and the mushrooms are tender. Serve immediately.

When buying meat for kabobs, look for boneless chicken breasts, which may be called cutlets or even supremes; both terms refer to breasts. The term "supreme" was coined years ago by chefs (notably Escoffier) who considered these fillets quite fancy. Supremes usually include both the small and large fillets from the breast half—as do most packages labeled "cutlets" or "breasts."

Thai-Style Chicken Kabobs   *Serves 6*

HEAT =

2 TO 2¼ POUNDS BONELESS, SKINLESS
   CHICKEN BREASTS, CUT INTO ABOUT
   THIRTY 1½-INCH CHUNKS

3 LARGE RED OR GREEN BELL PEPPERS,
   CUT INTO 1½-INCH PIECES

¼ CUP CANOLA OIL

¼ CUP FRESH LIME JUICE

2 TABLESPOONS SOY SAUCE

2 CLOVES GARLIC, FINELY CHOPPED

2 TABLESPOONS SHREDDED FRESH
   BASIL

3 TABLESPOONS SHREDDED FRESH
   CILANTRO

1 TABLESPOON PACKED LIGHT OR DARK
   BROWN SUGAR

VEGETABLE OIL COOKING SPRAY

SIX 12-INCH METAL SKEWERS

1. Combine the chicken and bell peppers in a shallow glass or ceramic dish.

2. Combine the oil, lime juice, soy sauce, garlic, basil, cilantro, and brown sugar in a small bowl, mixing well. Add to the chicken and bell peppers, tossing to coat. Cover and refrigerate for 30 minutes or up to 6 hours, letting the chicken come to room temperature before grilling.

3. Prepare a charcoal or gas grill: Lightly spray the grill rack with vegetable oil cooking spray. Light the coals or heating elements, and let them burn or heat until moderately hot.

4. Thread the chicken and bell peppers onto skewers, beginning and ending with the peppers. Drizzle some marinade over the skewers and discard the rest. Grill, covered, for 10 to 12 minutes, turning several times with tongs, until the chicken is cooked through and the juices run clear when the meat is pierced with a small, sharp knife. Serve immediately.

When skewered onto small bamboo skewers, chicken kabobs are great appetizers, welcome at any outdoor party. They can also be served at room temperature.

Chicken Satay

Serves 3 as a main course; serves 6 as an appetizer

HEAT =

1½ POUNDS BONELESS, SKINLESS
  CHICKEN BREAST, TRIMMED
½ CUP RICE WINE VINEGAR
⅓ CUP CREAMY PEANUT BUTTER
2 TABLESPOONS SOY SAUCE
2 TABLESPOONS FRESH LIME JUICE
1 TABLESPOON PACKED LIGHT BROWN
  SUGAR
1 TABLESPOON CHOPPED FRESH GINGER
2 OR 3 SCALLIONS, WHITE AND GREEN
  PARTS, CHOPPED
4 TO 6 BAMBOO SKEWERS
VEGETABLE OIL COOKING SPRAY

1. Cut the chicken on the diagonal into 1-inch-wide strips.

2. Whisk together the vinegar, peanut butter, soy sauce, lime juice, sugar, ginger, and scallions in a shallow glass or ceramic dish. Add the chicken strips, tossing to coat. Cover and refrigerate for at least 1 hour or up to 6 hours. Let the chicken come to room temperature before grilling.

3. Soak 4 to 6 bamboo skewers, depending on length and how you will serve the satay, in cold water to cover for 20 to 30 minutes.

4. Prepare a charcoal or gas grill: Lightly spray the grill rack with vegetable oil cooking spray. Light the coals or heating elements, and let them burn or heat until moderately hot.

5. Thread the chicken onto the skewers, spearing each strip at least twice so that they are secure. Grill for 10 to 12 minutes, turning 2 or 3 times, until the chicken is cooked through and the juices run clear when the meat is pierced with a small, sharp knife. Serve immediately.

The grill makes chicken salads special by providing the meat with a slightly smoky flavor.

Cold Basil Pesto Chicken Salad   *Serves 6*

HEAT =

2½ CUPS TORN BASIL LEAVES, PLUS
    EXTRA WHOLE LEAVES FOR GARNISH
2 CLOVES GARLIC, COARSELY CHOPPED
3 TABLESPOONS FRESHLY GRATED
    PARMESAN CHEESE
2 TABLESPOONS CIDER VINEGAR
½ CUP EXTRA VIRGIN OLIVE OIL
½ TEASPOON SALT
2 TO 2¼ POUNDS BONELESS, SKINLESS
    CHICKEN BREASTS, TRIMMED AND
    HALVED
VEGETABLE OIL COOKING SPRAY
1 SMALL HEAD RED LEAF LETTUCE
JUICE OF 1 LEMON

1. Combine the torn basil, garlic, cheese, and vinegar in the bowl of a food processor. Pulse 3 or 4 times to mix. With the processor running, slowly add the olive oil through the feed tube until the pesto is well mixed. (It will be more liquid than paste-like.) Season with salt.

2. Put the chicken in a shallow glass or ceramic dish and pour the pesto marinade over it, turning several times to coat. Cover and refrigerate for at least 3 hours and as long as 6 hours, letting the chicken come to room temperature before grilling.

3. Prepare a charcoal or gas grill: Lightly spray the grill rack with vegetable oil cooking spray. Light the coals or heating elements, and let them burn or heat until moderately hot to hot.

4. Lift the chicken from the dish, letting most of the marinade drip back into the bowl. Grill the chicken for 12 to 16 minutes, turning several times with tongs and brushing with the marinade once or twice during the first 5 minutes of cooking, discarding any remaining marinade, until cooked through and the juices run clear when the meat is pierced with a small, sharp knife. Discard the excess marinade.

5. Let the chicken cool, cut into bite-sized pieces, and chill for at least 1 hour.

6. Arrange the lettuce on a serving platter and sprinkle with lemon juice. Spoon the chicken over the lettuce, garnish with basil leaves, and serve.

This chicken salad is a composed salad, which means each ingredient is tossed with the vinaigrette separately before being assembled on a serving platter. Like all chicken salads, this can be partially made ahead of time and then served at room temperature.

Mediterranean Grilled Chicken Salad   *Serves 6*

HEAT =

SALAD

2 POUNDS BONELESS, SKINLESS
    CHICKEN BREASTS, TRIMMED AND
    HALVED

1 CUP WHITE WINE MARINADE
    (PAGE 237)

1 POUND SMALL RED POTATOES

½ POUND HARICOTS VERTS OR
    SLENDER GREEN BEANS, TRIMMED

VEGETABLE OIL COOKING SPRAY

FOUR TO SIX 12-INCH METAL SKEWERS

12 TO 14 CHERRY TOMATOES, HALVED
    OR LEFT WHOLE, DEPENDING ON SIZE

2 TEASPOONS CHOPPED FRESH
    TARRAGON, FOR GARNISH

VINAIGRETTE

¾ CUP EXTRA VIRGIN OLIVE OIL

¼ CUP WHITE WINE VINEGAR

2 TEASPOONS CHOPPED SHALLOTS

2 TEASPOONS DIJON MUSTARD

2 TEASPOONS CHOPPED FRESH
    TARRAGON

1. Make the salad: Place the chicken in a single layer in a shallow glass or ceramic dish and pour the marinade over it, turning a few times to coat. Cover and refrigerate for at least 1 hour and as long as 6 hours. Let the chicken come to room temperature before grilling.

2. Put the potatoes in a saucepan and add cold water to cover by several inches. Bring to a boil over high heat and cook for 10 to 12 minutes just until fork tender. Drain and cool. Do not overcook.

3. Blanch the haricots verts in boiling water to cover for about 1 minute. Drain and cool.

4. Prepare a charcoal or gas grill: Lightly spray the grill rack with vegetable oil cooking spray. Light the coals or heating elements, and let them burn or heat until moderately hot.

5. To make the vinaigrette, in a small bowl, whisk together the olive oil, vinegar, shallots, mustard, and tarragon. Season to taste with salt and pepper. Set aside.

6. Lift the chicken from the dish. Discard the marinade. Grill the chicken for 12 to 16 minutes, turning several times with tongs, until cooked through and the juices run clear when the meat is pierced with a small, sharp knife. Slice into thin strips.

**SALT AND FRESHLY GROUND BLACK
PEPPER TO TASTE**

7. Thread the potatoes on metal skewers and grill for about 5 minutes until lightly browned. Cut into halves or quarters, depending on their size. Transfer to a bowl and toss with about 5 tablespoons of vinaigrette.

8. Meanwhile, in a separate bowl, toss the haricots verts with 3 or 4 tablespoons of vinaigrette. In another bowl, toss the cherry tomatoes with 3 or 4 tablespoons of vinaigrette.

9. Assemble the salad by spreading the beans on a platter. Top the beans with the potatoes and then the chicken. Arrange the tomatoes around the chicken and sprinkle the salad with tarragon. Drizzle a little vinaigrette over the salad and serve.

Chicken and citrus fruit blend very nicely in a salad that can be served warm or at room temperature.

Grilled Chicken-Citrus Salad with Arugula *Serves 6*

HEAT =

½ CUP FRESH ORANGE JUICE

½ CUP FRESH GRAPEFRUIT JUICE

¼ CUP OLIVE OIL

3 TABLESPOONS ORANGE MARMALADE

1 TABLESPOON FINELY CHOPPED FRESH
   GINGER

2 TABLESPOONS CHOPPED FRESH
   CILANTRO OR FLAT-LEAF PARSLEY

SALT AND FRESHLY GROUND BLACK
   PEPPER TO TASTE

2 TO 2¼ POUNDS BONELESS, SKINLESS
   CHICKEN BREASTS, TRIMMED AND
   HALVED

VEGETABLE OIL COOKING SPRAY

1 NAVEL ORANGE, PEELED, WHITE PITH
   REMOVED

½ GRAPEFRUIT, PEELED, WHITE PITH
   REMOVED

3 SCALLIONS, WHITE AND GREEN PARTS,
   SLICED

1 LARGE HEAD RED OR GREEN LEAF
   LETTUCE

1 BUNCH ARUGULA

1. Combine the orange and grapefruit juices, oil, marmalade, ginger, and cilantro in a shallow glass or ceramic dish. Season with salt and pepper, whisking well. Pour half the mixture into a large bowl and set aside. Add the chicken to the dish, turning several times to coat. Cover and refrigerate for at least 1 hour and up to 6 hours, letting the chicken come to room temperature before grilling.

2. Prepare a charcoal or gas grill: Lightly spray the grill rack with vegetable oil cooking spray. Light the coals or heating elements, and let them burn or heat until moderately hot to hot.

3. Lift the chicken from the dish and let most of the marinade drip back into the dish. Grill the chicken for 12 to 16 minutes, until cooked through, turning several times with tongs; brush with any remaining marinade during the first 5 minutes of grilling. Discard any remaining marinade. The chicken is done when the juices run clear when the thickest sections are pierced with a fork or sharp knife. Set aside to cool slightly.

4. Holding the fruit above the bowl with the reserved marinade, separate the orange and the grapefruit half into sections, letting any juices collect in the bowl. Drop the sectioned fruit into the bowl and add the scallions. Toss gently. Cut the chicken into bite-sized pieces and add to the bowl. Toss to coat and season with salt and pepper.

3 RED RADISHES, TRIMMED AND THINLY SLICED

CHOPPED FRESH CILANTRO, FOR GARNISH

5. Arrange the lettuce and arugula on a platter and top with the chicken mixture. Garnish with radishes and cilantro and serve.

ASK THE BUTCHER

Which meats are best for marinating?

As you will see from the recipes in the book, we prefer marinating tougher cuts of beef and lamb, such as flank steak, round steak, and brisket, as well as lamb steaks. Cuts such as porterhouse steak and loin lamb chops are so flavorful that they don't benefit as much from marinades. On the other hand, pork is so mild and sweet, even tender cuts like tenderloin take to marinades deliciously. Chicken's natural mildness also makes it the perfect backdrop for a zesty or herbaceous marinade. When trying to decide what kind of marinade to pair with a type of meat, think of sweet, fruity flavors with pork, chicken, and game, herbaceous and mustardy ones with lamb, and red wine and herb mixtures with beef. But feel free to break each and every one of these rules to suit your taste! We do.

Classic combinations such as sundried tomatoes and pine nuts are perfect foils for mild-flavored chicken, here tossed with pasta for a salad that can serve as main course or as part of an array of dishes at a picnic.

Grilled Chicken Pasta Salad with Sundried Tomatoes and Pine Nuts   *Serves 6*

HEAT =

SALAD

1½ POUNDS BONELESS, SKINLESS
   CHICKEN BREASTS, TRIMMED AND
   HALVED

1 CUP WHITE WINE MARINADE
   (PAGE 237)

10 TO 12 DRY-PACKED SUNDRIED
   TOMATOES

1 CUP BOILING WATER

VEGETABLE OIL COOKING SPRAY

¾ POUND FARFALLE, COOKED AL DENTE

6 TO 8 WATER-PACKED ARTICHOKE
   HEARTS (FROM 14.5-OUNCE CAN),
   DRAINED AND SLICED

6 TABLESPOONS TOASTED PINE NUTS
   (SEE NOTE)

1 ROASTED RED BELL PEPPER (PAGE
   251), THINLY SLICED

1 ROASTED YELLOW BELL PEPPER (PAGE
   251), THINLY SLICED

2 TABLESPOONS CHOPPED FLAT-LEAF
   PARSLEY

1. Make the salad: Place the chicken in a single layer in a shallow glass or ceramic dish and pour the marinade over it. Turn a few times to coat, cover, and refrigerate for at least 1 hour and as long as 6 hours, letting the chicken come to room temperature before grilling.

2. Cover the tomatoes with the water in a large heatproof glass measuring cup and set aside to soak for 30 minutes. Drain, cool, and slice into slivers. Set aside.

3. Prepare a charcoal or gas grill: Lightly spray the grill rack with vegetable oil cooking spray. Light the coals or heating elements, and let them burn or heat until moderately hot.

4. To make the vinaigrette, whisk together the olive oil, vinegar, lemon juice, shallots, and parsley in a small bowl. Season to taste with salt and pepper. Set aside.

5. Lift the chicken from the dish. Discard the marinade. Grill the chicken for 12 to 16 minutes, turning with tongs several times, until cooked through and the juices run clear when the meat is pierced with a small knfe. Slice into thin strips.

VINAIGRETTE

¼ CUP EXTRA VIRGIN OLIVE OIL

2 TABLESPOONS WHITE WINE VINEGAR

1 TABLESPOON FRESH LEMON JUICE

½ TEASPOON CHOPPED SHALLOT

2 TEASPOONS CHOPPED FLAT-LEAF
   PARSLEY

SALT AND FRESHLY GROUND BLACK
   PEPPER TO TASTE

6. Meanwhile, in a large serving bowl, toss the pasta with about ⅓ cup of the vinaigrette. Add the slivered tomatoes, artichoke hearts, pine nuts, and chicken. Toss to mix. Add the roasted peppers and parsley. Toss again, adjust the seasonings, and drizzle with more vinaigrette to taste. Serve at room temperature.

note: To toast the pine nuts, spread them in a dry skillet over medium-high heat for about 4 minutes until lightly browned and fragrant. Shake the pan during toasting to prevent burning. Transfer to a plate to cool completely. Alternatively, roast the pine nuts in a roasting pan in a 350°F oven until lightly browned and fragrant.

here we live in the New York metropolitan area, chicken pizzas are extremely popular. We took a cue from local pizza parlors and developed the best chicken pizzas ever! Grilled chicken, grilled onions and peppers, barbecue sauce, and melted cheese come together in delicious harmony on top of little prebaked pizza crusts. If you have a favorite recipe for pizza dough and want to go all out, make your own crust; otherwise buy the prebaked ones at the supermarket. Have all components ready and lined up near the grill so that everyone can assemble their own pizzas just the way they like them. These make great appetizers, too, cut into wedges.

Mini BBQ Chicken Pizzas   *Serves 6*

HEAT =

2 POUNDS BONELESS, SKINLESS
    CHICKEN BREASTS

2 SWEET ONIONS, SUCH AS VIDALIA,
    PEELED AND HALVED CROSSWISE

1 LARGE RED BELL PEPPER, HALVED
    LENGTHWISE AND SEEDED

1 LARGE GREEN BELL PEPPER, HALVED
    LENGTHWISE AND SEEDED

½ CUP EXTRA VIRGIN OLIVE OIL

3 TABLESPOONS SPICY DRY RUB (PAGE
    242)

SIX 8-INCH MINI PREBAKED PIZZA
    SHELLS (SUCH AS BOBOLI)

VEGETABLE OIL COOKING SPRAY

1 CUP MADISON AVENUE BARBECUE
    SAUCE (PAGE 221)

1½ CUPS FRESHLY GRATED
    MOZZARELLA CHEESE

1. Put the chicken breasts, onions, and bell peppers in a shallow baking pan and drizzle with ¼ cup oil. Sprinkle the dry rub over the meat and vegetables. Lightly brush both sides of the pizza shells with the remaining ¼ cup of the oil.

2. Prepare a charcoal or gas grill: Lightly spray the grill rack with vegetable oil cooking spray. Light the coals or heating elements, and let them burn or heat until moderately hot.

3. Put the chicken, onions, and bell peppers, cut side down, on the grill. Cook the bell peppers for 8 to 10 minutes and the onions for 10 to 12 minutes. Turn both once or twice. When done, they will be a little charred and be crisp-tender. They will still hold their shape. Grill the chicken for 12 to 14 minutes, turning several times with tongs, until cooked through and the juices run clear.

4. Transfer the chicken and vegetables to a cutting board and let them rest for about 5 minutes or until cool enough to handle.

5. Slice the chicken into ¼-inch-thick strips and transfer to a small bowl. Toss with about ⅓ cup of the barbecue sauce and set aside, covered, to keep warm. Slice the peppers and onions and

**1½ CUPS GRATED MONTEREY OR
PEPPER JACK CHEESE**

**1 CUP ROUGHLY CHOPPED FLAT-LEAF
PARSLEY**

set aside separately, covered, to keep warm. Mix the two cheeses together.

6. Put the pizza shells, top side down, on the grill and toast for about 1 minute, just until warm. Remove from grill, turn right side up, and brush with the remaining barbecue sauce.

7. Divide the chicken, peppers, and onions among the pizzas. Lay the chicken on first and then top with the peppers and onions. Sprinkle each pizza with the parsley and then with the cheese.

8. Return the pizzas to the grill, cover, and cook for about 5 minutes, or until the cheese melts and the crust is browned and crispy. As the pizzas are done, transfer them to the cutting board and cut each in half or quarters with a sharp knife or pizza wheel. Serve immediately.

A chicken sandwich is even better when the chicken breast meat is grilled. Buy the best sourdough or kaiser rolls you can find—preferably from a bakery—or use the soft rolls called potato rolls or Portuguese rolls. Good bread is crucial for a good sandwich.

Grilled Summer Chicken Sandwich with Roasted Red Peppers *Serves 6*

HEAT =

3 BONELESS, SKINLESS CHICKEN
    BREASTS, TRIMMED AND HALVED

1 TABLESPOON FRESHLY CRACKED
    BLACK PEPPER

¼ CUP FRESH LEMON JUICE

2 TABLESPOONS COARSELY CHOPPED
    FRESH THYME OR TARRAGON

VEGETABLE OIL COOKING SPRAY

¼ CUP ROASTED GARLIC MAYONNAISE
    (PAGE 248), OR STORE-BOUGHT OR
    HOMEMADE MAYONNAISE

6 SOURDOUGH OR KAISER ROLLS,
    HALVED

6 LARGE LEAVES BIBB OR BOSTON
    LETTUCE

2 ROASTED RED BELL PEPPERS (PAGE
    251), CUT INTO STRIPS

SALT AND FRESHLY GROUND BLACK
    PEPPER TO TASTE

1. Cover the chicken breast halves with waxed paper or plastic wrap and, using a meat mallet or small heavy skillet, gently flatten the breasts to an even thickness of about ½ inch. Put the meat in a shallow glass or ceramic dish.

2. Sprinkle both sides of the chicken with cracked pepper, pressing gently so that it adheres to the meat. Pour the lemon juice over the chicken and sprinkle with thyme. Cover and refrigerate for at least 1 hour and as long as 4 hours, letting the chicken come to room temperature before grilling.

3. Prepare a charcoal or gas grill: Lightly spray the grill rack with vegetable oil cooking spray. Light the coals or heating elements, and let them burn or heat until moderately hot to hot.

4. Grill the chicken for 10 to 14 minutes, turning several times, until cooked through and the juices run clear when the meat is pierced with a small knfe.

5. Spread the mayonnaise on both halves of the rolls and place lettuce on the bottom halves of each roll. Top with strips of roasted red pepper. Place a chicken breast half on each sandwich, season with salt and pepper, and cover with the other half of the roll. Slice in half and serve immediately.

Here, we smoke an entire meal—chicken, sausage, and corn-on-the-cob—and is it good! If you have shelves in your smoker, stack the food. Otherwise, arrange it all together and let the hickory wood flavor the food as only it can. Of course, mesquite, apple wood, or another fruit wood would be fabulous, too. Serve this smoked mixed grill with crusty bread, sweet butter, sliced summer tomatoes, and assorted pickles. A simple summertime feast! Make sure to use uncooked sausage; we prefer spicy Italian sausages, but they're all good!

Smoked Mixed Grill   *Serves 6*

HEAT =

2 TABLESPOONS COARSE SALT

1 TABLESPOON DRIED THYME

1 TABLESPOON COARSELY GROUND
   BLACK PEPPER

1 TABLESPOON PACKED LIGHT OR DARK
   BROWN SUGAR

1 TEASPOON FINELY GRATED
   LEMON ZEST

6 BONELESS, SKINLESS CHICKEN
   BREAST HALVES

6 EARS SWEET CORN

3 POUNDS RAW HOT OR SWEET ITALIAN
   SAUSAGE LINKS

1. Mix together the salt, thyme, pepper, sugar and lemon zest in a small bowl. Evenly coat the chicken breasts with the seasoning rub, cover, and refrigerate for at least 4 hours and no longer than 8 hours.

2. Husk the corn, leaving a few layers of the inside leaves attached at the stem end. Thoroughly remove the silks. Pull the leaves back over the corn to cover the cob completely.

3. Prepare and preheat the smoker according to the manufacturer's instructions. We use a mixture of hickory wood.

4. Lift the chicken from the rub and rinse quickly under cool running water. Pat dry with paper towels, wiping most of the seasoning from the chicken.

5. If you have a smoker with shelves, put the sausage on the top shelf, the chicken in the middle, and the corn on the lowest rack. Otherwise, arrange them in your smoker in whatever fashion makes sense. Smoke for 1½ hours at 200°F, or until the chicken is cooked through when you cut it open.

6. Separate the sausage links, if necessary, and slice the chicken breasts. Remove the leaves from the corn. Put everything on a platter and serve.

Rock Cornish game hens are tiny birds that have caught on with Americans, often connoting elegant dining. The miniature birds were the brainchild of poultry breeder Jacques Makowsky, who crossed Cornish game cocks with Plymouth Rock hens at his Connecticut farm. Since their debut in 1950, the tender hens have rapidly grown in popularity.

Grilled Moroccan-Style Rock Cornish Game Hens   *Serves 4*

HEAT =

½ CUP PEANUT OIL

¼ CUP FRESH LEMON JUICE

2 TABLESPOONS CHOPPED FRESH
    CILANTRO

2 TABLESPOONS CHOPPED FLAT-LEAF
    PARSLEY

2 CLOVES GARLIC, MINCED

1 TABLESPOON SWEET PAPRIKA

2 TEASPOONS GROUND CINNAMON

2 TEASPOONS GROUND TURMERIC

2 TEASPOONS GROUND ALLSPICE

2 TEASPOONS MINCED FRESH GINGER

2 TEASPOONS MINCED LEMON ZEST

FOUR 1- TO 1¼-POUND ROCK CORNISH
    GAME HENS

VEGETABLE OIL COOKING SPRAY

1. Combine the oil, lemon juice, cilantro, parsley, garlic, paprika, cinnamon, turmeric, allspice, ginger, and lemon zest in a small bowl and stir until well mixed.

2. Put the hens in a shallow glass or ceramic dish and pour the marinade over them. Rub it over the hens and inside the cavities. Using kitchen twine, truss the hens. Cover and refrigerate for at least 6 hours or overnight, letting the hens come to room temperature before grilling.

3. Prepare a charcoal or gas grill: Lightly spray the grill rack with vegetable oil cooking spray. Light the coals or heating elements, and let them burn or heat until moderately hot.

4. Lift the hens from the dish. Discard the marinade. Grill, breast side down, for about 15 minutes. Turn and grill for 25 to 30 minutes longer, until the juices run clear when the thickest part of the meat is pricked with a fork or sharp knife, or when an instant-read thermometer inserted in the thickest meat registers 180°F. Let rest for about 5 minutes before serving.

Rock Cornish game hens are bred to be plump and all white meat—a combination that endears them to backyard chefs. Ask the butcher to split and flatten the hens for you or do it yourself. Treat these little treasures gently—they will flatten quite easily. We bathe them in a rich, coffee-based marinade, which turns them a light mahogany and infuses the mild meat with pleasant, slightly smoky flavor, a perfect backdrop for the pungent anchovy and olive oil rub. The result? Bold-tasting hens that sizzle with flavor when lifted from the grill.

Coffee-Marinated Rock Cornish Game Hens   *Serves 4*

HEAT =

FOUR 1- TO 1¼-POUND ROCK CORNISH
   GAME HENS

4 CUPS STRONG BREWED COFFEE, AT
   ROOM TEMPERATURE

VEGETABLE OIL COOKING SPRAY

2 ANCHOVIES OR 2 TEASPOONS
   ANCHOVY PASTE

2 TABLESPOONS OLIVE OIL

SALT AND FRESHLY GROUND BLACK
   PEPPER TO TASTE

1 TO 2 TABLESPOONS CHOPPED FRESH
   ROSEMARY

1. Split the hens down the backbone and using your hands, flatten them. Put them in a large, shallow glass or ceramic dish. Pour the coffee over them, cover, and refrigerate for 2 hours, letting the hens come to room temperature before grilling.

2. Prepare a charcoal or gas grill: Lightly spray the grill rack with vegetable oil cooking spray. Light the coals or heating elements, and let them burn or heat until moderately hot.

3. Combine the anchovies and oil in a small bowl and mix, mashing the anchovies with a fork, to make a paste.

4. Lift the hens from the coffee marinade and pat dry with paper towels. Rub the hens all over with the anchovy–olive oil mixture, inserting a little under the skin. Season with salt and pepper and sprinkle the skin sides with rosemary. Reserve about 1½ teaspoons rosemary for garnish.

5. Grill, skin side down, for about 15 minutes. Turn and grill for 25 to 30 minutes longer until the juices run clear when the thickest part of the meat is pricked with a fork or sharp knife, or when an instant-read thermometer inserted in the thickest meat registers 180°F. The skin should be browned and crisp. Let rest for about 5 minutes before serving.

Once you roast a turkey out of doors—even in the dead of winter—you will become a convert. The meat has a slightly smoky flavor that is hard to resist. We recommend fresh turkey, and preferably one that has been raised naturally. We suggest relatively small turkeys for outdoor grilling—those weighing 16 pounds or more do better in the oven. But 12- or 14-pound birds are spectacular cooked outside, and having the turkey on the grill frees up the oven for other dishes, including the dressing that many feel is essential when serving turkey.

It's important to keep the fire relatively cool, which is why we suggest putting an oven thermometer in the grill if yours is not equipped with one. If using a charcoal grill, you will have to add fresh coals to the fire every 45 minutes or so to maintain the heat. Keeping the vents only partially opened helps keep the fire low, too. We found that as in the oven, the turkey requires very little tending. The drip pan filled with water provides a nice, moist environment that makes it unnecessary to baste the turkey. If you prefer, add chicken broth and wine to the water for a little more flavor. But truth be told, we find this makes very little difference, as the overall taste of the bird is that of smokiness.

Roast Turkey On-the-Grill   *Serves 6 to 8*

HEAT =

VEGETABLE OIL COOKING SPRAY

ONE FRESH 12-POUND TURKEY

CANOLA OIL

SALT AND FRESHLY GROUND BLACK
    PEPPER TO TASTE

2 OR 3 CARROTS, COARSELY CHOPPED

1 LARGE ONION, COARSELY CHOPPED

2 CLOVES GARLIC, COARSELY CHOPPED

3 TABLESPOONS CHOPPED FLAT-LEAF
    PARSLEY

1 TABLESPOON CHOPPED FRESH THYME

1. Prepare a charcoal or gas grill, arranging the coals for indirect cooking (see page 7). Lightly spray the grill rack with vegetable oil cooking spray. Set a drip pan filled halfway with water under the area of the rack where the turkey will sit. Position an oven thermometer inside the grill, light the coals or heating elements, cover, and let them burn or heat until the temperature reaches 350°F. The coals should be moderately hot, but will cool down when the turkey cooks.

2. Rub the turkey inside and out with oil. Season the turkey inside and out with salt and pepper. Stuff the cavity with the carrots, onion, garlic, parsley, and thyme.

3. Set the stuffed turkey on the rack, breast side up, over the drip pan. Cover and grill for 2½ to 3 hours, approximately 12 to 15 minutes to the pound. Maintain the internal temperature of the grill at 300° to 325°F. Add fresh coals to the fire about every 45 minutes as necessary to maintain a moderate, constant heat. If using a gas grill, adjust the burners to keep the temperature even. The turkey is done when a meat thermometer inserted in the thickest part of the thigh registers 180°F and the juices run clear when the meat is pierced with a fork or sharp knife.

4. Transfer the turkey to a platter or cutting board and let rest for 15 minutes before carving. Discard the vegetables in the turkey's cavity.

Smoked turkey is a great favorite, whether served warm from the smoker or used later for sandwiches, salads, and snacks. We smoke a turkey breast rather than a whole bird for two reasons. First, most people like it best and second, it's easier to work with than a whole bird. If the butcher cuts the turkey breast for you and offers you the wings and backbone, grab them. Brine them with the breast if there is room in the pot, or smoke them without brining. Cut them into pieces, freeze them, and use them as you would smoked ham hocks or bacon to flavor baked beans, split pea soup, or winter greens. Start with a fresh turkey breast or a completely thawed frozen turkey breast.

Soaking the turkey breast in a simple brine adds a little flavor and a lot of moisture to the bird. Put the turkey in a large pot so that it has plenty of room and the brine can cover it by two or three inches. After 12 hours the turkey breast will have absorbed enough brine to be lovely and moist once it's smoked. You can leave the turkey in the brine for another 12 hours with no consequences, but much longer is not advised. Pat the turkey dry with paper towels before you smoke it.

We suggest serving this with our Chunky Cranberry Ketchup (page 235), which is also great on smoked turkey sandwiches. We also like to use this turkey for our club sandwiches on page 198.

Smoked Brined Turkey Breast   *Serves 6*

HEAT =

2 QUARTS WARM WATER

⅔ CUP COARSE SALT

½ CUP PACKED LIGHT OR DARK BROWN
   SUGAR

¼ CUP APPLE CIDER VINEGAR

1 YELLOW ONION, THINLY SLICED

1 RIB CELERY WITH LEAVES, THINLY
   SLICED

¼ CUP MINCED FRESH SAGE LEAVES OR
   2 TABLESPOONS CRUMBLED DRIED
   SAGE

1. Put the water in a pot large enough to hold the split turkey breast easily. Make sure the pot will also fit in the refrigerator (you could use two smaller pots or heavy resealable plastic bags and divide the brine and 2 sides of the breast between them). Add the salt, sugar, vinegar, onion, celery, sage, and cloves and stir until the salt and sugar dissolve and let cool to room temperature.

2. Submerge the turkey halves in the brine. They should be completely covered; if not, add more water. Cover and refrigerate for at least 12 hours and up to 24 hours.

3. Prepare and preheat the smoker according to the manufacturer's instructions. We used hickory wood but apple wood would be another good choice.

½ TEASPOON GROUND CLOVES

ONE 4- TO 5-POUND BONE-IN, SKIN-ON

TURKEY BREAST, SPLIT

CHUNKY CRANBERRY KETCHUP

(PAGE 235), FOR SERVING

4. Lift the turkey from the brine and pat dry with paper towels. Discard the brine.

5. Put the turkey breast halves on the rack of the smoker and smoke for 2½ to 3 hours at 225°F, until an instant-read thermometer registers 170°F. Remove the turkey from the smoker, slice, and serve with cranberry ketchup.

urkey producers have heeded the desires of consumers and stock the market with turkey parts, including ground turkey breast and boneless, skinless fillets. Ask the butcher to cut the fillets into 4-ounce cutlets for you, if necessary. And as with chicken roulades, the cutlets should be pounded to an even thickness. This facilitates rolling and even cooking on the grill.

Turkey Roulades with Fontina, Prosciutto, and Pesto Butter   *Serves 8*

HEAT =

PESTO BUTTER

¼ CUP UNSALTED BUTTER, SOFTENED

3 TABLESPOONS SUMMER PESTO (PAGE 229) OR STORE-BOUGHT BASIL PESTO

2 TABLESPOONS FRESHLY GRATED PARMESAN CHEESE

FRESHLY GROUND BLACK PEPPER TO TASTE

ROULADES

16 WOODEN TOOTHPICKS OR SMALL METAL SKEWERS

EIGHT 4-OUNCE BONELESS, SKINLESS TURKEY BREAST CUTLETS

SALT AND FRESHLY GROUND BLACK PEPPER TO TASTE

8 THIN SLICES PROSCIUTTO OR PARMA HAM (ABOUT 4 OUNCES TOTAL)

8 SLICES FONTINA CHEESE (ABOUT 4 OUNCES TOTAL)

OLIVE OIL

VEGETABLE OIL COOKING SPRAY

1. To prepare the pesto butter, combine the butter, pesto, and cheese in a small bowl. Mash with a fork until well mixed. Season to taste with pepper and scrape the butter onto a sheet of plastic wrap. Using your hands and the plastic wrap as guides, form the butter into a log about an inch in diameter. Wrap securely and refrigerate for at least 1 hour, until firm. Meanwhile, soak the toothpicks in water for about 30 minutes, if using to fasten the breasts closed.

2. To prepare the roulades, cover the turkey cutlets with waxed paper or plastic wrap and, using a meat mallet or small heavy skillet, gently flatten the cutlets into oval-shaped pieces about ¼ inch thick. Transfer the cutlets to a waxed paper–lined baking sheet. Season with salt and pepper. Place a slice of prosciutto on each cutlet, aligning the ham with the edges of the cutlet. Cut the pesto butter into 8 equal-sized pieces.

3. Place a piece of cheese and a slice of butter on the short end of each slice of prosciutto. Fold the prosciutto over the cheese and butter and then roll each cutlet into a neat package, tucking in the edges to enclose the stuffing. Secure each roulade with soaked wooden toothpicks. Leaving the roulades on the baking sheet, brush them with oil and refrigerate until ready to cook.

4. Prepare a charcoal or gas grill: Lightly spray the grill rack with vegetable oil cooking spray. Light the coals or heating elements, and let them burn or heat until moderately hot.

5. Grill the roulades, turning frequently with tongs, for about 10 minutes, or until lightly browned. Cover the grill and cook for 3 or 4 minutes longer until the butter and cheese begin to ooze from the roulades and the meat is cooked through and the juices run clear when the meat is pierced with a small, sharp knife. Serve immediately.

While turkey cutlets may be sold already packaged, for this recipe we recommend you ask the butcher to prepare them for you. Otherwise, they will be uneven and therefore difficult to slit and fill. The butcher can expertly cut them so that they are consistently about ½ inch thick and will also cut the pockets in the side of the cutlets. You could easily cut the pockets at home, but if the butcher is preparing the cutlets for you anyhow, why not ask? Two and a half pounds will yield six 5- or 6-ounce cutlets. Make sure you buy cutlets, not turkey tenders, which won't be cut thick enough for stuffing.

Cranberry-Orange Stuffed Turkey Cutlets *Serves 6*

HEAT =

3 TABLESPOON DRIED CRANBERRIES

4 TEASPOONS UNSALTED BUTTER

1 TABLESPOON MINCED SHALLOTS

3 TABLESPOON MINCED FLAT-LEAF PARSLEY

½ CUP PLUS 2 TABLESPOONS FRESH ORANGE JUICE

1 TABLESPOON MINCED FRESH SAGE LEAVES

1 TEASPOON MINCED FRESH THYME LEAVES

1 TEASPOON FINELY GRATED ORANGE ZEST

½ TEASPOON CELERY SEED

½ TEASPOON SALT

¼ TEASPOON FRESHLY GROUND BLACK PEPPER

1. Using a sharp knife or a mini food processor, chop the cranberries so that they are minced but still chunky.

2. Melt the butter over medium-low heat in a nonstick skillet. Add the shallots and sauté for 2 to 3 minutes, until softened. Add the parsley, 2 tablespoons of the orange juice, the sage, thyme, orange zest, celery seed, salt, pepper, and minced cranberries. Cook for about 1 minute, stirring, until heated through. Remove from the heat.

3. Stir the bread crumbs into the mixture. If the stuffing does not hold together, add another tablespoon or so of bread crumbs to the pan. You should have about ⅔ cup packed stuffing. Spread the stuffing on a plate to until cool enough to handle.

4. Meanwhile, cut a slit in the side of each cutlet using the tip of a sharp knife. Gently move the knife back and forth to widen the opening and make a lengthwise pocket in the cutlet.

5. Press about 1½ tablespoons of the stuffing into the pockets of each cutlet. You may not use all the stuffing, depending on

¾ CUP FRESH BREAD CRUMBS, PLUS
MORE IF NECESSARY (SEE NOTE)
6 TURKEY CUTLETS, EACH ABOUT ½
INCH THICK (ABOUT 2½ POUNDS
TOTAL)
SHORT BAMBOO OR METAL SKEWERS,
IF NEEDED
2 TABLESPOONS EXTRA VIRGIN
OLIVE OIL
VEGETABLE OIL COOKING SPRAY

the size of the pockets. If the meat tears or separates while filling, hold it together with a sturdy bamboo or short metal skewer. Weave it through the cutlet, lengthwise, in one or two places. If you use bamboo skewers, you can cut them to a manageable length, if necessary. Do not use toothpicks; they will break. This is not necessary unless the meat tears. In most cases the stuffing will not spill out of the pocket.

6. Lay the filled cutlets in a single layer in a shallow glass or ceramic dish.

7. Whisk together the remaining ½ cup of orange juice and the olive oil and then pour this over the cutlets. Cover and refrigerate for 30 to 35 minutes. (The acid in the orange juice firms the meat just enough to hold the cutlets together as they grill.)

8. Prepare a charcoal or gas grill: Lightly spray the grill rack with vegetable oil cooking spray. Light the coals or heating elements, and let them burn or heat until moderately hot.

9. Lift the cutlets from the dish and discard the marinade. Carefully lay each cutlet on the grill and cook for 3 minutes. Using tongs and a wide spatula, if necessary, turn them over and cook for 3 to 5 minutes longer, until the meat is cooked through and the juices run clear when pierced with a small, sharp knife. Serve immediately.

note: To make fresh bread crumbs, process the bread in a food processor or blender. For this recipe, use 2 slices of bread. You will make a little more than ¾ cup but because you may need a little extra, this is more than fine.

The bland flavor of turkey makes it a natural for boldly flavored marinades and the accompaniments that typically are served with fajitas—Tex-Mex food at its best. Boneless turkey breasts are great for fajitas. If you can't find them, look for turkey tenders, which are made from the flaps of meat under the breast. Or, if you would rather make these with chicken, use the small pieces of boneless, skinless chicken breast meat that are labeled "tenders."

Grilled Turkey Fajitas   *Serves 6*

HEAT =

¼ CUP FRESH LIME JUICE

2 TABLESPOONS PEANUT OIL

2 TABLESPOONS CHOPPED FRESH
   CILANTRO

1 TABLESPOON CHILI POWDER

1 TEASPOON GROUND CUMIN

½ TEASPOON CAYENNE

SALT AND FRESHLY GROUND BLACK
   PEPPER

2 POUNDS BONELESS, SKINLESS TURKEY
   BREAST CUTLETS OR TENDERS

VEGETABLE OIL COOKING SPRAY

TWELVE 7-INCH FLOUR TORTILLAS

1 MEDIUM TOMATO, SEEDED AND
   CHOPPED

½ AVOCADO, CHOPPED

¼ CUP CHOPPED SCALLIONS, WHITE
   AND GREEN PARTS

ABOUT 3 CUPS SHREDDED LETTUCE

CHOPPED FRESH CILANTRO, FOR GARNISH

SOUR CREAM, FOR GARNISH

BAJA-STYLE TOMATO SALSA (PAGE 233)
   OR HOT, HOT, HOT GRILLED SALSA
   (PAGE 234)

1. Combine the lime juice, oil, cilantro, chili powder, cumin, and cayenne in a shallow glass or ceramic dish. Season with salt and pepper, stirring well. Put the turkey in the dish, turning several times to coat. Cover and refrigerate for 6 to 8 hours, letting the turkey come to room temperature before grilling.

2. Prepare a charcoal or gas grill: Lightly spray the grill rack with vegetable oil cooking spray. Light the coals or heating elements, and let them burn or heat until moderately hot.

3. Lift the turkey from the dish. Discard the marinade. Grill the turkey for 10 to 14 minutes until cooked through and the juices run clear when the meat is pierced with a small, sharp knife, turning several times.

4. Meanwhile, wrap the tortillas in foil and place the packet on the outside edge of the grill and let the tortillas warm while the turkey cooks.

5. Cut the turkey into narrow strips and divide evenly among the warm tortillas. Top with tomatoes, avocado, scallions, lettuce, cilantro, and a dollop of sour cream and fold the tortillas around the filling. Serve with salsa.

Turkey tenders are widely sold in supermarket meat departments and from butcher shops. They are the tender flap of meat that lies directly under the turkey breast. If you prefer, cut the tenders from the turkey breast yourself. They can weigh as much as 12 ounces and should be cut in half lengthwise to make six-ounce "steaks." For even cooking, pound the tenders gently to an even thickness.

Grilled Turkey Steaks   *Serves 6*

HEAT =

2 1/2 POUNDS TURKEY BREAST TENDERS,
    CUT LENGTHWISE IN HALF

1 CUP DRY SHERRY

1/4 CUP FRESH LEMON JUICE

1 TABLESPOON GRATED ORANGE ZEST

2 TABLESPOONS HONEY

1/4 TEASPOON GROUND CLOVES

2 TABLESPOONS DIJON MUSTARD

1/4 TEASPOON CHILI POWDER

VEGETABLE OIL COOKING SPRAY

1. Place the tenders between sheets of waxed paper or plastic wrap and, using a meat mallet or small heavy skillet, gently flatten the breasts to an even thickness of about 1/2 inch.

2. Combine the sherry, lemon juice, orange zest, honey, cloves, mustard, and chili powder in a shallow glass or ceramic dish and mix well. Add the turkey steaks and turn to coat. Cover and refrigerate for at least 1 hour, letting the turkey come to room temperature before grilling.

3. Prepare a charcoal or gas grill: Lightly spray the grill rack with vegetable oil cooking spray. Light the coals or heating elements, and let them burn or heat until moderately hot.

4. Lift the turkey from the dish and pat dry. Discard the marinade. Place the turkey on the grill, cover, and grill for about 16 minutes, turning several times, until cooked through and the juices run clear when the meat is pierced with a small, sharp knife. Take care the turkey does overcook and dry out. Serve immediately.

This is a glorified and glorious club sandwich made with our smoked turkey and double-smoked bacon. We suggest roasting the tomatoes but you could grill them instead, or simply use luscious garden-ripe ones. Thick, crusty country-style bread that you slice yourself is key to this sandwich.

Smoked Turkey and Apple Wood Double-Smoked Bacon Club Sandwich   *Serves 6*

HEAT =

12 PLUM TOMATOES, HALVED

2 CLOVES GARLIC, SLICED

1 TEASPOON MINCED FRESH OREGANO

1 TEASPOON MINCED FRESH THYME

ABOUT ½ CUP OLIVE OIL

SALT AND FRESHLY GROUND BLACK
   PEPPER

18 SLICES COUNTRY-STYLE WHITE
   BREAD, EACH ABOUT ¾ INCH THICK

1½ CUPS MAYONNAISE, STORE-BOUGHT
   OR HOMEMADE

6 LARGE LETTUCE LEAVES

1½ POUNDS THINLY SLICED SMOKED
   BRINED TURKEY BREAST (PAGE 190)
   OR OTHER COOKED TURKEY BREAST

1 POUND APPLE WOOD DOUBLE-SMOKED
   BACON (PAGE 139) OR OTHER BACON

12 SLICES PROVOLONE CHEESE

SALT AND FRESHLY GROUND BLACK
   PEPPER

TOOTHPICKS OR SANDWICH PICKS

1. Preheat the oven to 225ºF.

2. In a large bowl, toss together the tomatoes, garlic, oregano, and thyme and add just enough olive oil to coat the tomatoes. Season to taste with salt and pepper. Set aside to marinate at room temperature for 5 to 10 minutes.

3. Spread the tomatoes, sliced sides up, on a baking sheet. Roast for 35 to 40 minutes, until they are lightly crusted and browned. Remove from the oven and set aside to cool.

4. In a large skillet, cook the bacon until crispy over medium-high heat. Drain on paper towels.

5. Toast the bread slices until golden. Spread each slice with mayonnaise. Top 6 of the slices with lettuce and then layer each with turkey, bacon, 1 slice of cheese, and 2 tomato halves. Season to taste with salt and pepper. Top each sandwich with another slice of bread, and layer on more mayonnaise, if desired, turkey, bacon, cheese, and tomatoes. Season to taste with salt and pepper. Top with a third slice of toast and press gently. Holding down each sandwich with your hand, cut in half or quarters. Secure the halves or quarters with toothpicks. Repeat with the remaining 5 sandwiches.

GAME AND GAME BIRDS

The grill is the most natural place to cook game and game birds. After all, man has been cooking game over glowing embers since the discovery of fire, and today, even with our sophisticated indoor cooking methods, the backyard grill is surprisingly similar to a primitive fire pit scraped from the packed dirt of a cave's entry. The ancient cooking method has not survived in vain, since, when properly handled, grilled game is delicious: delectably charred on the outside, juicy and tender on the inside, and with a vague smokiness augmenting its rich, gamy flavor.

By definition, the animals that fall in this category have better-developed muscle mass and eat a more varied and erratic diet than do animals raised domestically. This results in leaner meat that often is described as tasting "gamy." The gaminess pleases many folks and explains in part why thousands of Americans take to the woods, marshlands, and upland meadows in the fall and winter for hunting seasons. Much of the game eaten in the United States and Canada is the spoil of such sport, but a growing amount is raised on farms and preserves specifically for the retail market. Farm-raised venison, rabbit, duck, pheasant, and quail are all available. In fact, butchers and other retailers cannot sell game meat that is not farm-raised. Any game shot by hunters cannot be marketed commercially—it is for personal consumption only.

Farm-raised game and game birds retain many of their wild characteristics, however. Farmers will permit deer raised for venison to roam inside large fenced enclosures; ducks, pheasant, and quail, their wings clipped, are raised in open pens, as are rabbits. The natural environments provide most of the food, but these animals are also fed scientifically formulated feed designed to replicate the optimum diet they might find in the wild. They are slaughtered and butchered in safe, sanitary conditions and arrive at the retail market ready for consumers. Be sure to ask your butcher to prepare the game for the grill for you if you are not comfortable doing it yourself.

We find that most game benefits from oily marinades or at the very least a good rubbing with oil to keep it from drying out over the coals. We also like to pair the game with strong flavors that can stand up to its gusto. When cooking game and game birds, take care not to overcook the meat, and to maintain the fire at the correct temperature, which for the recipes that follow is moderately hot—neither sizzling nor cool.

Preparing Game and Game Birds for Grilling

When you get the meat home from the butcher or supermarket, immediately stow it in the coldest part of the refrigerator, which usually is the rear of the lowest shelf. Do not unwrap it; you do not want it to be unnecessarily exposed to the air, and keeping it wrapped in its original packaging is a good idea.

When you are ready to prepare the game for marinating, take it from the refrigerator and let it come to room temperature, which means leaving it on the counter for about 30 minutes. If it is a particularly hot, humid summer day, reduce the counter time. Pat the meat dry with paper towels and then marinate it, rub it with dry rub, or otherwise prepare it for the grill. We have not instructed you to pat the meat dry before marinating, rubbing, or otherwise preparing it in every recipe because it is universally appropriate whenever game is grilled.

Although a great deal of the duck consumed in this country is hunted during duck season, the duck you buy from the butcher or the meat counter will be farm-raised and carefully regulated. The most commonly sold variety is white Pekin, also known as Long Island duckling. Other kinds of duck commonly available are muscovy, domestic mallard, and moulard, which is a cross between muscovy and Pekin. Whole white Pekin ducks weigh from 4½ to 5½ pounds, have mild flavor and juicy meat, and are of a variety that originated centuries ago in China. Muscovy ducks are somewhat more flavorful than Pekins and may be smaller, too. Mallards are far smaller than either (from 1½ to 3 pounds) and are distinctively flavored with rich, dark meat. Moulards, larger than the white Pekin, are bred to be meaty and juicy, with good duck flavor. Any variety of duck would work well in these recipes, which call only for the duck breast, considered the finest cut of the bird. In this recipe, we serve the duck skin cooked until crisp (cracklings). The skin is sinfully delicious and the same technique employed here can be used in the recipe for Grilled Duck Breast in Grapefruit and Chipotle Marinade with Grapefruit-Avocado Salad (page 203).

Grilled Mustard Duck Breast with Cracklings   *Serves 4*

HEAT =

4 BONELESS SKIN-ON DUCK BREAST
   HALVES

1 TABLESPOON OLIVE OIL

1 TABLESPOON BALSAMIC VINEGAR

1 CLOVE GARLIC, MINCED

2 TEASPOONS DIJON MUSTARD

1 TEASPOON LIGHT OR DARK BROWN
   SUGAR

1 TEASPOON DRIED THYME

1 TEASPOON FRESHLY GROUND BLACK
   PEPPER

¼ TEASPOON SALT

1. Using your fingers and a small sharp knife, remove the skin from the duck breasts. Try to keep it in fairly large pieces. Wrap the skin tightly in plastic wrap and refrigerate until ready to cook.

2. Combine the oil, vinegar, garlic, mustard, brown sugar, and thyme in a shallow glass or ceramic dish. Season with pepper and salt. Stir well.

3. Trim the duck breasts of any remaining fat or tough connective tissue and pat dry with paper towels. Place the duck breasts in the marinade, turning several times to coat. Cover and refrigerate for 2 to 4 hours, letting the duck come to room temperature before grilling.

VEGETABLE OIL COOKING SPRAY

4 FIRM TART APPLES, SUCH AS GRANNY SMITH, CORTLAND, OR WINESAP, QUARTERED AND CORED

4. Preheat the oven to 375°F. Lightly spray a jelly roll pan or other shallow baking pan with vegetable oil cooking spray. Place the duck skin in the pan, outer side down, and spread it flat. Bake for about 20 minutes until browned and crisp. Drain on paper towels. Pour off all but 2 tablespoons of fat.

5. Raise the oven temperature to 400°F.

6. Place the apple quarters in a baking pan large enough to hold them snugly in one layer. Sprinkle the reserved 2 tablespoons of duck fat over the apples and toss to coat. Turn the quarters skin side down and bake for about 20 minutes, until just tender.

7. Prepare a charcoal or gas grill: Lightly spray the grill rack with vegetable oil cooking spray. Light the coals or heating elements, and let them burn or heat until moderately hot.

8. Lift the duck breasts from the dish. Discard the marinade. Grill the breasts, skin side up for about 5 minutes. Turn and grill for 3 to 4 minutes longer for medium-rare duck. For better-done meat, grill for a few minutes longer. Transfer the duck breasts to a cutting board and slice at an angle into wide, thin slices.

9. Meanwhile, cut the cracklings into thin slices or dice. Serve the duck meat with cracklings sprinkled over them and the apples alongside.

note: If the cracklings have softened when it is time to serve them, crisp them in a 200°F oven for about 10 minutes right before serving.

More than half of the ducks sold in this country are sold frozen, which is unfortunate because fresh duck tastes far better than frozen. Ask your butcher if he can get fresh duck for you—you won't be disappointed. If you buy frozen duck, let it thaw in the refrigerator for a day or two. When it is thawed, let it come to room temperature before wiping it dry with a paper towel and proceeding with the recipe.

Domestic ducks are marketed at ages between two and four months and so the consumer rarely has to worry about buying an old duck, which is tough and dry. If there is a question and if you have the opportunity to see the whole duck, look for soft pliable beaks, smooth legs, and soft webbing between the toes.

Grilled Duck Breast in Grapefruit and Chipotle Marinade with Grapefruit-Avocado Salad *Serves 4*

HEAT =

DUCK

1 CHIPOTLE CHILE IN ADOBO SAUCE, WIPED DRY (SEE NOTES)

½ TO 1 CUP CIDER VINEGAR

4 BONELESS, SKINLESS DUCK BREAST HALVES (SEE NOTES)

½ CUP FRESH GRAPEFRUIT JUICE

2 TABLESPOONS OLIVE OIL

2 CLOVES GARLIC, MINCED

1 TEASPOON DRIED OREGANO

¼ TEASPOON SALT

VEGETABLE OIL COOKING SPRAY

1. To prepare the duck, soak the chile, which has been wiped dry, for about 10 minutes in hot water to cover. Drain and transfer to a small glass or ceramic dish, cover with the vinegar, and set aside to marinate for at least 20 minutes. Drain and chop coarsely. You will have about 2 tablespoons of chopped chile.

2. Trim the duck breasts of any remaining fat or tough connective tissue and pat dry with paper towels. Score the skin side of the breasts in a diamond pattern.

3. Put the breasts in a shallow glass or ceramic dish. Combine the juice, oil, garlic, oregano, salt, and chopped chile in a bowl, stirring well. Add the marinade to the meat, turning to coat. Cover and refrigerate for 2 to 4 hours, letting the duck come to room temperature before grilling.

4. Prepare a charcoal or gas grill: Lightly spray the grill rack with vegetable oil cooking spray. Light the coals or heating elements, and let them burn or heat until moderately hot.

GRAPEFRUIT-AVOCADO SALAD

1 LARGE RED GRAPEFRUIT

½ BULB FENNEL, THINLY SLICED

1 TABLESPOON OLIVE OIL

SALT TO TASTE

1 LARGE AVOCADO, HALVED, PITTED,
    PEELED, AND SLICED

5. To make the salad, peel the grapefruit, trimming the white pith. Holding the fruit over a glass or ceramic bowl, slice the segments from the membrane, and let the juices drip into the bowl. Set the segments aside. Squeeze any juice from the membranes or peel into a small bowl.

6. Toss the fennel with 1 or 2 tablespoons of the grapefruit juice and the olive oil in another small bowl. Season with salt.

7. Sprinkle the remaining juice over the avocado slices to prevent discoloration. Cut the avocado slices crosswise. Arrange the fennel on a serving plate and top with the avocado and grapefruit slices.

8. Lift the duck breasts from the dish. Discard the marinade. Grill the breasts, skin side up, for about 5 minutes. Turn and grill for 3 to 4 minutes longer for medium-rare meat. For better-done meat, grill for a few minutes longer. Transfer the duck breasts to a cutting board and slice at an angle into wide, thin slices. Serve the duck slices alongside the salad.

notes: Chipotle chiles usually are sold canned, packed in adobo sauce, and are available in many supermarkets as well as Latin markets and specialty food stores. They are also available loose and dried, but are not as easy to find this way.

If you desire, reserve the duck skin and make cracklings, as explained in the recipe for Grilled Mustard Duck Breast with Cracklings on page 201. Serve them sprinkled over the duck slices.

Smoked duck breast is a classic and ours, lightly flavored as it is with raspberry vinegar and orange zest, is a keeper. Elegant, delicately flavored, and moist, the duck is wonderful served with wild rice and steamed vegetables, or sliced thin and topping a mixed green salad dressed with raspberry vinaigrette. It would be lovely served with a fruit chutney or, if you are in the mood to indulge yourself, sauté strips of sliced smoked duck breast in a nonstick pan and serve it with poached or scrambled eggs in place of bacon. You could even make a kind of eggs Benedict with it.

Smoked Raspberry-Scented Duck Breast *Serves 6*

HEAT =

6 BONELESS, SKIN-ON DUCK BREAST
　HALVES
1 LARGE NAVEL ORANGE
1/3 CUP SEEDLESS RASPBERRY
　PRESERVES
1/4 CUP RASPBERRY VINEGAR
2 TABLESPOONS COARSE SALT
2 TEASPOONS CAYENNE
1 TEASPOON MINCED FRESH GINGER
1/2 TEASPOON FRESHLY GRATED NUTMEG
PINCH OF GROUND ALLSPICE

1. Cut the whole duck breasts into separate breast halves. With a sharp knife, score the skin in a diamond pattern, slicing through the layer of fat but making sure not to cut the meat.

2. Carefully peel the orange so that only the colorful outer zest is used (you do not want white pith, which is bitter); cut the strips about 1 inch wide and as long as you can keep them. (Reserve the rest of the orange for another use.)

3. Mix together the orange strips with the raspberry preserves, raspberry vinegar, salt, cayenne, ginger, nutmeg, and allspice in a small bowl.

4. Lay the duck breast halves in a shallow glass or ceramic dish just large enough to hold them in a single, overlapping layer. Add the marinade and turn to coat. Cover and refrigerate for at least 4 hours and up to 12 hours.

5. Prepare and preheat the smoker according to the manufacturer's instructions. We used apple wood, but you could use cherry or hickory.

6. Remove the duck breasts from the dish and pat them dry with paper towels. Discard the marinade.

7. Lay the duck breasts on the smoker's rack, skin side up, and smoke for 1 hour at 200°F for medium-rare (140°F) to 1 hour and 20 minutes for medium (155°F). We prefer the longer cooking for smoked duck. Slice the duck and serve.

Pheasant are favorites of upland game hunters, but those at the butchers are farm-raised. Hens weigh less than cocks, which can weigh up to five pounds. The mild gaminess of pheasant welcomes the sweet-sour flavor of this very easy orange sauce, which is passed at the table. If you have a Microplane, use it to grate the orange zest. The finely grated zest adds deep orange flavor to the sauce.

Pheasant with Orange Sauce *Serves 4*

HEAT =

PHEASANT

ONE 2½- TO 3-POUND PHEASANT

1 TABLESPOON FINELY CHOPPED FRESH
    GINGER

1 TEASPOON CRUSHED CORIANDER SEED

1 TEASPOON COARSELY GROUND BLACK
    PEPPER

¼ CUP FRESH ORANGE JUICE

2 TABLESPOONS LIGHT SOY SAUCE

1 TEASPOON MOLASSES

VEGETABLE OIL COOKING SPRAY

SAUCE

2 CUPS FRESH ORANGE JUICE

1 CUP CHAMPAGNE OR WHITE WINE
    VINEGAR

½ CUP SUGAR

¼ CUP FRESH LEMON JUICE

1 TABLESPOON FINELY CHOPPED FRESH
    GINGER

1. Prepare the pheasant: Split the pheasant down the back along the backbone, taking care to keep the thigh meat intact, or ask the butcher to do this for you. Remove the backbone. Using a knife or poultry shears, cut through the top of the breast bone so that the breast can be flattened. Put the pheasant in a shallow glass or ceramic dish, spreading it open and flattening the breast slightly. Rub the pheasant inside and out with ginger, coriander, and pepper. Add the orange juice, soy sauce, and molasses and turn the pheasant to coat evenly. Cover and refrigerate for at least 6 hours or overnight, letting the pheasant come to room temperature before grilling.

2. To make the sauce, combine the orange juice, vinegar, sugar, lemon juice, and ginger. Bring to a boil over medium-high heat, stirring. Reduce the heat and simmer for about 10 minutes or until the sauce is reduced by half. Strain the sauce through a fine sieve and then return it to the pan. Add the chicken stock and orange zest and simmer for about 10 minutes longer, stirring, until the sauce is slightly syrupy. Serve warm or at room temperature with the pheasant.

3. Prepare a charcoal or gas grill: Lightly spray the grill rack with vegetable oil cooking spray. Light the coals or heating elements, and let them burn or heat until moderately hot.

½ CUP REDUCED-SODIUM CHICKEN
STOCK

2 TABLESPOONS FINELY SLIVERED OR
GRATED ORANGE ZEST

4. Lift the pheasant from the dish and discard the marinade. Put the pheasant on the grill skin side down, cover, and cook for 10 minutes. Turn the pheasant, cover, and cook for 10 minutes longer until the breast meat is cooked through and the juices run clear when pierced with a small sharp knife. Remove the pheasant from the grill and cut off the thighs and legs. Return them to the grill while the breast meat rests and cook, turning several times, for 4 or 5 minutes longer until cooked through. Serve immediately.

Pheasant is similar to chicken in size and conformation, although it is drier and stronger tasting. The meat on most birds is finely textured, firm, and plentiful.

Pheasant with Juniper, Sage, Fennel, and Cider Marinade   *Serves 4*

HEAT =

ONE 2½- TO 3-POUND PHEASANT

½ CUP CHOPPED ONIONS

½ CUP COARSELY CHOPPED PARSLEY STEMS

1½ TEASPOONS FINELY CHOPPED FRESH SAGE

6 WHOLE JUNIPER BERRIES, CRUSHED

½ TEASPOON CRUSHED FENNEL SEED

1 CLOVE GARLIC, CRUSHED

¼ TEASPOON BLACK PEPPERCORNS

½ CUP FRESH APPLE CIDER

¼ CUP OLIVE OIL

1 TABLESPOON APPLE CIDER VINEGAR

VEGETABLE OIL COOKING SPRAY

1. Split the pheasant down the back along the backbone, taking care to keep the thigh meat intact, or ask the butcher to do this for you. Remove the backbone. Using a knife or poultry shears, cut through the top of the breast bone so that the breast can be flattened. Put the pheasant in a shallow glass or ceramic dish, spreading it open and flattening the breast slightly. Rub the pheasant inside and out with onions, parsley, sage, juniper berries, fennel, garlic, and peppercorns. Add the cider, oil, and vinegar and turn the pheasant to coat evenly. Cover and refrigerate for at least 6 hours or overnight, letting the pheasant come to room temperature before grilling.

2. Prepare a charcoal or gas grill: Lightly spray the grill rack with vegetable oil cooking spray. Light the coals or heating elements, and let them burn or heat until moderately hot.

3. Lift the pheasant from the dish, wiping off and discarding any solid. Discard the marinade. Put the pheasant skin side down on the grill, cover, and cook for about 10 minutes. Turn the pheasant, cover the grill, and cook for about 10 minutes longer, until the breast meat is cooked through, feels springy to the touch, and the juices run clear when pierced with a small sharp knife. Remove the pheasant from the grill and cut the thighs and legs from the pheasant. Return the thighs and legs to the grill and cook, turning several times, for 4 or 5 minutes longer until cooked through. (Let the breast meat rest while cooking the dark meat.) Serve immediately.

These tiny birds can weigh from three-and-a-half to eight ounces, although for the best flavor, we suggest smaller birds. Their white meat is delicately flavored and quite skimpy; the dark meat is not worth thinking about since there is so little on the birds. Serve at least two quail per person, although if you are grilling for big eaters, consider three or more.

Grilled Quail with Raspberry-Cranberry Cumberland Sauce

Serves 4

HEAT =

QUAIL

EIGHT 3½- TO 4-OUNCE QUAIL

¼ CUP FINELY CHOPPED SHALLOTS

2 TEASPOONS FINELY CHOPPED FRESH
    ROSEMARY

FRESHLY GROUND BLACK PEPPER TO
    TASTE

½ CUP OLIVE OIL

¼ CUP RASPBERRY VINEGAR

8 SMALL BAMBOO SKEWERS

VEGETABLE OIL COOKING SPRAY

SAUCE

¼ CUP SEEDLESS RASPBERRY JAM

¼ CUP PORT WINE

1 TABLESPOON CHOPPED SHALLOTS

½ TEASPOON GRATED LEMON ZEST

½ CUP FRESH ORANGE JUICE

½ CUP FRESH CRANBERRIES

1 TABLESPOON SUGAR

PINCH OF CAYENNE

1. Prepare the quail: Using a small sharp knife or poultry shears, split each quail along the backbone, cutting through the ribs as close to the backbone as possible. Open the quails, skin side down, and cut partway through the breastbone. Flatten the quails with the flat side of a cleaver or the heel of your hand. Put the quails in a large, shallow glass or ceramic dish. Rub each bird inside and out with the shallots, rosemary, and pepper. Pour the oil and vinegar over the birds, turning them to coat evenly. Cover and refrigerate for 4 hours or overnight, letting the quail come to room temperature before grilling.

2. To prepare the sauce, in a small saucepan combine the jam, Port, shallots, and lemon zest. Bring to a simmer over medium-high heat. Reduce the heat and simmer gently for about 2 minutes. Add the orange juice, cranberries, and sugar, raise the heat to medium-high, and cook, stirring, for about 5 minutes, or until the cranberries burst and the sauce is slightly thickened. Season to taste with cayenne. Serve warm or at room temperature. (The sauce can be reheated just before serving.) Soak the bamboo skewers in warm water for at least 30 minutes.

3. Prepare a charcoal or gas grill: Lightly spray the grill rack with vegetable oil cooking spray. Light the coals or heating elements, and let them burn or heat until moderately hot.

4. Lift the quail, one at a time, from the dish, and place each bird flat, positioning the legs and thighs pointing inward to frame the breast. Discard the marinade. Using the bamboo skewers, skewer the quail so that they will hold together during grilling. Catch the outer skin of 1 thigh with a bamboo skewer and then weave it under the thigh bone, through the ribs and into the opposite thigh, under the bone, and out through the center of the skin. Cut the skewer with poultry shears so that it juts from the bird no more than 1 inch. Repeat with the remaining quail.

5. Place the quail on the grill, skin side down, and cover the grill. Cook for about 5 minutes, taking care the fire does not flare up or get too hot. Turn the birds and grill, covered, for about 5 minutes longer, until the breast meat feels springy to the touch and the meat is cooked through, golden brown on the outside and opaque throughout. Serve with the sauce.

To grill minute birds such as quail, it is a good idea to split them and spread them open so that they can lie nearly flat on the grill rack. They benefit from marinating—and will dry out quickly if overcooked.

Grilled Herb-Marinated Quail   *Serves 4*

HEAT =

EIGHT 3½- TO 4-OUNCE QUAIL

4 TO 6 CLOVES GARLIC, CRUSHED

2 TEASPOONS CHOPPED FRESH THYME

1 TEASPOON DRIED OREGANO

1 TEASPOON SALT

16 JUNIPER BERRIES, CRUSHED

½ CUP DRY WHITE WINE

½ CUP OLIVE OIL

VEGETABLE OIL COOKING SPRAY

8 SMALL BAMBOO SKEWERS

1. Using a small sharp knife or poultry shears, split each quail along the backbone, cutting through the ribs as close to the backbone as possible. Open the quail, skin side down, and cut partway through the breastbone. Flatten the quail using the flat side of a cleaver or the heel of your hand. Put the quail in a large, shallow glass or ceramic dish. Rub each bird inside and out with the garlic, thyme, oregano, salt, and juniper berries. Add the wine and oil to the birds, turning them to coat evenly. Cover and refrigerate for 4 hours or overnight, letting the quail come to room temperature before grilling.

2. Prepare a charcoal or gas grill: Lightly spray the grill rack with vegetable oil cooking spray. Light the coals or heating elements, and let them burn or heat until moderately hot. Soak the bamboo skewers in warm water for at least 30 minutes.

3. Lift each quail, one at a time, from the dish, and place each bird flat, positioning the legs and thighs pointing inward to frame the breast. Discard the marinade. Using bamboo skewers, skewer the quail so that they will hold together during grilling. Catch the outer skin of 1 thigh with a bamboo skewer and then weave it under the thigh bone, through the ribs and into the opposite thigh, over the bone, and out through the center of the skin. Cut the skewer with poultry shears so that it juts from the bird no more than 1 inch.

4. Place the quail on the grill, skin side down, and cover the grill. Cook for about 5 minutes, taking care the fire does not flare up or get too hot. Turn the birds and grill, covered, for about 5 minutes longer, or until the meat is cooked through. Serve immediately.

The venison loin is preferred for most culinary purposes, and certainly for grilling, although the haunch and saddle are good for moist indoor cooking, such as braising and stewing. Venison is leaner than other meat and so needs to be rubbed with oil before it is grilled. It also stands up very well to marinating. Try it with either White Wine Marinade (page 237) or Red Wine Vinegar Marinade (page 236). Venison loin steaks are all approximately the same size and weight.

Grilled Venison Loin Steaks with Red Wine–Herb Sauce *Serves 6*

HEAT =

6 BONELESS VENISON LOIN STEAKS, EACH ABOUT ½ INCH THICK

1 TEASPOON FINELY CHOPPED FRESH ROSEMARY

1 TEASPOON COARSELY GROUND BLACK PEPPER

2 TABLESPOONS OLIVE OIL

VEGETABLE OIL COOKING SPRAY

RED WINE–HERB SAUCE (PAGE 226)

1. Rub the venison steaks on both sides with the rosemary and pepper and put in a shallow glass or ceramic dish. Drizzle the olive oil over the meat, turning the steaks to coat. Cover and refrigerate for at least 2 hours or overnight, letting the meat come to room temperature before grilling.

2. Prepare a charcoal or gas grill: Lightly spray the grill rack with vegetable oil cooking spray. Light the coals or heating elements, and let them burn or heat until moderately hot.

3. Grill the venison steaks for about 3 minutes on each side for rare meat. Grill for a few minutes longer for medium-rare or medium. Serve immediately with the wine sauce.

Rabbits are widely eaten in Europe, but have been slow to catch on here—except among rabbit hunters. This is a shame as rabbit meat is tender with a lovely gamy flavor. All rabbit sold by butchers or in the markets are farm-raised. Some rabbits weigh as little as two pounds, although we sell larger ones that might weigh as much as four pounds. If necessary, buy two smaller rabbits to achieve the right weight for the recipe.

Rabbit with Herb and Mustard Marinade   *Serves 4 to 6*

HEAT =

ONE 3½- TO 4-POUND RABBIT

¼ CUP DIJON MUSTARD

¼ CUP OLIVE OIL

1 TABLESPOON CHOPPED FRESH THYME

1 TABLESPOON FINELY CHOPPED GARLIC

2 TEASPOONS GRATED ORANGE ZEST

2 TEASPOONS GRATED LEMON ZEST

1 TEASPOON FRESHLY GROUND BLACK PEPPER

VEGETABLE OIL COOKING SPRAY

1. Take the rabbit and sever the forelegs and hind legs from the body at the joints. Cut the center section, called the saddle, into 4 equal-sized pieces. (You can also ask the butcher to do this for you.) Put the pieces in a shallow glass or ceramic dish large enough to hold them in a single layer.

2. Combine the mustard, oil, thyme, garlic, orange and lemon zests, and pepper in a small bowl, stirring well. Pour the marinade over the rabbit, turning to coat. Cover and refrigerate for 4 hours or overnight, letting the meat come to room temperature before grilling.

3. Prepare a charcoal or gas grill: Lightly spray the grill rack with vegetable oil cooking spray. Light the coals or heating elements, and let them burn or heat until moderately hot.

4. Lift the meat from the dish. Discard the marinade. Grill the rabbit for about 10 minutes, turning often until browned on all sides. Cover the grill and continue to cook for about 8 minutes. Turn the meat and grill for 5 to 7 minutes longer, until lightly browned and cooked through and the meat is opaque when cut with a small knife. Move the smaller pieces of rabbit to the edge of the grill, if necessary, to prevent burning during cooking. If using a gas grill, reduce the heat a little to prevent burning. Serve immediately.

Rabbit is now quite easily available in supermarkets, although you may have to order it from the resident butcher. For grilling, we recommend cutting the rabbit into eight pieces. Uncooked rabbit meat is white, but when marinated and cooked, it turns dark.

Spicy-Marinated Grilled Rabbit

Serves 4 to 6

HEAT =

ONE 3½- TO 4-POUND RABBIT
½ CUP OLIVE OIL
2 TABLESPOONS CHOPPED FLAT-LEAF
   PARSLEY
1 TABLESPOON HOT PEPPER SAUCE
2 TEASPOONS MINCED GARLIC
1 TEASPOON DRIED ROSEMARY
½ TEASPOON SALT
½ TEASPOON FRESHLY GROUND BLACK
   PEPPER
VEGETABLE OIL COOKING SPRAY

1. Take the rabbit and sever the forelegs and hind legs from the body at the joints. Cut the center section, called the saddle, into 4 equal-sized pieces. (You can also ask the butcher to do this for you.) Put the pieces in a shallow glass or ceramic dish large enough to hold them in a single layer.

2. Combine the oil, parsley, hot pepper sauce, garlic, rosemary, salt, and pepper in a small bowl, stirring well. Pour the marinade over the rabbit, turning to coat. Cover and refrigerate for 4 hours or overnight, letting the meat come to room temperature before grilling.

3. Prepare a charcoal or gas grill: Lightly spray the grill rack with vegetable oil cooking spray. Light the coals or heating elements, and let them burn or heat until moderately hot.

4. Lift the meat from the dish. Discard the marinade. Grill the rabbit for about 10 minutes, turning often until browned on all sides. Cover the grill and continue to cook for about 8 minutes. Turn the meat and grill for 5 to 7 minutes longer, until lightly browned and cooked through and the meat is opaque when cut with a small knife. Move the smaller pieces of rabbit to the edge of the grill, if necessary, to prevent burning during cooking. If using a gas grill, reduce the heat a little to prevent burning. Serve immediately.

SAUCES, SALSAS, MARINADES, RUBS, AND OTHER CONDIMENTS

Nothing livens up a backyard meal like a full-flavored sauce, salsa, or other condiment. The right barbecue sauce, spicy salsa, or seasoned mayonnaise can make the difference between a bland meal and an exciting one. The same claims can be made for marinades, rubs, and pastes, which flavor the meat before grilling, providing herbal, citrusy, spicy, or sweet accents that happily mingle on our tongues when the meat is lifted from the grill.

Throughout the book, we incorporate marinades, rubs, and sauces in specific recipes, but just as often, we refer the reader to a recipe in this chapter. The distinction is made by the universality of the marinade or rub—we've tried to include the most essential, versatile, and adaptable recipes here. This does not mean you cannot use a marinade or rub you discover as part of a recipe with another kind of meat, but the formulas that follow here are particularly accommodating.

In ancient days, marinades were salty and were relied upon to preserve meat—but in the early twenty-first century, this is hardly necessary (although this ancient application does explain the origin of the word, with its root in the Latin word for the sea). We do not marinate all meat. In fact, high-quality, tender cuts such as sirloin, hanger steak, rack of lamb, and veal chops are best when minimally seasoned before grilling. Marinating is mostly used today to add extra flavor and, in some instances, to break down tougher cuts of meat.

Dry rubs and pastes are sometimes called "dry marinades," and as far as we are concerned, they are still the best-kept secrets to great grilling. As a rule, they are packed with flavor derived from chiles and whole toasted spices. The seasoning mixtures are rubbed into the meat; the meat is then refrigerated in a dish or resealable plastic bag and allowed to "marinate in its own juices." This happens because the spice, sugar, or salt in the dry rub attracts moisture from deep within the meat to its surface, where it mixes with the rub or paste, forming a wet, sticky coating with a wallop of flavor. For the best flavor, pork—particularly ribs—and bone-in chicken can be rubbed up to 24 hours before grilling, while chops and steaks should not be left for longer than 45 minutes at room temperature before they are grilled. During grilling, the dry rub forms an appealing crust on the meat, which is deliciously apparent in grilled meats such as spareribs.

Before pouring a marinade over meat or poultry, or before rubbing the spice mixture into the meat, pat the meat dry with paper towels. Put the food in a nonreactive dish (glass or ceramic is our choice), cover it with a lid or plastic wrap, and stow it in the refrigerator. As we have said, we also like to use heavy-duty resealable plastic bags, which are easier to store in a crowded refrigerator and easy to transport.

When, Why, and How to Marinate

Although some veteran grill cooks prefer to cook meat virtually unadorned and then liven it up later with sauces and salsas, we like to use marinades because they add both flavor and fun to the process. Marinades can be made from tantalizing combinations of herbs, spices, and other flavorings, and can get your mouth watering just thinking about them. As far as we're concerned, half the fun of planning a grilling meal is conjuring up the marinade.

Marinades work because of the acid present in them. Most commonly, this is wine, vinegar, tomatoes, or citrus juice. Theoretically, the acid breaks down fibers in the meat and tenderizes it, although the quality of meat available today makes this unnecessary. However, the acid also infuses the food with tangy flavor. Most marinades are accented, too, with wonderfully bright flavors provided by spices, onions, garlic, chiles, mustards, peppers, and similar ingredients. The small amount of oil found in most marinades serves a dual purpose—it lubricates the meat and adds moisture, and it serves as a flavor conductor.

The acid present in all marinades reacts with aluminum, which can impart a metallic taste to the food. Because of this, it is advisable to marinate all food in nonreactive containers. We prefer glass or ceramic, although some people marinate food in sturdy plastic containers with fitted lids, which work very well. Turn the meat several times to coat it well and then cover the dish with plastic or a lid. Heavy-duty resealable plastic bags work well, too, and make it easy to "fit" the marinating meat in a crowded refrigerator. During marinating, turn the meat several times, unless you feel confident it is totally submerged in liquid.

Marinades penetrate about one quarter of an inch into the food—they don't infuse the meat to its center—and because of this, long marinating rarely accomplishes better flavor than the minimum time suggested. In fact, after the first three or four hours, the food has absorbed as much of the marinade as it ever will. Longer marinating times are for convenience only. For example, we feel better organized when the meat and its marinade are successfully blended and tucked away in the fridge, leaving the remainder of the day free to tend to the rest of the meal.

Meat and poultry can stand up to long marinating, although boneless chicken breasts and pork tenderloins should not be left soaking for more than four to six hours or their consistencies will be mushy. If you are in a hurry, pour the marinade over the meat and leave the meat at room temperature for a short time (not longer than one hour). Never reuse a marinade and never serve it as sauce with the grilled food without first boiling it for at least five full minutes to kill any bacteria. If you want, brush a little on the meat during the initial stages of grilling so that it will cook along with the meat.

For safety, marinate food in the refrigerator, unless you are going to cook the meat within 30 minutes. Before grilling, let the meat or poultry come to room temperature—usually accomplished by letting it sit at room temperature for about 30 minutes.

We also strongly urge you to exercise caution when basting grilling meat or poultry with the marinade. We suggest doing so only during the first few minutes of cooking. You want to leave ample time for the heat of the fire to destroy any harmful bacteria lurking in the marinade, usually imparted by the meat during soaking. If you want to use the marinade as a sauce once the meat is cooked, be sure to bring the marinade to a rapid boil and then simmer briskly for at least five minutes first, or reserve a portion of unused marinade for serving with your meat if you like its flavor. When in doubt, discard the marinade after it has done its initial job of flavoring the uncooked meat or poultry.

Hot Pepper Sauces

Supermarket shelves bulge with bottled hot sauces. No longer are Tabasco and Frank's Original Red Hot the only choices. When they were, life was easier but not always inspiring. Now, the choices may be mind-boggling, but the mouthwatering variety makes cooking even more fun.

The category of Asian hot sauces is perhaps the most exciting. Bottles and jars of chili paste, chili-garlic sauce, and similar flavoring agents, most often imported from Thailand and Vietnam, are common condiments on tables throughout Southeast Asia and are showing up here in large numbers, too. They are prepared mixtures of vinegar, salt, and chiles, and sometimes include garlic, sugar, or both, and vary significantly in degrees of heat. Experiment with these delightful condiments. They'll add seductive interest to your cooking, particularly when making barbecue sauces and marinades.

Fresh or Dried Herbs?

We like to use fresh herbs when we cook, although there are times when dried are preferable or at least acceptable. Fresh herbs grow in profusion in the warm months of the year and are easy to find in the markets. You may even have lush basil, thyme, tarragon, and rosemary plants flourishing in your garden or in pots on the patio, ready for snipping when a recipe beckons. Fresh herbs are full of moisture and therefore do not burn during grilling as easily as dried.

Dried herbs are more intensely flavored. The rule of thumb is to use about a third as much of a dried herb as fresh: a teaspoon of dried for every tablespoon of chopped fresh. When adding dried herbs to a marinade, sauce, or any other preparation, rub it between your fingers or in the palm of your hand to release its essential oils. Store dried herbs in cool, dark cupboards and replenish them every six months, as they tend to go stale and lose flavor.

Although we call for specific herbs in our recipes, feel free to experiment with substitutions. Don't let the lack of cilantro, for example, dissuade you from making a salsa. Substitute parsley instead. Use thyme or chervil in place of tarragon; the flavor will be slightly different but the herb will still add great taste.

We sell a bottled barbecue sauce very similar to this one in our New York shop, which is on Madison Avenue near the corner of Eighty-second Street. It's great on beef, pork, or chicken. If you prefer hotter sauce, increase the amount of cayenne. Barbecue sauce is meant to be served with the cooked meat, not used as a marinade. However, you can slather it on chicken breasts or pork chops a few minutes before they are ready to come off the grill. If you do, then you can call it a "moppin' sauce."

Madison Avenue Barbecue Sauce

Makes about 1¾ cups

1 CUP TOMATO SAUCE

¾ CUP HONEY

¾ CUP SOY SAUCE

6 TABLESPOONS DISTILLED WHITE
   VINEGAR

¼ CUP LIGHT CORN SYRUP

3 TABLESPOONS WORCESTERSHIRE
   SAUCE

2 TABLESPOONS HOISIN SAUCE

½ TEASPOON CAYENNE

SALT AND FRESHLY GROUND BLACK
   PEPPER TO TASTE

Combine the ingredients in a nonreactive saucepan, stir, and cook over medium heat for about 30 minutes, until the flavors blend. Let cool and use immediately, or cover and refrigerate for up to 5 days.

Most barbecue sauce recipes for the home cook have a ketchup base, such as this one. Bottled ketchup is a boon for backyard chefs, because it can easily be doctored up in so many ways.

Quick Barbecue Sauce   *Makes about 1½ cups*

¼ CUP CANOLA OIL

4 CLOVES GARLIC, FINELY CHOPPED

1 CUP KETCHUP

¼ CUP CIDER VINEGAR

2 TEASPOONS HOT PEPPER SAUCE

4 TEASPOONS PACKED LIGHT OR DARK
   BROWN SUGAR

4 TEASPOONS DIJON MUSTARD

1. Heat the oil in a small nonreactive saucepan over medium heat. Add the garlic and cook, stirring, for 1 minute, or until fragrant. Take care the garlic does not burn. Add the remaining ingredients and stir to mix. Reduce the heat to low and cook, stirring occasionally, for about 15 minutes, or until thickened.

2. Let the sauce cool and use immediately or cover and refrigerate for up to 5 days.

Try this traditional-style sauce with any grilled beef—particularly roast beef or plain grilled steak.

Horseradish Cream Sauce *Makes about 1 cup*

1 CUP HEAVY CREAM

4 TABLESPOONS PREPARED
   HORSERADISH

1 TEASPOON SUGAR

1 TEASPOON DISTILLED WHITE VINEGAR

1. Using an electric mixer, beat the cream in a large bowl on medium-high speed until soft peaks form.

2. Combine the horseradish, sugar, and vinegar in a separate bowl and stir well. Fold the cream into the horseradish mixture. Serve immediately. This sauce does not keep well.

We love this with grilled steak or thick, juicy burgers. Use your favorite type of dried mushrooms, or a combination of different mushrooms.

Mushroom-Sage Sauce   *Makes about 1 cup*

½ OUNCE DRIED MUSHROOMS
   (SEE NOTE)

1½ CUPS BOILING WATER

2 TABLESPOONS OLIVE OIL

2 TABLESPOONS CHOPPED FRESH SAGE

2 SHALLOTS, DICED

4 OUNCES FRESH CREMINI
   MUSHROOMS, THINLY SLICED

4 OUNCES FRESH SHIITAKE
   MUSHROOMS, STEMMED AND THINLY
   SLICED

½ TEASPOON SALT

⅓ CUP HEAVY CREAM

1 TABLESPOON SHERRY

FRESHLY GROUND BLACK PEPPER TO
   TASTE

1 TABLESPOON FINELY CHOPPED
   FLAT-LEAF PARSLEY

1. Soak the dried mushrooms in a small bowl with the boiling water for 20 to 30 minutes. Lift out the mushrooms and gently squeeze to remove any excess liquid. Coarsely chop the mushrooms and reserve. Drain the liquid into another bowl, straining it through a coffee filter to remove any sandy grit. Set the liquid aside.

2. Heat the oil in a large skillet over medium-high heat. Add the sage and cook, stirring, for about 30 seconds, until sizzling and fragrant. Add the shallots and cook, stirring, for about 30 seconds, or until they begin to soften. Add the cremini and shiitake mushrooms, the reserved dried mushrooms, the reserved soaking liquid, and the salt. Stir until well mixed. Cover and cook for 3 or 4 minutes, until the mushrooms are soft.

3. Add the cream and sherry to the skillet and season with pepper. Bring to a simmer over medium-high heat and cook for 3 or 4 minutes, until the sauce is slightly thickened. Stir in the parsley and serve.

note: Dried mushrooms are sold in small amounts in most supermarkets. They may be a single type or a mixture of imported varieties and are sold in cellophane packages or plastic tubs. Any sort works here and adds deep, rich, earthy flavor.

A light, flavorful wine sauce is the perfect accompaniment for veal chops, but will enhance other mild grilled meats, too.

Merlot Wine Sauce   *Makes about 1½ cups*

3 CUPS OR ONE 750 ML BOTTLE MERLOT
   OR CABERNET SAUVIGNON

3 CUPS LOW-SODIUM BEEF OR CHICKEN
   BROTH

¼ CUP FINELY CHOPPED SHALLOTS

1 TABLESPOON CHOPPED FRESH THYME
   OR 1 TEASPOON DRIED

1 TABLESPOON UNSALTED BUTTER

SALT AND FRESHLY GROUND BLACK
   PEPPER TO TASTE

1. Combine the wine, broth, shallots, and thyme in a 2-quart nonreactive saucepan. Bring to a boil over high heat, reduce the heat, and simmer for 45 minutes to 1 hour until the sauce is reduced to about 1½ cups and has a thick, syrupy consistency. (The sauce may be made up to one day ahead to this point. Reheat before proceeding.)

2. Remove the sauce from the heat and whisk in the butter. Season with salt and pepper. Serve immediately.

This robust sauce perks up the flavor of stronger meats like game or beef.

Red Wine-Herb Sauce *Makes about ¾ cup*

2 TABLESPOONS OLIVE OIL

¾ CUP SLICED LEEKS, WHITE PART
   ONLY

½ CUP THINLY SLICED ONIONS

½ CUP THINLY SLICED CARROTS

2 CLOVES GARLIC, CRUSHED

½ CUP COARSELY CHOPPED PARSLEY
   STEMS

1 TEASPOON CHOPPED FRESH THYME OR
   ½ TEASPOON DRIED

¼ TEASPOON BLACK PEPPERCORNS

⅛ TEASPOON FENNEL SEED

1 SMALL BAY LEAF

2 CUPS DRY RED WINE

1 TABLESPOON PORT WINE

4 TABLESPOONS COLD, UNSALTED
   BUTTER

2 TABLESPOONS FINELY CHOPPED
   PARSLEY

SALT AND FRESHLY GROUND BLACK
   PEPPER TO TASTE

1. Heat the oil in a nonreactive saucepan over medium heat. Add the leeks, onions, carrots, garlic, parsley, thyme, peppercorns, fennel, and bay leaf and cook, stirring, for about 5 minutes, or until the vegetables begin to soften. Add the red wine, bring to a simmer over medium-high heat and cook for about 20 minutes, until the vegetables are very soft.

2. Strain the sauce through a sieve, pressing on the solids with the back of a spoon to extract as much liquid as possible. You will have about ¾ cup of liquid. Discard the solids.

3. Return the sauce to the saucepan, add the Port, and bring to a simmer. Cook for about 10 minutes until the sauce reduces to ½ cup.

4. With the pan set over medium-low heat, whisk in the butter, 1 tablespoon at a time. Make sure the each tablespoon is completely incorporated before adding the next. When the sauce is smooth and emulsified, stir in the parsley and season with pepper. Serve immediately.

Compound butters have long been used to punch up the flavor of sizzling hot, grilled meats, such as steaks and chops. They are easy to make: Simply mix a few herbs and other flavors into softened butter and then refrigerate until needed. During this time, the flavors infuse the butter. This one, made with horseradish, is perfect with thick grilled steaks.

Horseradish-Scallion Compound Butter *Makes about ½ cup*

½ CUP (1 STICK) UNSALTED BUTTER, SOFTENED

1 TABLESPOON PLUS 1½ TEASPOONS PREPARED HORSERADISH

3 SCALLIONS, GREEN PARTS ONLY, CHOPPED

½ TEASPOON SALT

1. Using a handheld electric mixer or in a mini food processor, blend the butter and horseradish until smooth. Add the scallions and salt and blend about 1 minute longer, until fully incorporated. Alternatively, mix the ingredients by hand.

2. Lay a piece of plastic wrap on the countertop. Scrape the butter onto the plastic, and using the plastic wrap as a guide, form the butter into a log about an inch in diameter. Fold the ends closed and refrigerate until ready to use.

We like to serve this cheese-flavored butter with steaks and lamb, both of which taste great with Gorgonzola.

Gorgonzola-Scallion Compound Butter *Makes about 1 cup*

½ CUP (1 STICK) UNSALTED BUTTER, SOFTENED

4 OUNCES GORGONZOLA CHEESE, CRUMBLED, AT ROOM TEMPERATURE

¼ CUP CHOPPED SCALLIONS, WHITE AND GREEN PARTS

1 TEASPOON COARSELY GROUND BLACK PEPPER

½ TEASPOON BALSAMIC VINEGAR

1. Using a handheld electric mixer or in a mini food processor, blend the butter and Gorgonzola until smooth. Add the scallions, pepper, and vinegar and blend for about 1 minute longer, until fully incorporated. Alternatively, mix the ingredients by hand.

2. Lay a piece of plastic wrap on the countertop. Scrape the butter onto the plastic and using the plastic wrap as a guide, form the butter into a log about an inch in diameter. Fold the ends closed and refrigerate until ready to use.

Pesto, which originated in Italy, has become one of the best-loved uncooked sauces in America, and is particularly popular in the summer when aromatic fresh basil is plentiful. Serve this with burgers, alongside grilled chicken, or toss it with cooked pasta for a great summer side dish.

Summer Pesto *Makes about 1 cup*

3 CUPS LOOSELY PACKED FRESH BASIL
   LEAVES
3 CLOVES GARLIC
$\frac{1}{2}$ CUP FRESHLY GRATED PARMESAN
   CHEESE
3 TABLESPOONS PINE NUTS
$\frac{1}{2}$ CUP EXTRA VIRGIN OLIVE OIL
SALT AND FRESHLY GROUND BLACK
   PEPPER TO TASTE

1. Combine the basil, garlic, and cheese in a food processor and process just until ground. Add the pine nuts and process until the nuts are finely chopped.

2. With the processor running, add the olive oil through the feed tube in a steady stream until the oil is absorbed. Season with salt and pepper. Serve immediately or press plastic wrap directly over the top, cover, and refrigerate for up to 1 day. Stir before serving.

At times, mustard is more welcome on burgers than ketchup or salsa. We like this on chicken and veal burgers.

Mustard Sauce   *Makes about ½ cup*

¼ CUP DIJON MUSTARD

2 TABLESPOONS WHITE WINE VINEGAR

1 TABLESPOON SUGAR

1 TEASPOON DRY MUSTARD

¼ CUP OLIVE OIL

1 TEASPOON HERBES DE PROVENCE
   (SEE NOTE)

Whisk together the mustard, vinegar, sugar, and dry mustard in a small bowl. Slowly add the olive oil, whisking constantly, until incorporated. Stir in the herbes de Provence. Serve immediately, or refrigerate for as long as 2 days. Whisk before serving.

note: Herbes de Provence are available in supermarkets, but if you cannot find them, use dried oregano, thyme, or a mixture of the two.

Across America, commercial salsas now outsell ketchup. The word simply means "sauce" in Spanish, and salsa can be made with any number of different ingredients. This one, made with fresh fruits and berries and given a little kick by jalapeños, is really good with sweet meats such as lamb and pork. But try it with burgers, too.

Minted Summer Fruit Salsa   *Makes about 2¼ cups*

1 CUP DICED STRAWBERRIES

1 CUP DICED MANGO

¾ CUP DICED KIWI

¼ CUP CHOPPED RED ONION

1 OR 2 JALAPEÑOS, SEEDED AND DICED

3 TABLESPOONS FRESH LIME JUICE

3 TABLESPOONS FINELY CHOPPED
   FRESH MINT

1 TEASPOON PACKED LIGHT BROWN
   SUGAR

Combine all the ingredients in a bowl and stir gently to blend. Serve immediately, or cover and refrigerate for several hours. Let the salsa come to room temperature before serving.

Mexicans are master salsa chefs, and this condiment is based on the green salsa that is served regularly in Mexico. Tomatillos are sometimes called "Mexican" or "green" tomatoes, although they are only distantly related to the common garden tomato. Small fruits covered with a papery husk that must be removed before use, tomatillos taste slightly acidic and herbal.

South-of-the-Border Tomatillo Salsa

Makes about 2 cups

8 TOMATILLOS (ABOUT ¾ POUND), HUSKED, WASHED, AND COARSELY CHOPPED

3 TABLESPOONS CHOPPED FRESH CILANTRO

2 TABLESPOONS CHOPPED SCALLIONS OR RED ONIONS

1 JALAPEÑO OR SERRANO CHILE, SEEDED AND CHOPPED

¼ CUP FRESH LIME JUICE

2 TABLESPOONS PEANUT OIL

½ TEASPOON SALT

SUGAR (OPTIONAL)

Combine the tomatillos, cilantro, scallions, chile, lime juice, oil, and salt in a glass or ceramic bowl and stir gently to mix. Adjust the seasonings, adding a little sugar if desired. Let the salsa stand for about 1 hour at room temperature to allow the flavors to blend. Serve or cover and refrigerate for as long as several hours. Let the salsa come to room temperature before serving.

This type of salsa, made with chopped tomatoes, bell peppers, and herbs, is a classic *salsa fresca*—which means it is not cooked. Serve this with just about any meat or poultry. We especially like it on burgers.

Baja-Style Tomato Salsa   *Makes about 2 cups*

1 POUND TOMATOES, CHOPPED

2 YELLOW OR RED BELL PEPPERS, SEEDED AND CHOPPED

1 CUP COOKED CORN KERNELS (SEE NOTE)

3 SCALLIONS, WHITE AND GREEN PARTS, FINELY CHOPPED

2 JALAPEÑO OR SERRANO CHILES, SEEDED AND CHOPPED

1 LARGE CLOVE GARLIC, MINCED

3 TABLESPOONS FINELY CHOPPED FRESH CILANTRO

1 TABLESPOON FRESH LIME JUICE

2 TEASPOONS CIDER VINEGAR

½ TEASPOON SALT, OR TO TASTE

Combine the tomatoes, peppers, corn, scallions, chiles, garlic, cilantro, lime juice, vinegar, and salt in a glass or ceramic bowl and stir gently to mix. Adjust the salt. Let the salsa stand for about an hour at room temperature to let the flavors blend. Serve or cover and refrigerate for several hours. Let the salsa come to room temperature before serving.

note: You can use frozen corn kernels, cooked and cooled. For better flavor, use leftover boiled summer corn, or, best yet, grill a few ears over hot coals or roast them in a very hot oven (400°F) until the husks blacken, which will take about 15 minutes and require turning several times. Let the corn cool and then slice the kernels from the cobs.

For those who like the richer, sweet flavor of grilled vegetables, this salsa is a real treat. The dried chiles make it nicely spicy. (Omit them if you prefer a milder condiment.) Try this with simple grilled chicken breasts, or use it to jazz up a burger or sirloin steak.

Hot, Hot, Hot Grilled Salsa   *Makes about 2 cups*

HEAT =

VEGETABLE OIL COOKING SPRAY

4 OR 5 RED OR YELLOW TOMATOES

1 RED ONION, CUT INTO 4 THICK SLICES

1 TABLESPOON OLIVE OIL

2 OR 3 CLOVES GARLIC, MINCED

3 TABLESPOONS CHOPPED FRESH
  CILANTRO

2 TABLESPOONS CHOPPED FLAT-LEAF
  PARSLEY OR FRESH MINT

1 OR 2 DRIED CHILES DE ARBOL OR
  OTHER HOT DRIED CHILE, TOASTED
  AND SHREDDED (SEE NOTE)

½ TEASPOON SALT

FRESH LIME JUICE (OPTIONAL)

1. Prepare a charcoal or gas grill. Lightly spray the grill rack with vegetable oil cooking spray. The coals should be moderately hot.

2. Rub the tomatoes and onion slices with olive oil. Place the vegetables on the grill and grill for 3 to 5 minutes until the vegetables are well marked, but not soft. Turn them often with tongs. Set aside until cool enough to handle.

3. Combine the garlic, cilantro, parsley, and chile in a bowl. Coarsely chop the tomatoes and onion and add to the bowl. Add the salt and a splash of lime juice, if desired. Stir gently and let the salsa stand for about 1 hour at room temperature to let the flavors blend. Serve, or cover and refrigerate for several hours. Let the salsa come to room temperature before serving.

note: To toast the chiles, place them in a dry skillet and cook over medium-high heat for about 1 minute, until lightly browned. Shake the pan during toasting to prevent burning. When cool, wearing plastic gloves to protect your skin, remove the stems and seeds and tear or shred the chiles with your hands. Be sure to wash your hands before touching sensitive areas such as eyes and mouth. The chiles can burn! Depending on your preference and the heat of the chiles, use 1 or 2 chiles.

We developed this to accompany the Stuffed Holiday Turkey Burgers on page 38, but liked it so much we also serve it alongside grilled turkey cutlets and grilled chicken.

Chunky Cranberry Ketchup

Makes about 1½ cups

½ CUP SUGAR

¼ CUP CIDER VINEGAR

1½ TEASPOONS MUSTARD SEEDS

1 TEASPOON SALT

1 BAY LEAF

PINCH OF GROUND CLOVES

1½ CUPS FRESH CRANBERRIES (ABOUT 6 OUNCES)

¼ CUP GOLDEN RAISINS

1 SHALLOT, MINCED

1. Combine the sugar, vinegar, mustard seeds, salt, bay leaf, and cloves in a nonreactive saucepan and bring to a boil over medium heat. Reduce the heat to medium-low and simmer for about 10 minutes.

2. Add the cranberries, raisins, and shallot and simmer, partially covered and stirring often, for about 15 minutes, or until most of the liquid evaporates and the ketchup thickens. Remove the bay leaf. Let cool to room temperature and serve at room temperature or chilled. If not using immediately, cover and refrigerate for as long as 2 days.

These classic marinades can be dressed up to suit your taste, but are just about perfect as they are. Use the red wine vinegar marinade on flank steak, blade lamb chops, or just about any red meat.

Red Wine Vinegar Marinade   *Makes about 1¾ cups*

1 CUP OLIVE OIL

½ CUP RED WINE VINEGAR

1 TABLESPOON WORCESTERSHIRE SAUCE

1 TABLESPOON DIJON MUSTARD

2 CLOVES GARLIC, CHOPPED

2 TABLESPOONS FINELY CHOPPED
SCALLIONS, WHITE AND GREEN PARTS

FRESHLY GROUND BLACK PEPPER TO
TASTE

Whisk together all the ingredients in a glass or ceramic bowl until blended. Adjust the seasoning. Use according to the recipe, or cover and refrigerate for as long as 2 days.

Use this elegant white wine marinade on chicken, veal, or any mild meat.

White Wine Marinade   *Makes about 1 cup*

½ CUP OLIVE OIL

¼ CUP DRY WHITE WINE

¼ CUP TARRAGON WHITE WINE VINEGAR

1 TABLESPOON CHOPPED FRESH
   TARRAGON OR CHERVIL

1 CLOVE GARLIC, MINCED

SALT AND FRESHLY GROUND BLACK
   PEPPER TO TASTE

Whisk together all the ingredients in a glass or ceramic bowl until blended. Adjust the seasonings. Use according to the recipe, or cover and refrigerate for as long as 2 days.

Toasting spices enhances their flavors. This marinade, which combines some of the piquant flavors we associate with Southeast Asia—cumin, cilantro, and garlic—is wonderful on chicken, beef, pork, you name it.

Toasted Cumin Marinade
Makes about 1½ cups

1 CUP CANOLA OIL

½ CUP FRESH LIME OR LEMON JUICE

1 TEASPOON TOASTED CUMIN SEEDS
(SEE NOTE)

2 CLOVES GARLIC, CHOPPED

2 TABLESPOONS CHOPPED FRESH
CILANTRO

SALT AND FRESHLY GROUND BLACK
PEPPER TO TASTE

Whisk together all the ingredients in a glass or ceramic bowl until blended. Adjust the seasonings. Use according to the recipe, or cover and refrigerate for as long as 2 days.

note: To toast the cumin seeds, spread them in a dry skillet and toast them over medium-high heat, shaking the pan to prevent scorching, for 1 to 2 minutes, until fragrant. Transfer the seeds to a plate to cool and stop the cooking.

This is an all-time favorite. We have recipes in the book that pair it with steak and with chicken, but it is great on pork, too.

Teriyaki Marinade   *Makes about 2 cups*

½ CUP LOW-SODIUM SOY SAUCE

½ CUP DRY SHERRY

⅓ CUP CANOLA OIL

6 TABLESPOONS RICE WINE VINEGAR

1 TABLESPOON SESAME OIL

¼ CUP FIRMLY PACKED LIGHT OR DARK
   BROWN SUGAR

2 TABLESPOONS CHOPPED FRESH
   GINGER

4 SCALLIONS, WHITE AND GREEN PARTS,
   SLICED

2 CLOVES GARLIC, MINCED

Combine the soy sauce, sherry, canola oil, vinegar, sesame oil, and sugar in a glass or ceramic bowl and whisk until the sugar dissolves. Add the ginger, scallions, and garlic and stir gently. Use according to the recipe, or cover and refrigerate for as long as 2 days.

Real maple syrup gives this fruity marinade just the sweetness it needs to enhance pork or chicken.

Maple Syrup Marinade   *Makes about 1½ cups*

1 CUP FRESH APPLE CIDER OR
   UNSWEETENED APPLE JUICE
⅓ CUP CIDER VINEGAR
3 TABLESPOONS REAL MAPLE SYRUP
2 TABLESPOONS PREPARED
   HORSERADISH
2 TEASPOONS WORCESTERSHIRE SAUCE
FRESHLY GROUND BLACK PEPPER TO
   TASTE

Whisk together all the ingredients in a glass or ceramic bowl until blended. Adjust the seasoning with pepper. Use according to the recipe, or cover and refrigerate for as long as 2 days.

note: If you prefer, substitute beer for the cider. The beer can be flat.

ry rubs are one of the best-kept secrets of backyard chefs. They can be made in batches and stored in a resealable plastic bag or small glass jar with the other spices in your cupboard. Rub them into the meat, refrigerate the meat, and let the rub draw the moisture from the center of the meat to the surface. The flavors penetrate the meat as it marinates in its own juices. This rub is made with four different types of pepper, which gives it a pleasingly sharp flavor. Try it on beef for the ultimate pepper steak. It also would taste good rubbed into lamb.

Peppery Dry Rub *Makes a generous ½ cup*

3 TABLESPOONS CHILI POWDER

2 TABLESPOONS FRESHLY GROUND
   BLACK PEPPER

2 TABLESPOONS PAPRIKA

2 TEASPOONS CRUSHED RED PEPPER

1 TEASPOON SALT

1 CLOVE GARLIC, MINCED

Mix the ingredients together in a glass jar or bowl. Cover and shake to mix. Refrigerate until ready to use.

Dry rubs can be made with any of your favorite spices—think of our formulas as blueprints for your own creations. Don't be shy when using one. Rub it liberally over the meat.

Spicy Dry Rub   *Makes about ⅓ cup*

2 TABLESPOONS CHILI POWDER

2 TABLESPOONS CAYENNE

1 TABLESPOON GROUND CORIANDER

1 TEASPOON CRUSHED RED PEPPER

SALT AND FRESHLY GROUND BLACK
  PEPPER TO TASTE

Mix the ingredients together in a glass jar or bowl. Cover and shake to mix. Store in a cool, dry place until ready to use.

When the meat is cooked, the dry rub, which has turned wet and sticky during marinating, becomes a delectable crust. This one is great on chicken and pork.

Sweet 'n' Spicy Dry Rub   *Makes about ⅓ cup*

2 TABLESPOONS PACKED LIGHT OR DARK
  BROWN SUGAR

1 TABLESPOON FINELY CHOPPED GARLIC

1 TABLESPOON DRIED MARJORAM

1 TABLESPOON SALT

1 TABLESPOON FRESHLY GROUND BLACK
  PEPPER

½ TEASPOON CAYENNE

¼ TEASPOON GROUND ALLSPICE

Mix the ingredients together in a glass jar or bowl. Cover and shake to mix. Refrigerate until ready to use.

This is a classic rub with its roots in India, where the whole spices are ground together in a mortar with a pestle. Rub it into chicken, pork, or lamb.

Garam Masala   *Makes about ¼ cup*

2 TABLESPOONS PLUS 2 TEASPOONS GROUND CARDAMOM

1 TABLESPOON GROUND CINNAMON

1 TEASPOON GROUND CLOVES

1 TEASPOON FRESHLY GROUND BLACK PEPPER

½ TEASPOON FRESHLY GRATED NUTMEG

Mix the ingredients together in a glass jar or bowl. Cover and shake to mix. Store in a cool, dry place until ready to use.

Rub this heady paste into pork, lamb, or chicken and let the meat marinate for a good long time—overnight is best. The Scotch bonnet peppers give the seasoning a searing heat as well as a sweetly aromatic quality that together provide the characteristic Jamaican taste. Cook jerked meat long and slow over moderately hot or cooler coals.

Jerk Seasoning *Makes about 1 cup*

½ CUP FINELY CHOPPED ONIONS

⅓ CUP FINELY CHOPPED SCALLIONS (4 TO 6 SCALLIONS), WHITE AND GREEN PARTS

¼ CUP FIRMLY PACKED FRESH THYME LEAVES AND TENDER STEMS

4 CLOVES GARLIC, FINELY CHOPPED

2 TABLESPOONS FRESH ORANGE JUICE

2 TABLESPOONS FRESH LIME JUICE

2 TABLESPOONS HOT PEPPER SAUCE MADE FROM SCOTCH BONNETS OR HABANERO CHILES, IF POSSIBLE, OR 1 TO 3 SCOTCH BONNET OR HABANERO CHILES, SEEDED AND MINCED, DEPENDING ON TASTE

1 TABLESPOON FINELY CHOPPED FRESH GINGER

2 TEASPOONS GROUND CORIANDER

2 TEASPOONS FRESHLY GROUND BLACK PEPPER

1 TEASPOON GROUND ALLSPICE

1 TEASPOON SALT

½ TEASPOON FRESHLY GRATED NUTMEG

½ TEASPOON GROUND CINNAMON

Combine all the ingredients in a small bowl and mix to form a coarse paste. Use immediately or transfer to a glass jar, cover, and refrigerate for as long as 1 month.

Lemongrass is an integral flavoring in much of the cooking of Southeast Asia and has found its way into American greengrocers and supermarkets, as well as Asian markets. It tastes slightly lemony and so provides lovely flavor to many preparations. It is long, slender, and pale green, and may be sold trimmed or not.

Asian-Style Lemongrass Paste

Makes about 1 cup

6 TABLESPOONS CHOPPED LEMONGRASS
(TAKEN FROM LESS FIBROUS INNER
LAYERS OF THE BULB PORTION OF
THE STALK)

3 TABLESPOONS PACKED LIGHT OR DARK
BROWN SUGAR

1 TABLESPOON PLUS 1 TEASPOON
MINCED FRESH GINGER

1 TABLESPOON PLUS 1 TEASPOON
FRESHLY CRACKED BLACK PEPPER

1 TABLESPOON MINCED GARLIC

1 TABLESPOON CUMIN SEEDS

Mix the ingredients together in a glass jar or bowl. Cover and shake to mix. Refrigerate until ready to use.

The addition of orange juice and water makes this more of a paste than a rub—although its texture lies somewhere between the two.

Curry Paste Rub *Makes about ¾ cup*

VEGETABLE OIL COOKING SPRAY

½ CUP CURRY POWDER

2 TABLESPOONS CHOPPED FRESH
GINGER

2 CLOVES GARLIC, CHOPPED

1½ TEASPOONS CRUSHED CORIANDER
SEEDS

3 TABLESPOONS ORANGE JUICE

2 TABLESPOONS WATER

SALT TO TASTE

1. Lightly spray a small skillet with vegetable oil cooking spray. Combine the curry powder, ginger, garlic, and coriander seeds in the skillet and cook over medium-low heat, stirring, for 2 or 3 minutes, until fragrant. Add the orange juice and water and stir gently until absorbed. The mixture will be dry and crumbly, although it should hold together in a mass. Season with salt.

2. Use immediately or transfer the rub to a covered container and refrigerate for up to 5 days.

Prepared mayonnaise becomes a palette for numerous culinary possibilities. Season it with roasted garlic, roasted peppers, or chopped herbs, as we have in the following three recipes.

Roasted Garlic Mayonnaise   *Makes about 1 cup*

2 WHOLE HEADS GARLIC

1 TEASPOON OLIVE OIL

1 CUP MAYONNAISE, STORE-BOUGHT OR
   HOMEMADE

1 TEASPOON LEMON JUICE

1. Preheat the oven to 400°F.

2. Remove the loose, papery outer skin from the garlic heads but do not separate them into cloves. Cut off the top ½ inch of each head. Rub each head with oil and wrap them in aluminum foil, making 2 packets. Set the packets on a baking sheet or in a baking dish and roast for 45 minutes to 1 hour until the garlic feels very soft when the packets are squeezed gently.

3. Unwrap the garlic heads and let them cool.

4. Squeeze the garlic from the cloves and transfer the garlic to the bowl of a food processor. Pulse 3 or 4 times until smooth. Add the mayonnaise and lemon juice and process until smooth and well combined. Serve immediately, or cover and refrigerate for up to 2 days.

Roasted Red Pepper Mayonnaise

Makes about 1¼ cups

2 ROASTED RED BELL PEPPERS (PAGE 251), COARSELY CHOPPED

1 CLOVE GARLIC, COARSELY CHOPPED

1 CUP MAYONNAISE, STORE-BOUGHT OR HOMEMADE

PINCH OF CAYENNE

Combine the roasted peppers and garlic in a food processor and process until smooth. Add the mayonnaise and cayenne and process just until combined. Serve immediately, or cover and refrigerate for up to 2 days.

Herbed Mayonnaise

Makes about 1 cup

1 CUP MAYONNAISE, STORE-BOUGHT OR
  HOMEMADE

½ CUP FINELY CHOPPED FLAT-LEAF
  PARSLEY

2 TABLESPOONS FINELY CHOPPED FRESH
  THYME

2 TABLESPOONS FINELY CHOPPED FRESH
  TARRAGON

2 TEASPOONS DIJON MUSTARD

Combine all the ingredients in a bowl and stir until well mixed.
Serve immediately, or cover and refrigerate for up to 2 days.

If a recipe calls for roasted peppers, follow this recipe through Step 3. Omit the salt and pepper, oil, and other flavorings. As an alternative to broiling, you may roast the peppers on the grill over a hot fire. To roast one or two peppers, skewer them on long-handled forks and char them over a gas flame.

The key to roasting peppers is to char the skin on all sides of the peppers and then to let the peppers steam during cooling. Do not peel the peppers under running water. The water dilutes the flavor. And do not worry if some charred bits of skin remain on the peppers. Use your fingers and a knife for peeling, rubbing off the skin as much as peeling it for the best flavor and texture.

Roasted Red or Yellow Bell Peppers in Olive Oil *Makes 4 peppers*

4 RED OR YELLOW BELL PEPPERS, HALVED, SEEDED, AND TRIMMED

SALT AND FRESHLY GROUND BLACK PEPPER TO TASTE

2 TO 3 TABLESPOONS EXTRA VIRGIN OLIVE OIL

BALSAMIC VINEGAR (OPTIONAL)

CAPERS (OPTIONAL)

1. Preheat the broiler. Line the broiler pan with foil.

2. Place the peppers, skin side up, on the broiling tray. Broil for about 15 minutes, turning, until the skin is charred and blistered on all sides. Transfer to a bowl and cover the bowl with foil or place in a paper bag and fold the top over to seal. Set aside to steam and cool for about 15 minutes.

3. Rub the charred skin from the peppers and cut the peppers into the size needed for a recipe, or if serving as a side dish, cut into wide strips.

4. Place the peppers on a platter and season with salt and pepper. Drizzle with olive oil. If desired, splash with vinegar and sprinkle with capers.

This slaw, inspired by some of the flavors used throughout Southeast Asia, adds bright flavor alongside burgers, grilled steaks, and pork chops. The crunchy cabbage and carrots marry with the soy sauce, sesame oil, lime juice, and cilantro to make this one of our favorite side dishes.

Asian Slaw   *Serves 6*

5 CUPS (ABOUT 1 POUND) FINELY
   SHREDDED GREEN OR RED CABBAGE,
   OR A MIXTURE
2 LARGE CARROTS, PEELED AND CUT
   INTO SMALL MATCHSTICK-SIZE
   PIECES
2 SCALLIONS, WHITE AND GREEN PARTS,
   CUT INTO 2-INCH-LONG THIN STRIPS
$\frac{1}{4}$ CUP CHOPPED FRESH CILANTRO
3 TABLESPOONS SOY SAUCE
2 TABLESPOONS TOASTED SESAME OIL
2 TABLESPOONS FRESH LIME JUICE
SALT AND FRESHLY GROUND BLACK
   PEPPER

1. Toss together the cabbage, carrots, scallions, and cilantro.

2. Whisk together the soy sauce, oil, and lime juice in a small bowl. Pour the dressing over the vegetables, toss, and set aside at room temperature for at least 30 minutes but no longer than 1 hour. Season to taste with salt and pepper. Serve at once or cover and refrigerate for up to 24 hours.

Cuts of Meat for Grilling

Throughout the book, we have taken care to explain which cuts of meat are best for different recipes, due to their qualities of size, tenderness, and composition. On the next pages are diagrams for beef, veal, lamb, and pork, which show the placement of the different cuts of meat. We also include tables covering the best cuts of meat for grilling for each animal (plus chicken, turkey, and game birds), along with shopping and grilling advice plus some alternative cooking methods that best suit the cut. Let these diagrams and tables assist you, as though your own personal butcher was right there beside you to answer your questions on the many cuts of meat out there, or to give advice on choosing the best cut of meat for your grilling needs.

Beef

CHUCK
- chuck steak
- flat-iron steak

RIB
- standing rib roast and rib steak
- short ribs

SHORT LOIN
- tenderloin roast and filet mignon
- shell roast and shell steak
- porterhouse steak
- T-bone steak
- club steak

HIP OR SIRLOIN
- sirloin steak
- tri-tip

ROUND
- round steak

BRISKET

FORESHANK

PLATE
- skirt steak
- hanger steak

FLANK
- flank steak

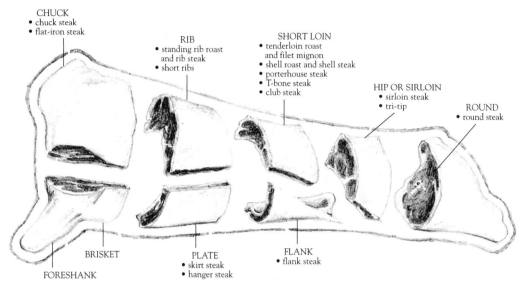

Beef carcass, divided into primal (wholesale) and retail cuts.

Veal

SHOULDER AND NECK

RIB OR RACK
- rib roast and rib chops

LOIN
- loin chops
- strip steak

ROUND (LEG)
- top round

FORESHANK

BREAST

FLANK

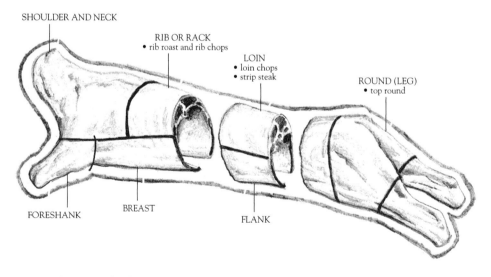

Veal carcass, divided into primal (wholesale) and retail cuts.

Lamb

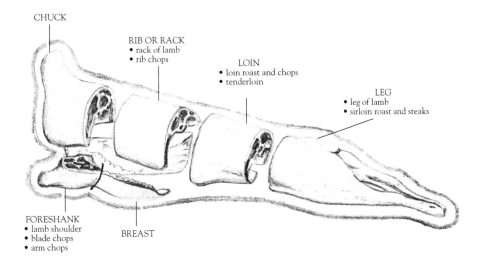

CHUCK

RIB OR RACK
• rack of lamb
• rib chops

LOIN
• loin roast and chops
• tenderloin

LEG
• leg of lamb
• sirloin roast and steaks

FORESHANK
• lamb shoulder
• blade chops
• arm chops

BREAST

Lamb carcass, divided into primal (wholesale) and retail cuts.

Pork

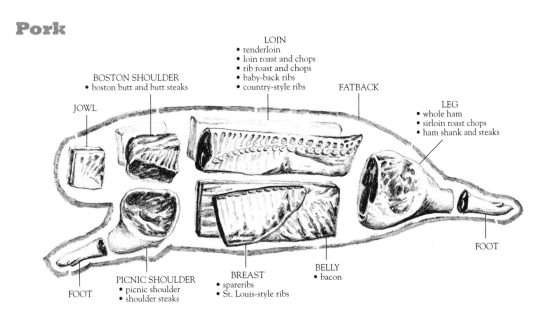

LOIN
• tenderloin
• loin roast and chops
• rib roast and chops
• baby-back ribs
• country-style ribs

BOSTON SHOULDER
• boston butt and butt steaks

JOWL

FATBACK

LEG
• whole ham
• sirloin roast chops
• ham shank and steaks

FOOT

PICNIC SHOULDER
• picnic shoulder
• shoulder steaks

FOOT

BREAST
• spareribs
• St. Louis-style ribs

BELLY
• bacon

Pork carcass, divided into primal (wholesale) and retail cuts.

Beef Cuts for Grilling *

Primal/ Retail Cut	Description	Recommended Size and Thickness for Grilling	How to Grill (or BBQ)	Other Cooking Methods
Short loin/ **Tenderloin roast** (also called filet)	The whole tenderloin is removed from the short loin before any other steaks are cut. It can be grilled whole or cut into large-sized *roasts*. (The head and tail ends are also excellent grilled as *steaks, tails, kabobs*, etc.)	A whole tenderloin weighs about 3.5 lbs. Tenderloin roasts range from 1–2 lbs. The *Châteaubriand* is a small roast (20–24 oz.) cut from the center of the tenderloin. Estimate 8 oz. per serving.	Roast on the grill using indirect heat.	Oven roast, broil, or pan broil.
Short loin/**Filet mignon** (also called tenderloin steak) and **tournedos**	The most tender cut of beef with a milder flavor than other steaks. Filets are cut from the center of the tenderloin; tournedos are small filets cut closer to the tail.	Filets range from 6–12 oz. and are 1–3 in. thick. Tournedos are generally 4 oz. and ½–¾ in. thick. 6–8 oz. per serving.	For steaks under 1¼ in. thick, grill using direct heat. Use indirect heat for thicker steaks.	Broil or sauté.
Short loin/ **Shell roast**	When the tenderloin has been removed from the short loin, the remaining portion of meat is called the shell. It can be cut into steaks or left in larger pieces to become roasts. A *boneless shell roast* is excellent for parties; it is very easy to slice.	A whole shell roast is about 8 lbs. and serves 10–14; half shell roasts are also available. 8–12 oz. per serving.	Roast on the grill using indirect heat.	Oven roast.
Short loin/ **Shell steak** (also called strip, New York strip, Kansas City strip, and strip loin)	Shell is the correct name for steaks cut from this section, although restaurants and butchers will call them by various other names, too. The steaks have fine marbling, hearty flavor, and toothsome texture.	Shell steaks can be cut to any thickness from ¾ in. for an 8-oz. steak to 4 in. for a massive 30-oz. double shell. Estimate 8 oz. for an average serving and up to 16 oz. for a large serving.	Rather than grilling individual steaks, try grilling a double-thick shell that will serve 2–3 adults, using indirect heat.	Broil or pan roast.

*See diagram, page 254.

Beef Cuts for Grilling *

Primal/ Retail Cut	Description	Recommended Size and Thickness for Grilling	How to Grill (or BBQ)	Other Cooking Methods
Short loin/ **Porterhouse steak**	Cut from the complete short loin, it includes a portion of shell and a portion of tenderloin. It comes from the section of short loin nearest the sirloin, resulting in a larger portion of tenderloin than found in the similar T-bone steak.	Porterhouse steaks can be cut 1¼–3½ in. thick. A 2-in.-thick steak will be 2–2½ lbs. and will serve 2 adults.	Grill using indirect heat. If steak contains a tail—a section of meat extending from the tenderloin—fold the tail back against the steak and secure with a small metal or wooden skewer for even grilling.	Broil or pan roast; pan broil cuts under 1¼ in. thick.
Short loin/ **T-bone steak**	Similar to the porterhouse but with a smaller section of tenderloin and a smaller tail. The T-bone steak comes from the center of the short loin, between the porterhouse and rib.	T-bone steaks can be cut from 1–3 in. thick. A 16-oz. T-bone is 1–1⅛ in. thick and considered an average serving.	See **Porterhouse steak.**	See **Porterhouse steak.**
Short loin/ **Club steak** (also called Delmonico, bone-in shell, and strip)	Smaller than the T-bone, club steak has the same large "eye" section of shell meat, but no tenderloin. Cut from the section of short loin nearest the rib end, the rectangular steak is delicious and tender.	Club steaks can be cut from 1¼ in.–2½ in. thick (14–20 oz.) and provide 1 large or 2 small servings. When shopping, look for meat that's finely textured with delicate marbling. If it seems coarse and contains fat chunks, it is not the quality you want.	Grill using indirect heat.	Broil or pan grill.

*See diagram, page 254.

continues

Beef Cuts for Grilling (continued) *

Primal/ Retail Cut	Description	Recommended Size and Thickness for Grilling	How to Grill (or BBQ)	Other Cooking Methods
Hip or Sirloin/ **Sirloin steak**	The sirloin is a large steak—a great summertime steak for feeding a crowd. Mostly available boneless, although some butchers (like Lobel's) also cut them the old-fashioned way, bone-in.	Sirloins range from 1–2 in. thick and weigh 2–4 lbs. A 2-lb. steak serves 4–6. If buying bone-in, look for a long, thin bone 4–6 in. long and 1 in. wide. Flat bone sirloins, cut closest to the porterhouse, are the fullest in body and flavor.	Grill using indirect heat.	Broil or pan roast; pan broil thinner cuts.
Hip or Sirloin/ **Tri-tip** (also called Santa Maria barbecue)	An economical, lean but flavorful cut that is tender and easy to prepare—ideal for the grill. Taken from the bottom sirloin, it makes a good alternative to skirt steak, and can be cubed for kabobs or sliced for stir-frys and satays. Cubed tri-tip is sometimes called *Santa Maria barbecue*—a favorite cut of vaqueros tending cattle on the range and the preferred cut among chili champions.	A whole tri-tip weighs about 2 lbs., yielding 4–6 servings.	Grill steaks over indirect heat. Slice across the grain to yield tender pieces. Be sure to check the graining as you go as the graining has a tendency to twist.	Broil.
Rib/**Standing rib roast**	Rib roasts are the most tender of all beef roasts, with juicy, well-marbled meat and a moisture-preserving layer of fat outside. They come four ways: 1. *Standing (bone-in) rib roast*—short ribs are attached but cracked; 2. *Half-standing rib roast*—short ribs are completely removed; 3. *Boned-and-tied standing rib roast*—short ribs removed, bones removed and then tied back in place, for easy removal again after cooking; 4. *Rolled (boneless) rib roast*—short ribs removed, bones completely removed, meat rolled and tied over outer layer of fat.	Roasts range from 3–14 lbs. 8–12 oz. per serving for a boneless roast and 16 oz. for a bone-in roast.	All four roasts are cooked similarly using indirect heat. When searing a boned-and-tied roast, turn frequently to avoid burning the strings that hold the roast together.	Oven roast.

*See diagram, page 254.

Beef Cuts for Grilling *

Primal/ Retail Cut	Description	Recommended Size and Thickness for Grilling	How to Grill (or BBQ)	Other Cooking Methods
Rib/**Rib steak**	Cut from the center of the rib section. Similar in appearance to club steaks (which they are sometimes sold as), rib steaks are less tender and have a full-bodied beef flavor, and should be less expensive. A boneless rib steak is often called a *rib-eye steak,* or *entrecôte* if the exterior fat has also been trimmed off. A bone-in rib steak that has an extended frenched rib bone is called a *cowboy steak.*	Bone-in rib steaks can be cut 1–2½ in. thick (16–28 oz.). Rib-eye steaks can be cut from ¾ in. thick (8 oz.) for an average serving to 2–2½ in. thick (18–22 oz.) for an extra large or two average servings.	Grill steaks up to 1¼ in. thick with direct heat; use indirect heat for thicker steaks.	Broil, grill, pan grill, or pan roast.
Rib/**Short ribs** (also called flanken)	These are cut from the ends of the rib roast and the plate. They contain layers of lean and fat with the flat rib bone.	German-style short ribs are cut in one- or two-rib sections 3–4 in. long. Korean-style short ribs are cut in strips of 4–6 bones ½–¾ in. thick. Estimate 16 oz. ribs per serving.	German-style short ribs are best smoked or barbecued using indirect heat. Korean-style ribs are best grilled over direct heat.	Short ribs make an exquisite boiled beef, enhance the flavor of soups, and are excellent braised.
Round/ **Round steak**	Round steak is cut from the rump (or top round) nearest the sirloin. It is oval in shape, with practically no fat; on the grill, it makes a fine *London broil*. Because it lacks marbling, round steak is not as flavorful or juicy as other cuts, but it has little waste and is an economical choice.	Round steak is cut 1–3 in. thick. The first three cuts from the sirloin end are best. Estimate 8 oz. per serving.	Marinate before grilling; grill using indirect heat.	Excellent for steak tartare.
Round/**London broil**	London broil is actually a term for any flat cut of meat that is marinated, broiled, or grilled, and cut at an angle against the grain. Beef labeled "London broil" generally comes from the top round, flank, or, as we do at Lobel's, the small end of the shell.	Depending on the cut, London broil will range from 1–3 in. thick. Estimate 8 oz. per serving.	Marinate before grilling. Grill cuts under 1¼ in. thick using direct heat, and thicker cuts using indirect heat.	Broil.

*See diagram, page 254.

continues

Beef Cuts for Grilling (continued) *

Primal/Retail Cut	Description	Recommended Size and Thickness for Grilling	How to Grill (or BBQ)	Other Cooking Methods
Flank/**Flank steak** (also called London broil)	The flank steak is a lean, flat muscle that comes from the middle section of the underbelly, beneath the loin and adjacent to the skirt. There is only one flank steak to a side of beef. Flank steak has a lovely flavor and tender texture when sliced thin against the grain.	Flank steaks are 1¼–1½ lbs. and 1¼–1½ in. thick. Estimate 8 oz. per serving.	To preserve meat's tenderness, marinate before grilling; grill quickly over direct heat to no more than medium-rare and slice crosswise, against the grain.	Broil.
Plate/**Skirt steak**	Skirt steak comes from the underside below the rib, adjacent to the flank. It has a slightly coarser grain, more marbling, and a more yielding texture than flank steak. It has a robust beefy flavor, and is the preferred cut for making fajitas.	Skirt steaks are uniformly ¾–1 in. thick and weigh about 1 lb. One steak serves 2–3.	Grill over direct heat to no more than medium-rare to preserve its tenderness.	Broil.
Plate/**Hanger steak**	A flavorsome, juicy, and tender cut popular with chefs and steak cognoscenti but hard to find. The hanger supports the diaphragm and "hangs" free of attachment to any bone. It consists of two long lobes of meat separated by a tough membrane that should be removed before grilling, separating the steak into two pieces.	A whole hanger steak is ¾–1 in. thick and about 1 lb. Serves 2.	Hanger steak is delicious grilled over direct heat just until rare, then sliced across the grain.	Broil.
Foreshank/**Brisket**	This popular cut from the breast accommodates a variety of treatments, including smoking low and slow to produce Texas-style barbecue. Look for Wagyu beef brisket, which has abundant marbling that bastes the meat from the inside and a substantial fat cap that bastes it from the outside (lower-grade briskets have leaner meat and a fat cap that varies in thickness).	A whole 9-lb. brisket will feed 18–20 adults. A *first-cut brisket* (the smaller portion of the cut) is comparatively lean, weighs about 4 lbs., and serves 8–10.	Brisket is best smoked low and slow to ensure tenderness. To barbecue it Texas style, smoke over mesquite for about 14 hours.	Braise, slow-roast in the oven over low heat.

*See diagram, page 254.

Beef Cuts for Grilling *

Primal/ Retail Cut	Description	Recommended Size and Thickness for Grilling	How to Grill (or BBQ)	Other Cooking Methods
Chuck/**Chuck steak** (also called blade chuck)	An economical cut that has well-developed flavor, but varies in tenderness. We consider the first three bones of the chuck section the most tender. They are adjacent to the rib roast and contain a sizable extension of the rib eye.	Chuck steaks are usually 1–1½ in. thick, 2–4 lbs., and will have varying amounts of fat. 8–10 oz. servings depending on fat content.	Grill cuts from the first three bones of the chuck section using indirect heat.	Braise or stew the less tender cuts from farther down the shoulder.
Chuck/**Flat-iron steak** (also called top blade)	Flat-iron steak is cut from the chuck shoulder in the forequarter. A rather inexpensive cut, it is relatively moist and tender with good beefy flavor. Sometimes a regional reference is added to the name: *Kansas City flat-iron, Chicago flat-iron, etc.*	Flat-iron steaks are 1– 1½ in. thick. Steaks are 6–8 oz., making them ideal for single-serving planning.	Grill cuts under 1¼ in. thick over direct heat and thicker cuts over indirect heat.	Broil; pan grill; braise; cut into cubes for kabobs or strips for stir-fries and satays.
ground beef	Don't buy pre-ground beef, which can come from any part of the steer, including the trimmings. Ask your butcher to grind beef to order. We recommend grinding one or a combination of these cuts: *round*, which has almost no fat; *chuck*, whose high fat content makes juicy burgers; *sirloin*, whose well-marbled texture makes tender, flavorful hamburgers; and *tail of porterhouse*, an especially flavorful cut available at our New York store and specialty butchers.	Burgers can vary in thickness, depending on weight. Palm-sized patties are typical. The average burger weighs 3–6 oz., and a big burger weighs about 8 oz. Lobel's Wyoming burgers weigh a pound each.	Grill over direct heat. Always use chilled ground beef: do not allow it to come to room temperature. Form the patties and then refrigerate until well chilled (30 minutes to overnight) before grilling.	Broil or pan broil burgers.

*See diagram, page 254.

Veal Cuts for Grilling *

Primal/ Retail Cut	Description	Recommended Size and Thickness for Grilling	How to Grill (or BBQ)	Other Cooking Methods
Loin/ **Loin chops** (also called veal porterhouse)	The equivalent of porterhouse steaks from mature beef cattle; identified by their T-shaped bones, with a large eye (strip) steak on one side and a portion of tenderloin on the other. The tail is usually trimmed off (see **Porterhouse steak**, page 257).	Chops 1–2¼ in. thick (14–18 oz.) are ideal for grilling. Estimate 2 servings per chop.	Grill using indirect heat.	Oven roast or broil.
Loin/ **Kidney chops**	These are similar to loin chops, but have a portion of veal kidney attached, as well as a tail (see **Porterhouse steak**, page 257).	Chops range from 1–3 in. thick (8–24 oz.). Estimate 8 oz. per serving.	Wrap the tail around the kidney and skewer to secure. Grill 1¼-in.-thick chops using direct heat. Grill thicker chops using indirect heat.	Bake, broil, pan roast, or pan grill.
Loin/ **Strip steak**	Veal strip steaks are an uncommon treat. Cut from the loin, near the rib, it is the strip side of a full loin chop, with no tenderloin (available *bone-in* or *boneless*). If cut from a mature animal, this would be the equivalent of a *club steak*.	Steaks 2¼–3 in. thick (12–14 oz.) are ideal for grilling. Estimate 1 large or 2 average servings per steak.	Grill using indirect heat.	Broil, pan grill, or pan roast.
Loin/**Loin kabobs**	Cut from a *boneless loin roast*.	Cubes should be 1¼–1½ in. square. Estimate 8 oz. per serving.	Threading each cube through two skewers spaced about ½ in. apart makes turning kabobs easy.	Broil.
Rib/**Rib roast** (also called rack roast)	The equivalent of a standing rib roast from mature beef cattle. As a bone-in roast, it is also called a *rack roast of veal*. Boneless, it is called a *boneless veal loin roast* and includes the tenderloin.	12–16 oz. per bone-in serving and 8 oz. per boneless serving.	(See beef **Standing rib roast**, page 258.)	Oven roast.

See diagram, page 254.

Veal Cuts for Grilling *

Primal/ Retail Cut	Description	Recommended Size and Thickness for Grilling	How to Grill (or BBQ)	Other Cooking Methods
Rib/ **Rib chops**	These chops are cut from the *rib roast* and are available *bone-in* or *boneless*.	A 1-bone chop is 1½–1¾ in. thick (about 14 oz.). Estimate 12 oz. per serving for bone-in and 8 oz. per serving for boneless.	Grill using indirect heat.	Broil, pan grill, or pan roast.
Round/ **Top round kabobs**	The round, or leg, is a relatively tender cut from the hindquarter. It is most often used for thin cuts like medallions or scaloppini. However, the round is also good for cutting into cubes for grilling.	Cubes should be 1¼–1½ in. square. Estimate 8 oz. per serving.	See **Loin kabobs,** page 262.	Broil.
Breast, Flank, Shoulder, Neck, and Foreshank	not commonly grilled			
Ground veal	Ground from cuts such as the *chuck, sirloin, round,* etc.	See **ground beef,** page 261.	Grill over direct heat. Always use chilled ground veal. Form the patties and then refrigerate until well chilled (30 minutes to overnight) before putting directly on the grill.	Broil or pan broil burgers. Mix with ground beef or pork for meatloaf.

*See diagram, page 254.

Lamb Cuts for Grilling *

Primal/ Retail Cut	Description	Recommended Size and Thickness for Grilling	How to Grill (or BBQ)	Other Cooking Methods
Loin/ **Loin roast**	Composed of the whole loin, including the eye (loin) and tenderloin separated by a T-shaped bone. Makes for a tender and dramatic roast for serving a crowd. A *double loin roast*, also called a *saddle of lamb*, consists of both loins joined by the breast bone.	A single loin roast with the breast bone removed weighs 2½–3 lbs. A full saddle weighs about 6 lbs. 8–12 oz. per serving.	Grill roast using indirect heat.	Oven roast.
Loin/ **Loin chops**	The tenderest lamb chops of all, made by cutting through the loin, these contain portions of eye and tenderloin separated by a T-bone. Can also have the kidney inserted below the tenderloin. When boned, trimmed, and rolled (sometimes with bacon), loin chops are called *noisettes*. Some chops will contain a "tail" (see **Porterhouse steak**, page 257).	Loin chops range from 1¼–1½ in. thick for a 5–6-oz. chop to 2½ in. thick for a 10-oz. chop. 1–2 chops per serving.	For chops over 1¼ in. thick grill using indirect heat.	Broil, pan grill, or pan roast.
Leg/ **Leg of lamb**	The leg is excellent grill-roasted. The hindmost section of the leg is called the *shank* and the front section is the *sirloin*. A whole leg comes three ways: 1. *Bone-in*; 2. *Boneless*, rolled and tied; 3. *Butterflied boneless*. The last can be laid flat and has a roughly uniform thickness, which facilitates grilling.	A whole leg weighs 7–9 lbs; boneless and butterflied boneless legs are 6–7 lbs. 8–10 oz. per serving. If a whole leg is larger than you need, ask to have a few sirloin steaks cut from the end to save for another meal.	Grill roast using indirect heat. A butterflied leg can be grilled flat and will cook much faster than the other leg cuts.	Oven roast.
Leg/ **Sirloin roast**	The thick sirloin portion of the leg (closest to the loin) makes a tender roast, and is a good size for small groups. Like the whole leg, it comes *bone-in*, *boneless*, and *butterflied boneless*.	A bone-in roast weighs 4–5 lbs.; a boneless or butterflied boneless roast weighs about 3½ lbs. Estimate 12 oz. per serving for bone-in, and 8 oz. per serving for boneless.	See **Leg of lamb**.	Oven roast.

See diagram, page 255.

Lamb Cuts for Grilling *

Primal/ Retail Cut	Description	Recommended Size and Thickness for Grilling	How to Grill (or BBQ)	Other Cooking Methods
Leg/ **Sirloin steaks** (chops)	The sirloin portion of the leg can be cut crosswise into steaks that are excellent grilled.	Sirloin steaks are usually large, 1–1¼ in. thick and weigh 12–18 oz. each. Allowing for center bone, 8–10 oz. per serving.	Grill using indirect heat.	Broil, grill, or pan grill.
Leg/ **Leg kabobs**	The most delicious lamb kabobs are cut from the leg. They can be cut from either the shank or sirloin section.	Cubes from 1–1½ in. are a good size for kabobs. 6–8 oz. per serving.	Marinate the cubes and string on a skewer with vegetables before grilling.	Broil.
Rib or rack/ **Rack of lamb**	The rib or rack section starts at the beginning of the foresaddle, in front of the loin. The rib contains no tenderloin, but the eye (loin) is delicious and tender when grilled, either as a rack or individual chops.	Each rack contains 8 rib chops. Estimate 4 chops per adult serving, 3 for smaller appetites.	Grill using indirect heat.	Oven roast.
Rib or rack/ **Rib chops**	The rib section can be cut crosswise into chops—single, double or triple, based on the number of bones they contain. We recommend grilling double or triple chops as they are easier to manage on the grill and, when sliced between the ribs, result in chops with a crusty exterior side and a juicy interior side.	A double-rib lamb chop is about 2 in. thick (6 oz.) and a triple chop is about 3 in. thick (9 oz.). 9–12 oz. per serving.	Grill using indirect heat. Single chops make great appetizers (the frenched rib bone makes a built-in handle), but grill them as double chops, then slice between ribs before serving.	Broil or pan grill.

*See diagram, page 255.

continues

Lamb Cuts for Grilling (continued) *

Primal/ Retail Cut	Description	Recommended Size and Thickness for Grilling	How to Grill (or BBQ)	Other Cooking Methods
Foreshank/ **Blade chops** (also called shoulder chops)	Cut from the beginning of the shoulder (the front leg) right after the rack. Blade chops are less tender than other chops, inexpensive and flavorful. They are meatier than arm chops.	These chops are typically 1 in. thick. 9–12 oz. per serving.	Can be cooked quickly over direct heat. For added tender-ness, marinate before grilling.	Broil, pan grill, or braise.
Foreshank/ **Arm chops**	These chops are cut from the lower part of the shoulder, near the shank, and have a small, round bone. Like blade chops, they are inexpensive but flavorful.	See **Blade chops.**	See **Blade chops.**	See **Blade chops.**

*See diagram, page 255.

Pork Cuts for Grilling *

Primal/ Retail Cut	Description	Recommended Size and Thickness for Grilling	How to Grill (or BBQ)	Other Cooking Methods
Loin/ **Tenderloin**	Pork tenderloins are removed from the pork loin in one piece, before any steaks are cut. Tenderloins are lean, with a mild flavor and tender texture, and ideal for the grill.	One whole pork tenderloin is 10–12 oz. and serves 2.	Grill over direct heat; tend to them carefully and turn frequently, as grilling takes only a few minutes.	Broil, pan grill, or pan roast.
Loin/ **Whole Loin**	The whole loin can be divided into the *loin roast*, nearest the leg, and the *rib roast*, nearest the shoulder. The loin roast comes bone-in. The rib roast can be prepared bone-in (called a *rack roast*) or boneless (called a *center-cut roast*).	A loin roast is 5–7 lbs. and yields 10–14 8-oz. chops. A rack roast is 5–7 lbs. and yields 10 8–10-oz. chops. A center-cut roast is about 6 lbs. and provides 12 8-oz. portions.	Grill using indirect heat.	Oven roast.
Loin/ **Loin chops**	Cut from the center of the loin roast, they consist of a nugget of tenderloin and a larger piece of the loin, separated by a T-shaped bone. Pork that is highly marbled (such as Kurobuta/Berkshire, Duroc, or heritage breeds) retains moisture well on the grill for a juicy result.	Chops are ¾ in.–1½ in. thick (8–12 oz.) and serve one. Thick chops are best for grilling to keep meat moist.	Grill using indirect heat.	Broil, pan grill, or pan roast.
Loin/ **Loin kabobs**	Cubes cut from the loin roast.	Cubes should be 1¼–1½-in. squares. 6–8 oz. per serving.	Marinate if using commercial (supermarket) pork to ensure a flavorful result.	Broil, pan grill, or pan roast.
Loin/ **Rib chops**	Cut from the rib section of the loin.	See **Loin chops**.	See **Loin chops**.	See **Loin chops**.

*See diagram, page 255.

continues

Pork Cuts for Grilling (continued) *

Primal/ Retail Cut	Description	Recommended Size and Thickness for Grilling	How to Grill (or BBQ)	Other Cooking Methods
Loin/ **Baby-back ribs**	If you remove the rib bones from a *rib roast*, you have a rack of baby-back ribs. These are the most lean and tender pork ribs because of their proximity to the loin.	A full *slab* of baby-back ribs will contain 13 rib bones, while a *rack* of baby backs will contain 10–13, depending on how the loin was cut. 4–5 ribs per serving.	Their generally uniform shape and length make them easy to grill using indirect heat.	Broil or oven roast.
Loin/**Country-style ribs**	Cut from the section of the loin nearest the shoulder (usually the first 6 ribs of the loin), these meaty ribs are composed of a portion of eye (loin) meat attached to a portion of baby-back rib. The remaining portion of eye is sold separately as *boneless loin chops*.	Country-style ribs are available in 6-rib sections or as individual 1-in. chops. 2–3 ribs per serving.	Unless they will be slow-cooked in a smoker, country-style ribs are often parboiled before grilling. This helps tenderize them and reduces grill time. Grill using direct or indirect heat.	Broil, oven roast, or braise.
Breast/ **Spareribs**	Spareribs are characteristic for their bowed shape, because the brisket bone (breast bone) is left attached. Best smoked low-and-slow over hickory, although there are myriad other ways, including Chinese and Korean methods.	A full *slab* of spareribs contains 13 ribs, while a *rack* will contain 10–13 ribs, depending on how the loin was cut. 2–3 servings per slab or rack.	If you don't have a smoker, partially roast roast spareribs in a 350°F oven and finish on the grill, adding barbecue sauce near the end to caramelize it.	Oven roast, then finish under the broiler.
Breast/ **St. Louis-style ribs**	Essentially *spareribs* with the brisket bone removed. The result is a slab or rack of ribs that is squared off and uniform in length end to end.	See **Spareribs**.	See **Spareribs**.	See **Spareribs**.

See diagram, page 255.

Pork Cuts for Grilling *

Primal/ Retail Cut	Description	Recommended Size and Thickness for Grilling	How to Grill (or BBQ)	Other Cooking Methods
Belly/ **bacon**	Pork belly can be used fresh; salted to make salt pork; or cured, smoked, or cured and smoked to make bacon (including pancetta). Bacon can be wrapped around lean meat like filet mignon, pork tenderloin, shrimp, scallops, fish, chicken, etc., before grilling.	Slice bacon ⅛ in. thick for wrapping around small foods (kabobs, etc.) before grilling; slice ¼ in. thick for wrapping steaks or draping on fish when grill roasting.	If you have a smoker, you can make smoked pork belly, which can be used much like bacon. To make actual bacon from fresh belly, you need to cure the meat several weeks prior to smoking.	Pan fry, pan grill, or microwave.
Boston Shoulder and Picnic Shoulder/**Whole Shoulder**	The whole shoulder comprises both the Boston Shoulder and the Picnic Shoulder. It usually comes with the skin left on and it may or may not include the whole *shank*. Grill-roasted Whole shoulder has a taste and juicy texture reminiscent of a roasted pork loin.	A whole shoulder, including the *shank*, is 15–18 lbs. Allowing for large bones, estimate 12 oz. per serving.	Grill roast low-and-slow over indirect heat, or smoke to an an internal temperature of 160°F if slicing, or 190°F for pulled pork.	Oven roast.
Boston Shoulder (also called Boston butt)	This is the top half of the whole shoulder, available *bone-in* or *boneless*. Smoked low-and-slow for hours, Boston butt is the favorite cut among pit masters everywhere for authentic pulled pork barbecue.	A Boston butt typically weighs 6–8 lbs. Estimate 12 oz. per serving.	See **Whole shoulder**.	Slow roast in the oven; braise.

*See diagram, page 255.

continues

Pork Cuts for Grilling (continued) *

Primal/ Retail Cut	Description	Recommended Size and Thickness for Grilling	How to Grill (or BBQ)	Other Cooking Methods
Boston Shoulder/ **Butt steaks**	Cross-section slices of *Boston butt*.	Butt steaks are usually ½–¾ in. thick (6–8 oz.). Estimate 1 steak per person.	Unless you have high quality, well-marbled pork, butt steaks can be tricky to grill because they are lean. Marinate before grilling.	Broil, pan fry, or pan grill.
Boston Shoulder/ **Butt kabobs**	Cubes cut from the *Boston butt*.	Cut cubes into 1¼–1½- in. squares. Estimate 8 oz. per serving.	Marinate before grilling, because they tend to be lean.	Broil.
Picnic shoulder (also called picnic ham)	This is the bottom half of the whole shoulder, usually found bone-in, including part of the *shank*. Can also be used to make pulled pork. See **Whole shoulder**.	A picnic shoulder weighs 9–12 lbs. Allowing for bones, estimate 12 oz. per serving.	See **Whole shoulder**.	See **Whole shoulder**.
Picnic shoulder/ **Shoulder steaks**	Shoulder steaks are streaked with fat and pockets of meat. A good, inexpensive cut for grilling.	Relatively thin steaks are best, ¾–1 in. thick for a quick grill. Estimate 1 steak per person.	Grill over direct heat.	Broil.
Leg/ **Whole ham**	Essentially the whole rear leg except the foot, from sirloin end to shank end.	The whole ham is one size, 20 lbs. or more.	Best smoked or grill roasted low-and-slow.	Oven roast or braise.
Leg/ **Sirloin roast**	The front or top part of the ham. Has a high ratio of lean meat in relation to bone and fat.	A whole *bone-in sirloin roast* is 8–10 lbs. Estimate 12 oz. per serving.	Best smoked or grill roasted low-and-slow.	Oven roast or braise.
Leg/ **Sirloin chops** (also called ham butt)	Cross-section chops cut off the sirloin roast.	Chops, which tend to be lean, should be about 1 in. thick (8–10 oz.) to ensure they stay moist while grilling. Estimate 1 chop per serving.	Marinate and grill using indirect heat.	Braise.

*See diagram, page 255.

Pork Cuts for Grilling *

Primal/ Retail Cut	Description	Recommended Size and Thickness for Grilling	How to Grill (or BBQ)	Other Cooking Methods
Leg/ **Ham shank**	The rear part of the ham between the sirloin and the foot. Although the ham shank has a meaty end, it contains more bone and less meat than the sirloin. It is excellent smoked.	The ham shank is 10–15 lbs. Estimate 12 oz. per serving.	Best smoked or grill roasted low-and-slow.	Oven roast or braise.
Leg/ **Ham steaks**	Cross-section steaks cut off the ham shank.	Steaks should be 1–1½ in. thick (up to 1½ lbs.), which easily serves 2.	Marinate. Grill thick steaks using indirect heat. Baste or mop frequently with vinegar-based sauce. Apply sweet sauce only during the last 10 minutes of grilling to prevent burning.	Braise.
Foot, Jowl, and Fatback	not commonly grilled			

*See diagram, page 255.

Poultry and Game Birds for Grilling

Bird/ Type or Cut	Description	Recommended Size and Thickness for Grilling	How to Grill (or BBQ)	Other Cooking Methods
Chicken/ **Poussin**	The youngest chickens, relatively lean.	Each weighs about 1 lb. and serves 1.	Grill roast whole, split, or butterflied (Tuscan style) using indirect heat.	Oven roast whole; broil splits.
Chicken/**Rock Cornish Game Hen**	A breed of domestic chicken that has a savory, slightly stronger flavor than chicken, but not as strong as partridge or quail.	Each weighs 1½–3 lbs. and serves 1–2.	See **Poussin**.	See **Poussin**.
Chicken/ **Fryer or Broiler**	Chickens between 8 and 13 weeks of age. Cut in half, these are packaged as split broilers.	Each weighs 3–5 lbs. Estimate ¼ to ½ chicken per serving.	Great choice for making beer-can chicken. See **Poussin**.	See **Poussin**.
Chicken/ **Pieces**	For grilling, look for *chicken pieces* rather than *cut-up chicken* or *quartered chicken*. These will have been separated at the joints and will lie flatter for even grilling.	Skin-on chicken is preferable for grilling: In addition to adding flavor, it protects the meat, helps it retain juices, and takes on any char instead of the meat (it can always be removed after grilling).	Grill over direct heat. Chicken thighs can stand higher direct heat than chicken breasts, and will stay moister during grilling. Use a marinade or oil-based baste for boneless, skinless breasts.	Stew, fry, or deep fry.
Chicken/ **Roasters**	Larger, older chickens that are bigger and plumper than fryer/boilers. Usually sold whole.	Each weighs 6–7 lbs. and serves 6–7.	Ideal for grill roasting whole, split, or butterflied (Tuscan style) using indirect heat.	Oven roast.
Chicken/ **Capon**	Castrated male chickens 8–9 months old. Plump and ideal for grill roasting because of their higher fat content. Usually sold whole or cut into whole bone-in breasts.	Capons weigh about 10 lbs. and serve 10–12.	If a turkey is too big to consider grilling, a capon will do very nicely.	Oven roast.

Poultry and Game Birds for Grilling

Primal/ Retail Cut	Description	Recommended Size and Thickness for Grilling	How to Grill (or BBQ)	Other Cooking Methods
Turkey	Hens (female) and tom (male) turkeys differ mainly by weight, not by tenderness of the meat. Hens are usually sold whole; toms are frequently sold as turkey parts, including wings, thighs, drumsticks, whole breasts, and breast cutlets, also known as turkey steaks.	Hens weigh up to 16 lbs.; toms usually weigh over 16 lbs. Estimate 16 oz. whole or cut-up turkey per serving.	Grill roast whole turkey or turkey parts using indirect heat or smoke.	Oven roast whole and parts; grill or broil turkey cutlets.
Duck	Usually sold whole. Legs and breasts, including *skinless, defatted breasts*, can be found at specialty butchers and meat departments.	Most breeds are 5–7 lbs. Because of the high percentage of fat and bone, estimate 3–4 servings per duck.	Grill roast using indirect heat. Even the leanest ducks will render a good amount of fat while they cook. Consequently, a drip pan must be placed directly below the duck. Keep a bulb baster nearby to remove excess accumulated fat from the pan.	Oven roast, braise.
Goose	Usually sold whole. Goose has a moist texture and a rich, robust taste similar to dark-meat turkey or duck.	A goose typically weighs 10–12 lbs., but can be up to 25 lbs. Estimate 1 lb. of goose per serving.	See **Duck**. Make sure drip pan sits under the entire length of the bird.	Oven roast, braise.
Pheasant	Usually sold whole. Meat is finely textured, firm, and plentiful. Wild pheasant meat is lean and can have a pronounced gamy taste; farm-raised meat has a milder flavor.	Hens weigh 2½–3 lbs.; cocks weigh up to 5 lbs. Estimate 1 lb. of pheasant per serving.	Usually split for grilling.	Oven roast, braise.
Quail	Usually sold whole. Tender, mildly flavored, and lean, quail do not yield a lot of meat per bird.	Quail weigh about 5–7 oz. Estimate 2 or more quail per serving.	Quail are best split and marinated for grilling as they are lean and dry out easily if overcooked.	Broil or sauté splits.

Index